Early to Rise

Early to Rise

A Sussex Boyhood

BOB COPPER

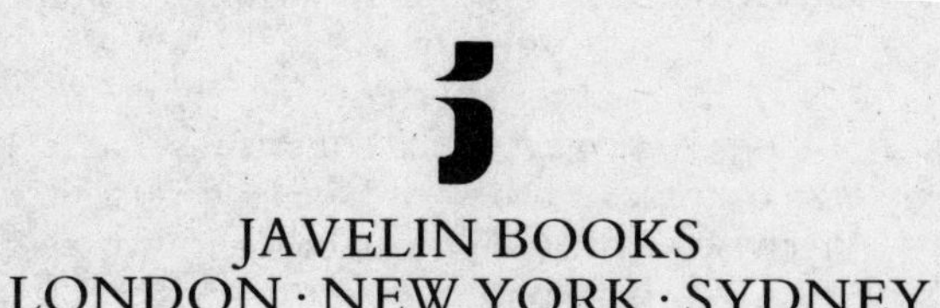

JAVELIN BOOKS
LONDON · NEW YORK · SYDNEY

First published in the UK 1976 by Book Club
Associates by arrangement with William Heinemann Ltd.

This Javelin Books edition first published 1988
Artillery House, Artillery Row, London SW1P 1RT

Distributed in the United States by
Sterling Publishing Co., Inc.,
2 Park Avenue, New York, NY 10016

Distributed in Australia by
Capricorn Link (Australia) Pty Ltd,
PO Box 665, Lane Cove, NSW 2066

British Library Cataloguing in Publication Data

Copper, Bob
  Early to rise : a Sussex boyhood.
  1. Rottingdean (Sussex)—Social life and
  customs   2. Folk-songs, English—England
  —East Sussex
  I. Title
  942.2'56   DA690.R814

ISBN 0 7137 2026 3

Printed and bound in Great Britain by The Guernsey
Press Co. Ltd.,
Guernsey, C.I.

To Ben Copper

The story on pages 68–70 first appeared in
Sussex Life Magazine.

To Ben Copper

The story on pages 68–70 first appeared in
Sussex Life Magazine.

Contents

List of Illustrations

between pages 118–119

Part I
★ ★ ★
Early to Rise

Chapter One

As the early morning sun climbed steadily up to a steeper angle, the slanting rays struck the surface of the water, and shattered into a thousand splinters of light that went dancing down into the shimmering depths of the sea like shoals of tiny, mercurial fishes. Of other signs of fishes in the sea there were none and we sat there with our lines dropping almost perpendicular to the sea-bed where the temptingly-baited hooks dangled with no effect.

The tide was at the stage which we used to call 'slack-water', an almost tideless period that occurs on this part of the coast about twenty minutes before and again twenty minutes after high tide. Whatever the technical details, however, it was considered to be a time when the fish 'went off the bite'.

From where we lay at anchor in the small dinghy, the white chalk cliffs hugged the shoreline in a long, low, undulating line, and the gently swelling front-hills of the South Downs sloped gradually northward to the skyline. The air was motionless and quiet, and the oil-calm, tideless water stretched away southwards into a distance where the colours of sea and sky blended so completely that it was quite impossible to imagine where the one ended and the other began.

'You never don't wanna be afeard o' dyin', me ol' buddy boy,' said Bob suddenly. Actually the thought had not crossed my mind and I wondered what had prompted him to choose such an unexpected subject to break the silence between us. Then I heard it too. The deep, sonorous tolling of the big bell in the church tower some mile and a half away on shore. It was the death-knell and its single note clonging out at minute intervals carried clear across the water, bringing the news of a death in the village during the night. My attention having been focused in that direction, I could hear, too, in the intermittent silences, the cawing of rooks in the elms opposite the church and I wondered which home had seen the drama of death.

'Somebody back there must've turned their toes up las' night,' old Bob went on, expertly rolling a cigarette with one hand—a trick he had learnt years before on horse-back on the plains of Patagonia—while retaining his grip on the fishing line with the other. Placing one end of the cigarette to his lips, he nibbled off the loose strands of tobacco, spat them into the sea and, taking a Vestas match from his waistcoat pocket, struck it into flame with his thumb-nail, lit up and inhaled deeply.

'That's the fate that's gotta come t' all on us sooner or later.' He spoke slowly with long, reflective pauses, spacing his sentences or sometimes breaking a sentence clean in two. 'But you don't wanna go worryin' y' head about that. For when they put y',' his watery, brown eyes looked directly into mine from under the heavy, dark balcony of his brow, 'in that li'l ol' box, boy, an' cart y' up the churchyard, you're only goin' back t' where y' came from in the first place—wherever that is!'

After a considerable smoke-indulgent silence, he continued, 'Has it ever occurred t' you, ol' buddy boy, that before that ol' mid-wife holds y' up be the ham-strings an' knocks a li'l o' God's sweet air into y' lungs,' he waited, as if giving me time to absorb the picture he had drawn, 'you've already bin dead f'r a million years—in a manner o' speakin'?'

My eleven-year-old head was quite incapable of grasping his argument, but I remember being intrigued and that may have marked for me the start of many vague ponderings upon the imponderable. We dream of deities and give them strange-sounding names; we dress them in celestial pomp, surround them with a heavenly host and weave about them an elaborate pattern of theological supposition. Yet only in the song of the skylark, the crashing of waves on a storm-swept shore and the firm grip of the hand of friendship do we find any reassurance that they exist.

Our codes and creeds are based on faith and optimism and, undismayed by the lack of any suggestion of existence before birth, we cling eagerly to comforting theories of a life after death. But the period in time, the location and individual circumstances in which we find ourselves first drawing breath, seem to be the results of some hideous lottery. 'Tinker, tailor, soldier, sailor, rich man, poor man, beggar man, thief.'

By an astonishing stroke of good fortune, I fell to earth in southern England and first saw the light of day through the narrow casement of a farm-worker's cottage in the small village of Rottingdean on the Sussex coast. It was January 1915. These were the dark and threatening days of the Great War, just at the time when the first Zeppelins were dropping their bombs on the east coast. The nation's precious currency of male vigour was being squandered on the fields of Ypres, and the threat of 'bad news from the front' hung like a bat-winged spectre over practically every home in the country. In my earliest recollections, however, I was only vaguely aware of it all and accepted the fact that adult whisperings at the tea-table of trench-warfare, gas-attacks, shell-shock, sunken ships and missing uncles were all part of the mysterious world of grown-ups which was remote, grave, and sinister.

Although no precise details imprinted themselves on my childish mind, I remember a pervading feeling of apprehension: a built-in awe of marching boots, troops of trotting horses and gun-limbers, albeit British, as being part of that dreaded, dominating situation known as war. Cartoons, seen in newspapers, of Prussian guards impaling babies on their blood-wet bayonets as dispassionately, apparently, as they would pick up a pickled onion on the end of a fork, did nothing to dispel these fears which persisted for some time after the war had ended.

We were early to have electric light in the cottage and after dark, the bulb and shade over the sink in the scullery, when not actually in use, flung a shadow on the ceiling when the kitchen door was open that bore a remarkable resemblance to the Kaiser's helmet. This made a visit to the tap for a drink of water or, subsequently, to the pail under the sink, something to be avoided, except in direst necessity. And after we had climbed the steep stairs to the bedroom and the bedside candle had been snuffed out, the frightened dreams would return, exaggerated out of all proportion.

But though our village suffered like any other and the black diamond patch or arm-band was worn as a badge of bereavement on far too many sleeves, we as a family were lucky enough to be practically untouched by the war.

My grandfather, who had worked for the same farmer for well over forty years, had just handed over the job of farm bailiff to my father, Jim. His oldest son, my uncle John, was established as head shepherd, which in a farming area that was predominantly sheep-country was one of the most important posts to be had. My father, eager to taste the novelty and excitement that enlistment appeared to offer and being, perhaps, like thousands of others, ignorant of the full implications of war, made several attempts to join the army, but in view of his special knowledge and experience in farming was turned down each time. We were therefore fortunate enough to be spared the agony and suspense of the separations that so many families suffered.

Life went on, then, very much the same as it had for centuries. The speed of transport, the speed of thought and speech, the speed of progress, was still geared to that of the horse and cart. Not so much the brisk, high-stepping pace of a pony and the spinning wheels of a well-sprung gig, as the slow, ponderous progress of the shaggy-fetlocked shire and the rumbling and crunching of iron-shod wagon wheels on flint-metalled roads.

Having never been subjected to any of the reforms that had wrought so much change in the industrial world, the agricultural policies of the area—indeed the country—and even the methods of working had changed little over the years. There was in fact a marked antipathy to change in our village which seemed to indicate a general feeling of contentment among the majority of the male population of the village.

While this picture contrasts sharply with the poverty and privations of the near-starving rural communities in other areas of England, it is not to say that life was easy. The back-breaking, shirt-soaking nature of farm work in those days, when muscle-power from man and horse was the only motive power, demanded practically all the energy a man could muster to carry him through his working day. In return, he had the use of a cottage, a garden in which he could grow a good deal of his food and keep half-a-dozen hens and a few, a very few shillings each week to purchase for his family those further bare necessities of life that had to be bought from the butcher, baker and general stores.

The pinching poverty of his lot, the heavy grind of hard, repetitive work and exposure to all winds and weathers often twisted his body and rheumaticky joints into something far short of 'God's own image' but, nevertheless, of the village men of my father's and grandfather's generations, many of whom I got to know extremely well, there were a good number of fulfilled and well-adjusted people.

Sons followed their father's trade or calling without question, for it was considered to be the natural order of things and there still existed a long line of continuity in the patterns of living and established habits in thought, word and deed. With fishermen on the foreshore casting their nets by hand, shepherds watching their flocks on the hillside and sowers flinging their seed to the rhythm of their stride, scenes of Biblical simplicity were part of everyday life.

*   *   *

It is inevitable, I suppose, that one's very earliest recollections are predominantly concerned with life at ground level. I recall even now a world confined to the kitchen floor of the cottage which was covered with green parquet-patterned linoleum referred to as oil-cloth. The structural features that were every bit as prominent in that world as the Post Office Tower is today, were the underside and legs of a stout, white-wood table that my father had made soon after his wedding in 1908, and four varnished, spindle-backed chairs with turned legs, all except one of which bore under their seats a label marked 'Ibex'.

The most approachable inhabitant of this world was the dog, Bingo who, apart from being one of the most affable members of the household—particularly during the working day when the rest had so much to do—was the only being I consistently met on equal terms and at eye-level. Much of each day, it seems, was spent in his company lying curled up beside him while he twitched and grumbled in his sleep in the throes of some canine dream of cornered rats, fleet-footed hares or coveys of partridges whirring over the stubbles.

The rest of the family were more familiar from the waist down. Mother during the morning was an ankle-length skirt of dark serge, protected in front by a coarse apron of hessian tied round the waist with white tapes, which whisked about busily from one job to another, propelled by two sensible black shoes. They would carry her up and down the stairs to clean and dust the bedrooms and make the beds and make multifarious journeys into the garden to feed the hens and gather eggs, hang out the washing, dig a root or two of potatoes, cut a cabbage or fetch a bucket of coal or an armful of logs to feed the hungry mouth of the kitchen-range. She seemed to be continually scurrying about in defiance of any principles of time and motion.

As dinner-time approached, while she still moved in an unapproachable aura of bustling industry, tantalizing smells of steak and kidney pudding, stewed apple and custard and other aromas reduced Bingo and me to a state of drooling supplication. Sometimes manna was dropped from heaven by flour-encrusted fingers in the form of apple-peelings for me, rejected beef gristle for my friend, or a large bowl out of which we would share the remains of a cake-mixture, sultanas and all, scraped with a wooden spoon.

After dinner, mother settled down to 'snatch forty winks', that puzzling adult expedient for avoiding the use of the word 'sleep', which at any other hour than night-time was looked upon as something approaching sloth. I, sworn to utter immobility and silence, sat and watched house flies buzzing round the sticky fly-paper suspended from the lamp-shade and tried to will them away from their impending glutinous fate. Later she would disappear into the bedroom to re-emerge as a blue cotton dress and floral pinafore which moved more leisurely and gracefully about upon shoes slightly more dressy in style, pointed of toe and with what were called, I think, 'Louis' heels.

The afternoon was an altogether more composed and restful period of the day, when I would be lifted on to a comfortable lap and into a maternal presence that had seemed quite inaccessible earlier in the day. It was a soft, warm period of reassuring looks and comforting words and the faint, unobtrusive perfume of Cuticura toilet soap and those little powder-impregnated papers—her only concession to the use of cosmetics—that mother tore from a booklet to take the shine off her nose.

Our little session of soothing tunes and rhymes would be broken only by my sister's door-bursting arrival home from school. She was four years older than me and seemed very grown-up. Pink-cheeked and breathless beneath the fly-away brim of a black velour hat she brought into the cosy seclusion and privacy of the little room a breath of bustle and mystery of the outside world and was overflowing with tales of what had been going on at school. Tommy Sayers had been caned for pinching apples from the headmaster's garden and that 'Queeny' Parnell had been and had her hair bobbed and

Marcel-waved and, brazen hussy (mother's observation), had taken to wearing lipstick.

Father usually made an appearance about tea-time which was heralded by a great deal of banging and foot-scraping outside before his actual arrival indoors. Having deposited in the corner of the scullery by the copper his perks for the day, a mess of rape greens, a sack of tail-corn for the chickens or a brace of rabbits—for he seldom returned home empty-handed—he would stand for a while, framed in the kitchen doorway, as if to allow time for the mutual appreciation of his homecoming to take full effect.

To me, from the level of the hearth-rug, he was a pair of huge hob-nailed boots and corduroy trousers tied in beneath the knees with leather straps called 'yorkers' and again at the waist by a stout leather belt with a large, rectangular brass buckle, but which actually relied for suspension upon a pair of heavy leather-thonged braces. His entrance introduced a feeling of family completion and set the scene for an entirely different atmosphere.

Bingo's barked greeting accompanied by ecstatic wrigglings and tail-wagging at the sight of his master were cut short by a stern instruction, 'Box!' whereupon he would retire dutifully to his sack-upholstered bed in the corner, lie down with his chin resting on the edge and watch father's every move.

Father was seated again at the end of the day in his favourite fireside chair. After removing his boots and placing them on the hearth to dry, he would rub his feet together, as a grass-hopper does his hind legs, to remove the chaff and barley-beards that clung to the hand-knitted stitches, then, stretching his legs out before him and wiggling his toes he would throw back his head and let off a great sigh of satisfaction. 'Aaaa-agh! We got round ag'in, then.' Something attempted, something done, he had indeed earned a night's repose.

Taking off his yorkers to hang them on the special nail under the mantelshelf beside the slate on which he wrote the farm orders for the following day, and reaching for his

slippers, he would wipe his sweat-damp forehead and settle
down to a large mug of tea before going into the scullery for
a great, sploshing wash under the brass tap at the sink,
puffing, snorting and blowing the air through his lips with a
bubbling sound as if he was grooming a horse. Wetting a
comb under the tap he would part his hair and smarm it
down on either side, then lift the front up into a smart and
fashionable quiff. 'How's that then?' he'd say, turning to us
with a caricatured grin. 'Tapolene, that is. The poor man's
macassar-oil!' Then he would take up his place at the table.

As the man of the house, in those days, was the only wage-
earner and source of income, his physical welfare was a
matter of great importance and so it naturally followed that
father was the best-fed member of the family. For a start, his
was the largest plate and on it were placed the choicest pieces
of meat, the middle-cut of the suet pudding, the biggest
potatoes, the roundest and firmest of brussel sprouts, the
whitest part of the cauliflower or the shapeliest carrots. As
mother brought his dinner in from the scullery and set it
down before him towering high above a moat of rich, brown
gravy, it gave off delicious clouds of steam that made us
wish we hadn't had ours at midday and still had some to
come.

Like any other job he tackled, father went about eating a
meal in a brisk and workmanlike manner. With the exception
of a dusting of salt and pepper, he spurned the use of condi-
ments and maintained that 'hunger was the best sauce'. His
cutlery was highly individual. The inscription on the handle
of the heavily-plated fork named its owners as 'The Pullman
Car Company Ltd.' and his wooden-handled knife had a
broad blade of pliable steel shaped rather like a miniature
kukri with which, despite maternal mutterings of dis-
approval, he would shovel up green peas by the mouthful or
scrape every vestige of gravy from his plate when the meal
was finished. He had found the knife in the swill when he
had been feeding the pigs so it had probably come from the
kitchens of one of the big hotels in Brighton and somehow

found its way into the pig bucket. No meal for father would have been the same without it and we had to give it special treatment on the knife-board on cutlery-cleaning day.

With the meal over, he would turn his chair to the fire and sometimes take me on his knee, while I explored the contours of his face, which long exposure to wind and weather was beginning to etch into countless wrinkles like sand on the foreshore at low tide. It was a familiar and re-assuring landscape, the generously proportioned nose, the unobtrusive moustache, the tiny warts at the corners of the eyes and, most intriguing of all, the pupil of the right eye that was shaped like a tiny key-hole.

Evenings were not the dull affairs some younger people may imagine them to have been. Father was the type of man who could never sit idle. Though his day's work on the hills had left him physically tired, he would spend the evenings, particularly in winter, making rabbit-nets or mending watches and clocks and I was always perfectly content to sit and watch. He once made a most unusual bird-cage for a favourite bullfinch named Joey. Joey had a very smart appearance with a russet-red breast, a grey back and a neat, black skull-cap and with his engaging ways became almost like one of the family. The cage was so designed that he was unable to get to either his seed or water without considerable initiative and effort. The seed was contained in a small, four-wheeled trolley at the lower end of a sloping runway about six inches long and was attached to the wires of the cage by a fine-linked chain. Joey soon discovered that the only way to get a meal was to raise the trolley up the runway by pulling the chain with his beak and holding it fast to the perch with one of his claws to prevent it running back. On the opposite side of the cage he got his water in a similar manner through a hole in the floor of an over-hanging balcony by hauling on a chain attached to a small, silver thimble which rested in a jar of water directly beneath. He appeared to enjoy working for his living and after a cropful of rape-seed or crushed hemp washed down with a thimbleful of water he would send forth

a burst of trilling song or pipe a bar or two of some tune
father had painstakingly taught him.

Like as not, while busily engaged on the job in hand, while
mother's knitting-needles clicked away busily on the other
side of the hearth, father would break into song himself,
often with one of his own father's old songs.

> Sometimes I do reap and sometimes I do mow
> At other times to hedging and to ditching I do go
> There's nothing comes amiss to me from the harrow to the plough
> That's how I get my living by the sweat of my brow.
>
> When I get home at night just as tired as I be
> I take my youngest child and I dance him on my knee
> The others come around me with their prittle prattling toys
> And that's the only pleasure a working man enjoys.

It really was remarkable how closely cottage life at that
time still resembled that depicted in those old songs many of
which, even then, were well over a hundred years old.

As children we had our favourite songs and preferred
those which gave father an opportunity to clown, like 'When
Shall We Get Married?' This is best sung as a duet in conversation style but father, of course, took both parts and sung
the repetitive reply by the betrothed lady, 'O-oh, couldn't
we have something bettah?' in an over-posh and exaggerated falsetto which reduced us to tears of laughter. Other
favourites which lent themselves to burlesque were, 'The
Fox' with a very sibilant 'Mrs S-shlipper S-shlopper' jumping
out of bed, 'The Parson and the Pig', and 'Corduroy' with
the disastrous consequences following a 'dose of salts'.[1]

My grandfather, into whose cottage we had moved on the
death of Granny, travelled round to various parts of the
country to live for periods with each of his children in turn,
but he always regarded the cottage at Rottingdean as his
home and much of his time was spent there. Although he was
in his seventies, his presence was still a positive and influential

[1] *See* pp. 216, 218, 220, 222.

force in the household. Kindly and genial, his firm, self-assured manner left no room for doubt as to his views on matters as diverse as whether the fourteen-acre gratten at Man-and-Mare should be put down to oats or mangolds next year, or if the 'spotted-Dick pudden' that we had had for dinner could have done with another handful of raisins.

But to me he was a pair of sturdy, corduroyed knees, slightly swollen with the rheumatism that kept him pretty much confined to his chair. Up on to those twin pillars of the family stronghold I was, from time to time, allowed to clamber; this was an exciting experience for Grandy was a heavy-handed man with an organ-like voice and a pat on the head from him bore an alarming resemblance to a clout round the ear, while the deep diapason even of childish patter to his grandson had a thrilling and somewhat terrifying effect.

Grand-dad was a man of the soil, and as earthy as a sack of potatoes. His old tweed jacket, threadbare at the cuffs and facings and faded across the back from the sunshine and showers of many seasons, was still as tough as canvas and as serviceable. Though sagging at the shoulders over a slightly shrunken frame, the revers at the level of the waist had long since failed to meet and a loop of leather bootlace was necessary to link the button-hole to the button. Its predecessor, of uncertain but very early vintage, lay in rags at his feet yet in spite of it all was still doing a useful daily service.

This was in the age when nothing was wasted, and along with other discarded garments it had been cut into narrow strips some five inches long and woven into a sacking base made out of an old chaff-poke to provide a comfortable and hard-wearing hearth rug about six feet by three. Grand-dad's jacket, which was a pepper-and-salt mixture tweed, formed the neutral background upon which a geometrical pattern had been worked in red and navy-blue. The red was all that remained of a Life Guard's tunic and the blue of a policeman's trousers, both of which had been worn by rather more obscure relatives on the distaff side of the family back in the 1870's and '80's. It was somehow fitting and entirely in character with the simple elements that made up cottage life to have as much family history woven into something that was not only decorative but also useful at the hearth.

Life, to a great extent, seemed to revolve around the fire in the kitchen-range. It was the source of coal-glowing cheer, in front of which the whole family huddled on cold winter nights. While the north-east winds moaned down the stairway like a drunken flautist at a funeral and the draughts whistled under the ill-fitting doors, we sat with freezing calves while our shins itched with the heat. It was the provider of hot meals and it heated the bricks which, wrapped in blanket, we carried up to bed to warm the icy sheets. When rain made out-door drying impossible, it dried the weekly wash. Indeed it was the universal provider of so much comfort and sustenance that it was given the devoted care and attention of a minor god. From daily applications of Zebo and a great deal of 'elbow grease', it shone like ebony in startling contrast to the pristine whiteness of the hearth-stone around which, like a small altar rail, stood a burnished steel fender.

I spent so many happy hours on that old hearth rug that I sometimes wonder if my future was being influenced, and that the Life Guard's tunic, the policeman's trousers and Grand-dad's old country jacket were somehow getting into my blood. For it so transpired that my love of the countryside has been every bit as real and important a part of life as my years of service in the Life Guards and the Police Force—perhaps even more so.

That this is to some extent an idealized account of the domestic scene, I have not the slightest doubt. It nevertheless recreates the kind of atmosphere that prevailed for by far the greater part of the time of childhood, and one that has remained in my mind with extraordinary clarity for the better part of sixty years.

Chapter Two

If the itinerant trades-people who called to offer their wares on the back doorstep were ambassadors of the world at large, then the world was indeed, as father used to say, 'a rum ol' place'. They were certainly of importance to me as being the only evidence of human life outside the immediate domestic circle and those who called regularly I remember with remarkable clarity.

There are certain people whose demeanour is so positive, whose prevailing mood—be it joyous or sad—so dominant and contagious, that they appear to move about in an aura of either sunshine or cloud, into which one is inadvertently admitted on meeting them. They seem, particularly in retrospect, to have carried their own weather about with them.

Whenever Mr Hook, under a storm-cloud of melancholy, shuffled along the brick path at the back of the cottages and dumped down his baskets of dried fish with an exaggerated air of resignation and despair, it always seemed to be raining. As he stood there in his oilskins, bemoaning his lot and intermittently assuring mother that the smoked haddock he held spread before him like some huge, yellow butterfly was 'dee-licious an' eats like 'am', I would stand wide-eyed; while the rain pelted down, I would watch the string of small diamond beads that ran around the turned-down brim of his sou-wester and the large solitaire that trembled under the tip of his beak-like nose, wondering which would be the first to drip on to our prospective dinner. But while I felt a good deal of sympathy for poor Mr Hook and his unhappy fate, it was, nonetheless, something of a relief to see the door shut again on the cold and wet, and watch his bent figure retreating into the dismal, grey distance with a basket in the crook of each arm.

If, for no apparent reason on an otherwise perfectly still day, there was a sudden stirring of leaves in the ivy on the cottage wall and the hollyhocks in the flower bed started to sway elegantly like eastern dancers, it most probably signalled the approach of Midget, the milkman. He would burst round the corner like a sudden squall wearing a smile as white as a button-hole of daisies. Brisk of step, bright of eye, his brown boots and leather leggings gleaming in the sun, he would stride up to the door swinging his pail and making the measures inside churn about till you thought the contents must surely turn into butter. Setting it down on the step he would ladle out the milk into the jug held by mother, chatting furiously all the while, and always add 'a little drop for the cat' who was already lapping at the spillage that had dribbled down on to the bricks during the transaction. It was all over in a matter of seconds and in no time at all he was back on the float, slapping the reins on his horse's flanks and trotting off down the road whistling a shrill and gleeful tune to the rhythm of the clopping hooves. His visit was short and sharp, like the proverbial donkey's gallop, but the morning was all the brighter for his calling.

Only too well aware of my propensity for roaming away from the cottage, up the white chalk road and out into the wicked larger world, mother hit upon the idea of shutting me up in the chicken-run 'out of harm's way'. An additional advantage to this precaution was, I feel, that I was also out of her way while she went about her daily chores.

It would be peaceful sitting there with my back against the nesting box and the time never dragged. Two or three lop-eared inhabitants of the rabbit-hutches nearby would be thrown in for further companionship and, sharing the morning with company in which I was so heavily out-numbered by furred and feathered kind, I often found myself choosing whether to identify with one or the other.

Sometimes Mr Jones, the greengrocer from Brighton, would appear round the end of the row, looking like a nineteenth-century undertaker, in a three-quarter morning coat of black box-cloth and an aged bowler hat frayed at the brim and greening slightly on top, like a sprinkling of moss on a tarred gatepost. He would throw an armful of cabbage leaves and carrot tops over the wire fence, clucking like a hen announcing a new egg and snapping his fingers in encouragement to the rabbits, but ignoring my presence so completely that I sometimes wondered if my fantasies had been fulfilled. After dealing with mother at the back door, he would come back, his gentle grey eyes twinkling and his dark moustache bristling into a smile as he took a juicy William pear from his pocket and passed it through the gate. 'There y'are, young fella me lad,' he'd say, 'did y' think I'd forgotten y'?' and faith in my existence as a human being was restored.

There was Mr Rumbold who, in his way, was one of the last of the travelling packmen of old. True his pack was contained in two gigantic and much-used cardboard suitcases posing as leather, but the astonishing array of pinafores, blouses, socks, shirts, handkerchieves, ties, braces, pullovers, and tweed caps he had to offer would have stocked a small shop.

He was tall and angular with a wide big-toothed smile and wore pince-nez glasses with very thick lenses which reduced his eyes to the size of a ferret's. His doorstep manner and patronizing humility were as well-worn and threadbare as his dress. With his greasy-banded, grey Homburg and winged collar, his long black, waisted overcoat and grey spats worn over black boots, he had a certain shabby stylishness, as if he might have been 'something in the city' in Edwardian London. His arms were disproportionately long, as though from constantly carrying the burden of his stock-in-trade from door to door.

On Saturday afternoons we could look forward to a visit from the 'Penny Lady' who offered many of the miscellany of items she carried in her basket for that modest sum. Reels of cotton, cards of darning wool, packets of needles and pins, buttons, lengths of elastic, bars of toffee or chocolate, bull's eyes and acid drops bagged up in penn'orths and the un-forgettable gob-stoppers, those huge, globular confections that precluded speech while sucking was in progress and changed colour as they slowly diminished in size towards the centre.

She always seemed a little breathless on arrival and glad to set her basket down after the steady climb out of the village to where we lived at Northgate. Her complexion and animated look, framed by a coronet of tight pin-curls under the brim of a not particularly memorable hat, must have been the envy of many ladies of more distinction.

But the weekly caller to whom my attention was inclined more fondly was Uncle John who looked in about tea-time on a Monday to pay the Slate and Tontine clubs. These were voluntary savings and sickness benefit schemes, run by the landlords of the local pubs, and Dad would take Uncle John's subscriptions to save him a journey to the pub later in the evening. Coming straight off the downs where he had been all day tending his flocks Uncle John brought into the tiny kitchen not only the smell of Cooper's No. 1 sheep dip and St Bruno tobacco, but also a breath of the big, open hill country where he spent all his working days and his tales, told in a leisurely way yet with great enthusiasm, smacked of that country where the wind whistles through the bents and the gorse and stunted blackthorn lay their backs to the sea. He would tell how 't'would be two-an'-twenty year agoo come May' when they 'dag' lambs from the snowdrifts 'up 'Oxeysocks' or how he had once met a colony of rats on the move.

'We wuz comin' 'ome up along Smuggler's Track one evenin'—about October time as I recall—th' ol' sun wuz jes' a-gooin' down an' 'twuz gittin' a li'l dusky-like under th' 'ill, when prensly th' ol' dawg stops sudden-like and stands stock still. Whumperin' an' tremblin' from 'ead t' tail 'e wuz. "What's up then, mairt?" I sez.'

Fosh, who lay on the cornsack that served as a doormat, looked up at his master, as if he remembered the occasion well.

'Then over th' brow o' th' 'ill I sees this big, dark patch, like a damn grut pool o' treacle, slowly pourin' down th' steep side 'ill. It 'ad me guessin' fer a bit, I can tell ye, but as it got a li'l closer I could see 'twas thousands 'pon thousands o' rats, movin' along like an army an' leavin' a swathe o' trodden grass behin' 'em as they went.

'I've never sin th' ol' dawg s' upset afore. 'E kinda cowered down at m' fit with 'is back arched, tail tucked tight up between 'is legs an' 'is eyes stickin' out of 'is 'ead like organ stops—an' I 'ad the wind up a notch or two, I dun't mind tellin' ye.

'But they went past us about five an' twenty yards away t' th' east'ard an' there was so many an 'em that took th' best part o' twenny minutes for 'em t' pass. I should think they was makin' f' 'Arvey's Crawss, be th' way they wuz 'eadin' an', thinks I t' meself, ol' 'Steady Pettit's in f' a load o' trouble if they are. Never sin anythin' like it afore nor since, 'ave we, mairt?' he said to Fosh.

As the stage of my little world extended, so the players increased both in number and variation of character. In the appropriate season, Mr Sallis would drive along the cliff-top road, sitting with his legs dangling over the side of a flat-topped cart loaded with a slippery, silver heap of mackerel, herrings, or sprats that had been beached at Brighton that morning. The two-wheeled vehicle lurched along behind his briskly trotting pony while a bucket swayed crazily from the axle underneath and a great block of ice in the fish pile slithered about from side to side threatening to spill some of the cargo overboard.

Mr Sallis always wore a well-washed, blue denim jacket and a flat, tweed cap which sat like a plate above his round, red, benign countenance. As he made his interrupted journey up the High Street, stopping first this side and then that as housewives came to their cottage doors with dishes or plates and a 'few ha'pence' in their hands, he would be followed, like the Pied Piper of Hamelin, by half the children in the village cadging a piece of ice and, after them, a host of nondescript cats irresistibly attracted by the fishy aromas that trailed behind him.

For the children this was more of a game than anything else, for even the lucky ones were doubtful about their good fortune when rewarded with an unmanageable chipping from the block which they could just about cram into their mouths. Tasting unmistakably of fish and garnished liberally with herring scales, it would render them speechless for a while as they stood aside wrestling with the miniature iceberg between their freezing jaws and spitting out the fish scales one by one.

Charlie appeared only in summertime, shuffling slowly along the line of inattentive faces in the queues on the cliff-top for the buses back to Brighton reciting, in a soft and pleasant voice, extracts from Kipling, Shakespeare or Spenser. He dragged a withered leg behind him and held the arm on the corresponding side across his chest. The knuckles on the hand were swollen and blue, even on the hottest day, and the useless fingers protruded from a ragged woollen mitten like thin, red sausages. He constantly inclined his head towards the sky, his watery, pale-blue eyes looking towards heaven, it seemed, for the help that was so slow in coming on earth. Slowly, reluctantly, pennies and halfpennies were extracted from holiday pockets and purses, and dropped into the grimy palm of his good hand, but the response was meagre and existence on such a pittance must have been a struggle.

His features were thin and sad and there was a wax-like and ethereal quality about his almost hairless face which brought to mind those dispirited expressions seen in early stained-glass windows. He was ragged and not on very good terms with soap and water, yet had preserved a gentleness of manner and politeness which betrayed a cultured background.

In quiet periods between performances, he was a source of wonderment to village children towards whom his attitude was that of a gentle and slightly ingratiating uncle. He addressed us all as 'Dear' and found it easier to express himself in verse than in ordinary conversation. He drew his inspiration from the most diverse of sources.

Was the morning springlike?

> . . . The year's at the spring,
> And day's at the morn;
> Morning's at seven;
> The hillside's dew-pearled;
> The lark's on the wing;
> The snail's on the thorn:
> God's in his heaven—
> All's right with the world!

Did someone yawn?

> . . . And sleep that sometime closes sorrow's eye
> Steal me a while from my own company . . .

Did a small girl shake her head in play?

> . . . Amarantha, sweet and fair
> Ah, braid no more that shining hair. . . .
> Do not, then, wind up that light,
> In ribands, and o'er-cloud in night,
> Like the sun in's early ray
> But shake your head and scatter day.

His knowledge of poetry was inexhaustible. He was a walking *Palgrave's Golden Treasury*.

His recitations, though inaudible to anyone more than ten paces away, were delivered with a great deal of feeling and expression and in a cultured accent which, outside church, was strange to our rustic and untutored ears and there was something strangely compelling about them that sent shivers down the spine. The flow of words and cadences of expression had the same thrilling effect as the tremendous, rolling chords of the organ voluntary in church on Sunday.

Until I heard the magic of Charlie's recitations, poetry and romance had seldom been conveyed to me in words. It was the sights and sounds of everyday life that more frequently opened the gateway into Elysian fields of dreaming and imagination. Lying face down on the grass, gazing into the scarlet eye of the pimpernel; watching the laborious progress of a snail on a stone or turning on my back to watch the skylark hover like a smut from a chimney against the deep blue infinities of the sky, I felt a compulsive and indefinable affinity with the surrounding moods of nature.

But in Charlie's poetry the spell came from the words themselves, in spite of the fact that much of what he spoke was not understood. His eloquence alone was enough to capture me. Charlie, poor, pathetic, hobbling Charlie, this shambling scarecrow with the golden tongue, was to initiate me into the delights of poetry. To this tatterdemalion with the soul of a bard, I shall be eternally grateful.

Chapter Three

My first exploratory excursions into the countryside beyond the confines of the garden were made on foot, alone and without mother's knowledge. Up the path that led over the bank opposite and into the meadow, my footsteps would lead me, tracing an indeterminate track through the buttercups.

Mother knitted me a scarlet woollen jersey which, amid the sea of greens, browns, and duns of the terrain, shone out like an errant poppy in a cornfield and whenever my absence from the cottage or the garden was discovered, a quick reconnaissance from the attic window would usually reveal a small red dot in the far distance and peace of mind would be restored.

The red jersey also became known to the carters and farm-hands, and often a detour would be made to pick me up. Thrown up into a wagon or on to a horse's back I would be carried home and dumped somewhere near the cottage door. This same red jersey was once the means of saving my life. It was a story I heard often repeated.

The day had started normally enough, with my father up soon after five to give him time to feed his ferrets and enjoy a reflective smoke in the garden before work in the harvest field and the heat of the day began. They were cutting a twelve-acre piece of winter wheat up at the Compt and hoped to get it finished and shocked up before nightfall.

He was out and away from the cottage before anyone else was up and by half past six was up on the hill where the carters were driving the binders round and round the field in ever decreasing, concentric swathes. Each machine was drawn by three horses and as the corn was cut, the rotating blades of the sweeps knocked it back on to the table from which it was elevated, on a moving canvas sheet, up into the binding and knotting mechanism. At regular intervals, a neatly butted and tied sheaf was shot out to the newly-cut stubble and in time these were picked up and stacked together, ears uppermost, in groups of eight or so, known locally as shocks, to dry in the sun and wind.

In the field's high south-west corner, where the stacks would be eventually built, and where you could look down the valley to the sea, wooden trestles had been set up upon which the cutting knives could be sharpened, This was a full-time job for one man, as they were changed frequently and regularly and he would also fit new, individual triangular sections or blades on to a knife to replace those that may have been accidentally broken on stones or such.

Here also, leaning on its shafts, stood a two-wheeled tip-cart which had been drawn up by one of the horses that morning carrying several spare sets of knives, the horses' nose-bags with their midday feed and a box of tools and an oil can for on-the-spot repairs. In the shade of the cart, the men had left their jackets, waistcoats and the frails. These were plaited straw baskets containing their food and bottles of cold, milkless tea which, alas, only in appearance resembled the beer that moistened the thirsty throats of the harvesters of times gone by.

Leaning against one of the cart wheels was Dad's double-barrelled shot-gun, taken along specifically to capture a dinner or two as the rabbits started to bolt when the standing corn had diminished so in area as not to offer them sufficient cover. The day was fine and as the sun climbed higher the larks sang and work in the field went on apace.

Back at home, left pretty much to my own resources, the morning began to drag. Teasing the cat with a piece of string and a cockerel's tail-feather had palled and I had grown tired of dabbling in the water-butt trying, rather belatedly, to rescue a drowned blackbird and watching those extraordinary little scarlet aquatic worms that live in such places, go looping down into the green, weed-grown depths like animated interrogation marks.

I sat on the doorstep and looked at my companion, a rather dilapidated, much-loved wooden doll who was my constant companion at the time. It was indeed 'a poor thing but mine own' and had known better and more exciting times. Dad had made it many years before and it was the type of dancing doll which, in days gone by, used to cause a great deal of fun and merriment in the taprooms. Crudely carved out of oak, it was merely a head and trunk, rather like a peg-top stuck on top of the thick half of a parsnip, to which were attached arms and legs double jointed at the shoulders, elbows, hips and knees. In its hours of fame on a Saturday night down at the Black Horse, dressed as a sailor-boy, it would have been held by a light cane inserted in a hole in the small of the back so that its feet just rested on the end of a thin, springy board which protruded between the wide-spread knees of the performer who sat on the other end of the board anchoring it down to his chair. When the board was tapped with his free hand it caused the doll to do a vigorous and eccentric dance to the rhythm of a song or an accompany-ing concertina. It must have earned Dad many a free pint of beer.

But its days of public-house performances were over. It had long since lost its clothing and any facial features that may at one time have been painted on had completely worn away, robbing it of any vestige of personality. Its feet had been broken off and, had it not been for the hole above its kidneys, it would have been impossible to tell which way it was facing.

If I had expected inspiration from my companion as to how to pass the morning, I was to be disappointed. He lay there sprawled inelegantly on the brick pavement and offered no suggestion whatever.

It was about this time that the notion of going off to find

Dad first occurred to me. Having once decided, it was only a matter of minutes before I had picked an apple from the Worcester Pearmain trained against the garden wall and set off, pulling a four-wheeled wooden trolley which bumped and rattled over the rough, chalk road, with the doll slumped back uncomfortably inside, one wooden arm trailing over the back.

The white, deeply rutted road climbed steeply on to the open down but, having reached the crest of the hill, veered away in the wrong direction, so to pursue my search it was necessary to branch off on an overgrown and little-used path along which I found it impossible to drag the trolley. Reluctantly I had to abandon it, having tucked it well out of sight under a gorse bush and, taking my wooden friend by the arm, I journeyed on.

My objective was really no great distance away in ordinary terms but it was certainly further away than I had ever been before and scaled down to match the size of my short legs, it was a pretty daunting undertaking.

When the men in the cornfield stopped for dinner and sat around under shocks to eat their 'bait' and enjoy a smoke, they could see down the valley, on the nearside of the long undulating line of Funnell's hedge, a large rectangular field known as Kennels Laine. It had grown a remarkably good crop of rye well over six feet high, the cutting of which was to be their task on the following day.

Arch Holder interrupted his meal for a while, a piece of cheese impaled on the blade of his knife poised in mid-air. 'There's a fox or something ha-coming through that 'ere rye down there. The one that was haround after my chicking laas' night, hi shouldn't wonder,' he said in an assumed accent, hinting of work other than that with rough farm labourers, although everyone knew that most of his working life had been spent in the fields. 'Hi'm a very light sleeper, y'know, an 'abit formed when hi was a young man ha-workin' for the Customers and Hexercise down at New'aven 'Arbour. Hand when you form an 'abit in hearly life, hit's a job to get it hout of your cistern,' he went on, in an orgy of malapropisms.

'Wal, hi 'eard this 'ere noise, y'know, an', thinks hi to meself, 'ullo, we've got a stranger hin our mist and on goin' to the window I sees Charlie meandering hup the garden path just as large has life. Han' that's 'im now, a-comin' through that rye down there, hi lay a crown.'

'I can't see no fox,' said someone.

'You watch down there,' said Arch, 'where hi'm a-pointin'.'

Sure enough, on looking closer and watching carefully, a gentle movement in the rye could be discerned. The day was quiet and still without the slightest movement in the air so the possibility of the rye swaying in the breeze could be discounted. Then it was noticed that the movement followed a determined line slowly approaching in their direction.

'Yeah, that's Maas' Reynolds, all right,' said Dad, and got up and loaded his gun. 'Kip quiet, all an ye, and I'll 'ave 'im as soon as 'es near the edge of the fiel'.'

'Give 'im a barrel for me, Jim, will you?' said Arch.

They waited and though they could actually see nothing, the path being taken through the field was betrayed by the movement of the ears of rye. They followed its progress expectantly remaining absolutely still and silent. As it neared the field's boundary Dad raised the gun, his finger on the triggers, watching intently for the first glimpse that would tell him to fire.

Gradually something was appearing through the thick screen of growing stalks but—he hesitated. It wasn't, he thought, moving quite fast enough for a fox and as it grew plainer there was a distinct showing of colour. A funny thing—a fox isn't that red! Sorta scarlet. Could it be—? He lowered the muzzle and waited.

Seconds later, I emerged into the open, blinking in the bright sunlight with the wooden doll dangling from one hand. Exclamations of disbelief came from the men. 'Wal,

I'm buggered!' 'That were a close 'en, Jim!' Dad put the gun down with a prayer.

I walked up and stood by old Arch as he sat there, leaning back against a shock, his corduroyed legs stuck out in front of him and his great, well-dubbined boots sticking up enormously from the hard, stubbled ground. The small hob-nails which patterned the soles in groups of three and the tips and pelts were burnished to silver by constant wear on the dry earth.

On his lap, laid on a red and white handkerchief that served as a sort of table-cloth, were the remains of half a coburg loaf and a ninety-degree wedge of a spherical, red-skinned cheese. In his left hand, he held smaller pieces of each from which he methodically cut mouth-sized portions with the sharp blade of a bone-handled knife. He cut always with the blade moving towards his thumb which was protected from the cutting edge by a piece of crust known as a 'thumb-piece'.

He looked at me with piercing eyes from under the brim of a straw hat that threw his forehead and sandy eyebrows into shade. His eyes were the palest blue I had ever seen. The lower half of his face was in the sun, and his blond moustache and the three-day growth of whiskers on his chin glistened like the bristles of a brass-wire brush. The dividing line between light and shade cut horizontally across his face somewhere just below the bridge of his nose but as he moved his head in talking, it shifted up and down and the vermilion tip of his nose, now in shadow, now in brilliant sunlight, shone intermittently like a flashing danger signal.

'Come on 'ere an' sit down halong o' me,' he said. 'Hi reck'n that must be your lucky day, me boy.'

He cut first a large portion of bread and then a piece of cheese corresponding in size and crammed them into his mouth then started to masticate in a business-like manner. Thirty-two bites to every mouthful we were always told around the meal-table at home, but with Arch's habit of over-loading the hopper I should have thought one hundred and thirty-two would have been nearer the mark.

'Y'know,' he continued, 'good luck is hall you want in this 'ere life, without it you can't make much 'eadway. Without it this morning, me boy, you wouldn't be sittin' 'ere ha-talkin' to me hat this 'ere moment.' He spoke with an immoderate and inappropriate use of aspirates in a curious mixture of local dialect and pseudo-genteel. 'Now you take this 'ere grain o' wheat.' He stuck his knife in the ground, picked up an ear of wheat and rubbed it between his palms then winnowed away the chaff by blowing gently through his cupped hands. Singling out one of the grains he held it towards me and pointed out the tiny crescent-shaped mark at one end of the crease down the middle. 'Now, that there is an 'orse-shoe, han where there's an 'orse-shoe there's bound t' be luck. Now lookin' haround this 'ere field, hi shouldn't 'esitate t' say that there's millions of 'em—not countin' those on the 'orses themselves. An' hi reck'n there's an 'ole lot o' luck haround 'ere this morning, too.'

I was not at all sure what he was talking about, only that in some extraordinary way the horse-shoes on the wheat-grains had saved my life. But Dad was more practical. 'Don't you believe it, neighbour,' he said, 'it was that red jackut. If it 'adn't a' bin f' that, I'd let the boy 'ave it—both barrels.'

When Arch climbed stiffly to his feet and returned to work with the rest of the men, I lay back with my head on his jacket which was warm with the sun and had a reassuring, masculine smell about it of rough tweed, straw and tobacco. The sun shone down full in my face and even with my eyes tight shut the light penetrated my eyelids in a hot, red haze. The voices of the men and the whirring of the binders faded into oblivion and I fell into a shallow sleep to dream of horse-shoes, grains of wheat and a forest of cornstalks reaching up to where gigantic ears of rye waved overhead against a scarlet sky.

Chapter Four

Until about the turn of the century the peaceful, plodding pace of life to which the human frame had been geared since the beginning of time, was obviously dictated by the limitations of the speed of horse-drawn traffic. But there was something in that steady pace that entered a man's heart and made for a leisurely frame of mind and a general lack of haste in decision and action. This tenor of life bred people who moved about graciously and found time to feel as well as to think and these qualities are now in danger of joining the growing list of lost arts, for the very nature of speed precludes gentle thought or graceful movement.

Time was, though it is hard to believe, when a journey of even a few miles was anticipated and planned several days ahead, when the steady progress along the dusty road allowed time to greet a fellow worker in the field, to hear the sound of bird song, to smell the sweet-briar in the hedgerow, to laugh and even to sing. The journey was just as important as the destination and there was an affinity with the travellers of all the ages that have ever been. He who has ridden on a wagon-load of hay behind a team of horses over the chalk-ruts of a downland track has ridden with Caedmon, for to have heard the sound of hooves and jingle of harness and felt the wagon lurching beneath you is to have travelled for a while in Anglo-Saxon England.

We cannot turn the clock back to 1919. The motor car is now inescapably with us, but there is no reason why we should not count the change in our pockets to see what we have paid for the privilege of having it.

'Git th' boy out in th' road jest afore eight on We'nsdy mornin', an' 'e kin 'ave a trip t' Lewes.' Dad was talking to mother between mouthfuls of his evening meal. 'Edwin an' Chollie'll be goin' awf t' the rail-'ead witha couple o' waggin'-load o' 'ool. They kin pick young Ron up at Klondyke an' it'll make a good day out f' th' boys.'

Lewes, the county town, was about ten miles distant by road and I couldn't believe my luck. I hardly slept a wink that night thinking about it—and even less the next night. On Wednesday morning I could hear the wagons even before they left Court Farm yard, a quarter of a mile away down by the church, and when they appeared round the corner of High Wall, my heart leapt.

Piled high to well above the corner-poles with bales of wool, the two wagons sailed into view like tall ships in line. Each one was drawn by three horses hitched up in tandem with the carters, Charlie Goddens and Edwin Pettit, walking at the lead-horses' heads. They both wore blue denim jackets and carried brass-bound whips over their shoulders and came proudly up the road out of the village towards Northgate with a sense of purpose that was lacking in the work-a-day trips within the limits of the village or farm. This seemed to be transmitted to the horses who held their heads high as if they knew that this was a once-a-year journey and felt privileged that they should be selected for the job.

These wagons contained the fruits of the local flock-masters' harvest. Baled and sewn up in hessian, the recently shorn fleeces were on their way to the manufacturing towns of the midlands to be made into blankets and clothing. A short month or so before, they had been 'makin' that ol' mutton sweat' up on the chalk-hills of the south country.

'Wey!' cried Charlie to the leading team, as they drew level with the cottages where we stood waiting, and with a rattle of trace-chains and an impatient flinging about of heads the horses pulled to a halt. Standing on the shafts, he took me from mother and chucked me up on top of the load as high as the cottage eaves and I found myself bouncing on the huge mattress of bales and looking in through the attic window from which, standing in my night-shirt, I had so lately been looking out. Dad's pigeons, a mixed bunch of tumblers, blue-rocks and fan-tails, strutted tenderly about on pink feet skidding on the sloping tiles and rummaging in the creeper and rambler roses which were draped over the dormer window like a shawl. Then with an exchange of waving farewells worthy of a departure to Australia, we moved off, Charlie keeping up a continuous, one-sided conversation with his team, 'Gid up, Traveller—Jim, you long-faced old sod, pick 'em up then. You gotta long way to goo yet. Move on, there, move on.'

Two hundred yards along the road we stopped to pick up cousin Ron and, being that much older than I, he grabbed one of the ropes by which the bales were securely lashed down and shinned up it like a shell-back. Then off we went at a steady four miles an hour down the familiar road, past New Barn where the mellow tiles of the roof, ranging in colour from brick-red to mauve and stained in places with the yellow and orange of lichen, shone in the morning like Joseph's coat. Past the pond around which earlier in the year coltsfoot had sprouted from the flooded footprints of drink-ing cattle and frogspawn had lain under the grass banks like skeins of under-cooked tapioca, and on up into the open country beyond.

At the top of St Mary's hill, we left the last of the houses behind us. The road levelled out a bit and Charlie and Edwin dropped the perfunctory show of ceremony that had marked their exit from the village, stuck their whips up beside the corner-poles and sat side-fashion on the wagon shafts. Charlie lit his pipe, settling down for the long journey ahead and wisps of smoke wafted up to where we in splendid, elevated isolation, lay couched in five-star luxury, watching the surrounding country slowly revolve on either side. The horizons slid gently forwards while roadside banks and hedge-rows fell behind. The morning sun climbed steeply towards its zenith, baking the fields to pale gold and scabious, toadflax and ladies' bedstraw made every meadow bank a garden. The day was loud with larksong and the merry-go-round of our little world was turning slow, sweet and peaceful.

Somewhere along the road, Ron remembered the gooseberries which he had filched from the bushes at the end of Uncle John's garden before he left home. He put his hand into his trouser pocket to discover a messy poultice of split-skins, juice and seeds where they had been squashed in his clambering up the rope. 'Gaugh!' he grimaced, pulling the pocket inside out and scraping it clean with the blade of his jackknife. 'Shouldn'ta nicked 'em, I reckon,' he went on philosophically. Then his eye caught mine and with a wry grin, 'Good job I snatched awf a few peas an' stuck 'em in t'other'n, wadn't it?'

From his other pocket he pulled out a handful of green pea pods and shared them out equally. Then we lay looking down over the front of the load to where Charlie sat beneath us, while intermittent clouds of blue smoke appeared from under the wide brim of his nodding hat. Ron dropped an empty pea-shuck down and it landed plumb in the middle of the dented crown. There was a considerable pause then a horny hand reached up and took the shuck down to where it could be examined and after an interval of several seconds it was tossed to the roadside.

Empty pea-shucks continued to fall from heaven at regular intervals while we carried on our feast up aloft. Some bounced from Charlie's shoulders into the roadway, others remained where they fell in the crown or on the brim of his hat and when this happened the response was always the same. The hand reached up, took it down for closer inspection and eventually discarded it with an aplomb and self-assurance that appeared to accept the fact that pea pods dropping from the sky and landing on your hat in the middle of the Sussex downland on a hot morning in July was the most natural thing in the world.

We stopped outside the Swan at Falmer and while the

horses stood patiently in the road munching and nuzzling their nose-bags, the carters went inside. They presently re-appeared and, having handed up a couple of bottles of stone ginger and Brighton biscuits to Ron and me, sat down in the shade of the porch and had their bait.

Charlie had an old-fashioned face. That is to say he had a face that was totally uninhibited by any thought of how it looked to other people. It was a mobile, elastic face which was an open window into his heart. It laughed, scowled, coughed, spat, belched, wept, yawned and in short did all the things that a human face was intended to do. At that moment, it was golloping back mouthfuls of beer and great chunks of cold meat pie and reflecting in its bright blue grinning eyes the intense pleasure its owner was experiencing in doing so.

'Right, best start makin' tracks, I reck'n,' it said presently, and we were soon off on the road again.

Just before we came to Lewes, we passed the grim, grey walls of the prison where, Charlie told us 'all naughty boys finishes up'. We looked at each other meaningfully, for there was something in his tone which made us feel that we were carrying a whole bellyful of guilty secrets as well as the peas we had just gobbled up. 'Don't you ever let on about them goose-gogs, will y'?' hissed Ron.

About mid-morning, with the nearside, hindermost wheels of the wagons locked and riding in skid-pans, we rattled and skidded down the steep hill to the railway goods yard, leaving two shiny marks trailing behind us on the road surface like snail-tracks. After the ropes had been slacked off, the wagons were unloaded by half a dozen glum-looking men, who shuffled about disconsolately, speaking infrequently and, even then, unintelligibly. They were dressed in dark blue overalls with large red circles in the middle of the back and they dragged the bales off the wagons with vicious-looking metal hooks which were alarmingly like that which protruded from the cuff of Captain Hook's empty sleeve.

'You'd better be'ave y'salves, you young 'uns,' said Charlie out of the corner of his mouth, 'these 'ere cheps be Germans. They lives in the prison up yonder.'

Germans! The very word struck terror into the hearts of both of us and as we scrambled from one bale to another on the load, like mice in a diminishing corn-stack, keeping as far away as we could from the slashing hooks, our hearts pounded like steam-hammers in our chests and the hair bristled on the backs of our necks. To be so physically close to the bogies that had so frequently haunted our dreams was a terrifying experience and, although the war had been over for some little while, we felt as exposed as if we were in the front line on active service.

At last the unloading was complete and we cowered in the corner of the empty wagon, praying for the moment when we could set off for home. When we at last took the road, the prison buildings looked even more sinister and we crouched down under the side of the wagon out of the sight of spying German eyes.

On the open road again we breathed more easily and lay down on a few old empty sacks, an amenity with which every wagon was equipped, and seemed to pass down a long, tree-canopied corridor. The afternoon sun flickered down through the leaves overhead and the rumbling of iron tyres and the hypnotic rhythm of hooves on the flint road made sleep hard to resist.

'Shan't be long now 'fore we're 'ome, ol' kiddy,' Ron's voice broke into my dreaming. ''Tis all down 'ill from 'ere.' And at tea-time, greeted by a cloud of sweet, syrupy steam, I walked in through the open scullery door. Mother was making strawberry jam.

Chapter Five

At this time, about 1920, the village was just emerging from the insularity it had enjoyed ever since it had been a small Anglo-Saxon settlement. Little more than twenty years before, it had been a self-contained community practically untouched by influences from the outside world, which was regarded in a vague and uninterested way by the locals as being somewhere over the hills to the north. Any town from London to Leeds, from Oxford to Edinburgh, was referred to as being 'somewhere up the back o' Lewes'.

The various branches of the Beard family, whose ancestors lay in the walled-in, sacred patch known as the Quakers' burial ground just to the north of the church, occupied the large eighteenth-century properties around the green and generation after generation, the same few families of workers lived in the cottages in the High Street. There were only a handful of surnames and they cropped up regularly in the register of births in the church vestry and on the headstones in the grave-yard and if, as might be suggested, we had been exposed to the risks of congenital idiocy through excessive intermarriage, we had at least inherited a legacy of self-sufficiency and contentment of mind seldom met with in the wider context of modern urban life.

There were a couple of small racing stables facing the green and a few longshoremen who lifted a precarious living from the sea, but it had always been farming which provided by far the biggest proportion of work for the employable male population. There were three thousand acres of downland farmed from the village and to keep this in 'good heart' reqiured the efforts of nine four-horse teams, two teams of eight bullocks or oxen, and sixty to sixty-five men and boys employed full-time.

Until just after the Great War, the village of Rottingdean continued to lie entirely contained in the narrow valley that ran down to the sea, snuggling down out of the worst of the winds like a brood of young partridges nested in a disused wheel-track. It is only in more recent times that the buildings have spread outwards and upwards over the bare downs and broken the smooth, maternal skyline of the hills. But even now, every road or trackway out of the village climbs steadily so that after five minutes walking in any direction you can look back down on to the dwellings clustered round the church and green and the wide expanse of sea. Outwards in every other direction, lies the great open hill-country. Fold after fold of undulating land patterned geometrically with the grey-greens and duns of pasture and fallow, the yellow of mustard, the pale-blue of a flax field or the rich bronze and gold of harvest-time. If Norfolk resembles a chess-board, as they say it does, then this part of Sussex is like a patchwork quilt thrown on a bed occupied by two fat ladies.

Walk to the cliff-edge here and look out to sea into the face of the prevailing wind. Taking a line between the tip of Cherbourg and St Catherine's Point on the Isle of Wight, the next landfall—over three thousand oceanic miles away—would be the coast of Florida. Here the south-west wind comes bounding ashore like a homing sailor, swaggering up the High Street snatching hats from unsuspecting heads and lifting modest hemlines. Round the chimney pots he dances, whistling under the eaves, drumming with soft fingers on the window panes, shaking the tree tops and sending cloud shadows racing away madly over the hills beyond.

But if you would feel the pulse of the village, sit on the green on a hot summer afternoon. Here, within sight of the white-railed pond and the stark, black windmill on the hill, listening to the church clock strike the hours away, you will quickly find yourself in tune with days gone by.

Close by stood the village pump from which 'Butty' Bowles used to fill the donkey-drawn water-cart to take round to the villagers at $\frac{1}{2}$d a bucket. Near the chestnut tree was where the children used to gather on May mornings and dance round the maypole with garlands of flowers to the tune of fiddles. Up the narrow lane the tall, erect figure of Len Avery, the butcher's man, used to be seen making his way to one or another of the big houses with a delivery of meat. With one corner of his blue-and-white striped apron tucked into his belt and a sharpening steel swinging from his waist, he carried on his shoulder the shallow, wooden tray peculiar to his trade. Shaped like an elongated version of a skate's egg-case—empty specimens of which were so frequently washed up on the foreshore—it would be piled high with an array of cuts and joints that would delight the eye and whet the appetite of even the least carnivorous, with a string of coarse-cut sausages hanging down the back like the tail of a kite.

In those days, the butcher's shop lay in quiet seclusion just off the High Street in the lane that took its name from the trade—Butcher's Lane. The house where the butcher lived and to which the shop was attached was then, and still is, known as Whipping Post House and a pollarded horse-chestnut a few yards from the front door marks the spot where once long ago stood the stocks and whipping-post used for the correction of village malefactors.

I remember afternoons when ducks stood one-legged on the grassy banks of the pond drowsing in the shade of the elms while swallows, with incredible speed and skill, swooped down to pick flies from the placid surface of the water leaving only the faintest rings of ripples to mark their passing. On the other side of the green just outside the churchyard lych-gate, a disconsolate mare with ribs showing like a plate-rack would often be seen standing patiently in the shafts of a rubber-tyred brougham, nuzzling the chaff in her nose-bag, her only reward for the four-mile journey from Brighton. The bowler-hatted cabby, leaning back against the shafts and idly flicking away flies from his horse's head with the lash of his whip, sneaked a quick draw on his clay pipe while his fares, two elderly ladies in picture hats carrying parasols, went into the church to look at the Burne-Jones windows. This was the heart of the village and on days like these it was beating slow and steady.

But the mood could change suddenly and drastically. Adjoining the butcher's shop were the stables and slaughter-house and at weekly intervals on killing day, the atmosphere would be charged with impending death. Men with sticks and ropes could be seen forcing a bolt-eyed steer in towards its pole-axed doom. Constantly bellowing in panic and protest with its hooves slipping and sliding in the brick-paved yard it would fight every inch of the way in complete contrast to the pen of lambs who shuffled, in dumb bewilderment, to their unsuspected fate. For a short while the tempo quickened and the afternoon would be hideous with the shouting of men, the barking of dogs and the cries of dying beasts.

Here within a radius of a hundred yards, the whole microcosm of village life was enacted. From baptismal font to funeral bier, from maypole to whipping-post, these old flint walls and ancient elms have encompassed it all.

Small wonder that painters and poets alike who came here to live were inspired to produce from palette and pen some of the best works of the period about the turn of the century. John Drinkwater wrote:

The days are sweet at Rottingdean
And very sweet at Rottingdean,
Where leagues of downland travel north and southward leagues of sea,
A sea that flashes blue and green,
With purple flashes thrown between,
And downs that gather up the songs of all the winds that be . . .

The rest of the shops, apart from the butcher's, all lay in the narrow High Street although they formed only a small portion of the whole and most of the buildings were tiny flint and cobble cottages. There was something about shops and shop-keepers in the days of which I am writing—and village shops in particular—which made them altogether personal and friendly and, compared with the brisk, business-like visits to the supermarkets of today, shopping was a pleasant social occasion.

In mid-afternoon while the menfolk were still at work and before the bigger children had come spilling out of the school-doors like beans from a split sack, running, whooping and flooding the street with waves of pent-up exuberance, there was a period of calm and quiet when mothers could be seen making their leisurely way from shop to shop. They paraded the High Street in their afternoon clothes, with their youngest in high-wheeled perambulators and the toddlers holding hands and trailing along behind. The actual shopping was often rather perfunctory and of secondary importance, for there were frequent long pauses to stop and gossip. Had you heard that little Tommy So-and-so had 'gone down with mumps'? That Mrs Somebody had run off with some chap from Brighton? Or how about poor old George Snudden who fell off a scaffold and broke his ankle? Very high? Well, no—that was the funny thing—the board was only one-brick high off the ground when it happened.

It was a pleasant time of day with the housework of the morning done and when the older women, dressed in the styles of earlier days, held conversations with their neigh-bours across the road and were only very occasionally interrupted by a passing car or farm wagon. In summer they sat in kitchen chairs on their doorsteps knitting or busy with needle and mending-thread. Through the polished panes of narrow casements draped with white lace curtains, cats could be seen curled up asleep beside the potted cyclamen or geranium which, in many cases, shared the window-sill with jam-jars full of pale, yellowish liquid in which small blobs of yeast culture surfaced and sank with monotonous regularity like restless balls of cotton-wool. This was 'bee-wine' in the making and so called because the fluffy pieces of yeast were known as 'Jerusalem bees'. They were 'fed' on sugar and after a week or two in a warm window, the water, with which the process had been started, was miraculously turned into wine and all for the price of a few spoonsful of sugar. It was a craze that swept the southern counties in the twenties and, in fact, 'bee-wine', I think, was known throughout the country.

On wet days when the wind came funnelling up the street from the sea, bringing daylong periods of drenching rain, the street would be practically deserted and only the one or two women to whom a trip to the shop was imperative were to be seen. With their prams hooded and aproned against the weather, they shuffled along beneath large umbrellas held aslant into the wind like shiny black beetles, taking care to avoid gutter-pipes gushing out water on to the narrow brick and cobble-stone pavements, and threading their way between potted aspidistras placed outside to drink the rain that fell all too freely from the grey skies overhead.

The shops themselves differed widely in character and atmosphere and this depended as much upon the shop-keepers or assistants as on the nature of their wares. In the grocery store there was the pleasant and all pervading aroma of tea, cheese, bacon, spices, soaps, polishes and all the other things in stock. Yet none was sufficiently predominant as to be identifiable save, of course, the unmistakable fragrance of coffee-beans being ground by hand in the huge green coffee-mill with the brass, funnel-shaped hopper on top and heavy, iron fly-wheel at the side. A double-tiered row of biscuit tins ran the entire length of the front of the counter, their labels as various and colourful as all the flags of the League of Nations. Petit Beurre, Marie, Rich Tea, Thin Arrowroot, Breakfast, Digestive and Ginger Nuts were all there for the asking.

Behind the counter in the deep drawers of a heavy mahogany shop-fitting with turned legs and pillars and inset, bevelled mirrors, were kept sultanas, currants, raisins, cinnamon, root-ginger, candied peel, cloves, sugar, tea and cocoa and standing on the floor in clean sacks, the mouths of which were opened wide and rolled back to display the contents, rice, sago, tapioca, split peas, butter beans, dried figs and apple-rings. Mr Richardson moved gravely about from one job to the next, weighing up the goods in the gleaming brass scales and shooting them from the scoop into neat, conical bags which his deft fingers could make with a couple of quick turns and a flick of the wrist from squares of coarse, blue paper stacked near the scales for the purpose. He wore a clerical grey, alpaca jacket which was the mark of proprietorship and seemed to match his mood, and a rather heavy, greying moustache, clipped in a perfectly level line across his upper lip, bristled beneath his nose. He was a man of few words, but in any case would have had a job to have made himself heard against the flow of chatter from the loquacious Jim who presided over the cheese and bacon counter on the opposite side of the shop.

Here the counter was topped with a large slab of white marble on which Jim, wearing a long white apron hooked to the uppermost button of his waistcoat and with his spotted bow-tie slightly awry, would slap and bash chunks of delicious deep-golden butter into neat blocks with his wooden butter pats and a lot of overt display and showmanship. 'There you are lady,' he would say, 'butter fit for a queen.' Or he would cut a wedge of cheese from the block with a thin wire attached to the cheese-board or peel off a few pink rashers from a bacon joint on the patent slicing machine, wrap the purchase expertly in grease-proof paper and tie it with thin 'sugar' string which he pulled from an ornamental, caste-iron holder suspended like a lantern from the ceiling over his head. All the time he kept up a continual flow of patter. 'Right then, here we are. Butter, bacon and back-chat. My goodness how your little boy do grow. He's got his father's nose—God help him. Now let's see, that'll be ninepence ha'penny. Nine and a half'll mak y' laugh—two and a half out of a bob.'

Across the street, a few feet above ground level, was a small shop which boasted on its lintel that it had been 'established over 100 years'. Climbing a short, steep flight of steps and opening the yellow-painted door, which set a small bell tinkling madly behind it, you found yourself in the baker's shop. You would, most probably, also find yourself alone, but not for long. Summoned by the frantic ringing, Mrs Hilder, the baker's wife, would appear from a room at the back smiling affably and wiping her hands on a clean, white cloth. There was always a friendly greeting with kind personal enquiries as to how the world was treating you or 'how were your father's legs or mother's cough' for she had a detailed knowledge of her customers' private lives and knew, also, whether they preferred a well-baked cottage loaf or a pale coburg.

Climbing a short, steep flight of steps, you found yourself
in the baker's shop.

In the shop window were trays of fleed cakes, currant buns, doughnuts and plum-heavies and on the shelves behind the counter were rows of glass jars containing bull's-eyes, aniseed balls, humbugs, sticks of barley sugar and acid drops. The top shelf was reserved for bags of flour. There were tin trays on the counter from which she broke with a small hammer pieces of creamy toffee or 'black jack' a kind of treacle toffee which was also known as 'stick jaw'.

Complimentary observations about the health or appearance of each customer or her offspring were served up as a matter of course with each purchase and favourite children were given a sweet from one of the jars. One proud mother, it was said, was once let down rather badly by a precocious son who, having been lifted on to the counter to deliver a recitation, started off in fine style, 'Little Tommy Tucker sang for his supper . . .' But then, forgetting his lines and to the embarrassment of his mother fell into a repetitive chorus of '. . . bugger, bugger, bugger, bugger' until a parental hand was clamped firmly over his mouth bringing the recital to a summary and untimely conclusion.

Daily the morning air was sweetened with the smell of new-baked bread coming from the bakehouse at the end of the narrow passage between the shop and the Black Horse next door. Having extracted the new batch from his oven with a long-handled wooden peel and knocked the loaves from their tins with hands mittened in old yeast bags, in the process whetting the appetites of half the village, Mr Hilder would prepare to set off on his rounds. The bread would be loaded into a smart, two-wheeled hand-cart, painted green with a white top and lined out in gilt, with a hook on the front to take the large basket in which he carried the loaves from door to door.

Each day at noon precisely the barrow, with Mr Hilder holding the handles and following along behind, seemed to find its way to the foot of the steps that led up into the public bar of the Queen Victoria and there it would stand unattended for some fifteen or twenty minutes. A lady resident from one of the big houses, who was not in favour of a man 'moistening his clay with ale', however long and hard he had worked in the forenoon, once enquired, 'Why is it,

Hilder, that I see your barrow outside the Queen Victoria every morning?'

'Wal, ma'am,' said the baker, 'that's 'cos I can't get her up the steps and in the bar along with me.'

Though we never went into the tailor's shop, the silent and solitary gloom of the world in which he appeared to live seeped out even through the closed door. 'R. Trowbridge, Bespoke Tailor', written in faded and dusty gilt letters on a black, wire-gauze screen at the back of the window, announced the nature of the owner's trade, but it was quite superfluous. The hacking jackets, riding breeches and blue serge suits, in various stages of manufacture with chalk marks and tacking stitches still in evidence, which were draped over the top obliterating the text, told just as clearly what he did for a living.

Looking through the window into the dimly lit interior, you could see the hump-backed, bearded figure of Mr Trowbridge sitting like a gnome cross-legged on the wide, mahogany counter surrounded by bales of suiting and rolls of buckram and striped cotton lining material, with a tape-measure draped round his neck like the parson wore his vestments in church on Sunday. He sat there eternally, it seemed, peering over his steel-rimmed spectacles at the work in hand and stitching away with rhythmic, figure-of-eight movements of his right hand or licking the end of the thread and holding the needle to the light of the window the better to see the eye. Almost invariably denied the power of speech by the row of pins held firmly between his lips, he could, nonetheless, make himself clearly understood when he tapped smartly on the inside of the window with a thimbled finger and waved his intolerance of small boys pressing their noses to the glass outside and watching him work. Poor Mr Trowbridge seemed to live a lonely and unenviable existence.

Nell Tuppen was a bright and busy little person and as pert as a wren, despite her seventy-odd years. Her sharp, brown eyes missed nothing and as she spoke, you were aware that her look flickered about your face, from your eyes to your forehead and to the corners of your mouth, searching it seemed for a frown or the beginnings of a smile or the slightest sign of expression which might have betrayed your reaction to what she was saying.

She had been at the 'paper shop' for as long as most people could remember and combined the business of newsagent and stationer with that of selling small fancy goods. There were fishing lines, shrimp nets, buckets and spades, small wooden sailing boats with sharp tin keels, colourful Japanese paper parasols and all manner of useless articles of souvenir pottery to catch the eye of the few visitors who made a brief appearance during the summer.

On the other side of the shop were displayed plants, bulbs, seeds and various small garden requisites, and on slatted wooden shelves stood pots of cyclamen, pelargoniums, begonias and calceolarias all raised in the greenhouse in the large garden at the back of the shop. They were all attractive in their way, but the specimen which usually claimed the attention of small visitors to the shop was a 'sensitive plant' which responded to the slightest touch of a grubby finger and contracted its outspread, pinnate leaves into a closed position, like fingers held lightly together in prayer.

Miss Tuppen's interest in botanical matters was also carried further and on a Sunday afternoon in summer she might be seen walking primly up one of the tracks that led on to the hills on a secret mission. She cherished the closely-guarded knowledge of where, in the right season, rare wild orchids could be gathered and her trim, diminutive figure, stepping lightly along the rough, chalk tracks in the wide open downland, with a veil covering her pale face and fastened under the chin and a tightly-rolled silk sunshade on the crook of her arm, looked frail and incongruous.

That evening as she tripped up the path from the lych-gate to the church door in time for evensong with the hem of her skirt brushing the daisies on the grass verge and her prayer-book and hymnal clutched in a white-gloved hand, the lapel of her brown, waisted costume would boast a single bloom of a ram's-horn, a bee- or fly-orchid or even that often sought but seldom found prize of downland, a man-orchid. The names by which these orchids were known to most of us sprang from the shape and appearance of the flowers. Both bee- and fly-orchids looked exactly like those two insects and the flowers of the man-orchid bore a distinct resemblance to the human form. But Miss Tuppen would probably have known them by their Latin names.

As the villagers grew most of their own vegetables in their gardens and potatoes, for the farm-workers at least, were grown on farm land, there was little reason to visit the greengrocer's except for the occasional purchase of oranges, lemons, bananas and such fruit as could not be raised at home. Frank 'Crowey' Mockford who, like a number of other local tradespeople, had inherited the business from his father, followed his father's example of going off along the coast road to Brighton Market with his pony and cart at four a.m. every weekday. He returned with a wide variety of fruit and vegetables mostly to satisfy the sophisticated fancies of the gentry, and chicory, endives and asparagus rubbed shoulders with the simple vegetables of a more home-spun taste. By eight o'clock, the shop would be open ready for business and as you stepped in through the low doorway on to the scrubbed brick floor, the indigenous, earthy smell of potatoes, cabbages and onions was spiked with the sharp, exotic fragrance of citrus fruits, pineapples and pomegranates from afar.

Frank, again in the paternal pattern, kept a few pigs up in Park Place, an area of spare ground which opened out behind the cottages on the west side of the High Street, and this ensured that no vegetable matter was wasted and also accounted for the periodic appearance of half a pig hanging from a hook in the low ceiling-beam amongst the hands of bananas and strings of onions. He was also a keen sportsman, hiring the shooting rights of a considerable area of the downs, and frequently a pile of rabbits, paunched and hamstrung, would lie on the floor in a corner at ninepence a time. 'Pick where you like—you can always get threepence back on the skin.'

There was a warm feeling of insularity where everyone knew everyone else and the tradespeople catered for individual tastes and preferences. With the exception of 'Crowey's' occasional pigs and rabbits, they also stuck to their own trades and it was all faintly reminiscent of a game of Happy Families where life was still pursued in that easy-going and affable manner to which many of us look back so wistfully.

Chapter Six

On looking back, one of the most extraordinary features of village life even as late as the twenties was the small compass in which it was carried on. It is all the more remarkable at the present time when so many of us commute daily to and from work distances which would, at that time, have been unthinkable and then, as if to satiate some uncontrollable craving for movement and an irresistible urge to get away from home, fly halfway round the world to spend our holidays. But in those days, villagers were often bred, baptised, book-taught, betrothed, bedded, boarded, and buried all within hailing distance of the cottage which had seen their birth and many would never have occasion to travel beyond the perimeter of land that could be seen from the top of a haystack.

Our home was situated in that part of the village known as Northgate, implying that there was at one time or another a toll-gate across the road there although I have never come across any other evidence to support this theory. We lived in the northernmost of a row of four flint cottages which had been built in the early 1890's as an adjunct to Challenors, the main farm of the village, and Dad, who was then a boy of about ten years, proudly claimed that he had been the first person to spend a night under its roof. This was not strictly true, as it was still in the course of erection at the time and the rafters at night were covered with a large tarpaulin so, to be precise, the roof was not complete. But at least it can be said he was the first to spend a night within its walls.

No. 1, as it was designated, was built specifically for the

use of Grand-dad, who as farm bailiff, would be expected to use the front room as a parlour-cum-office in which to meet the various corn-chandlers, vets, agricultural merchants and suppliers of farm machinery with whom he had dealings. To compensate for this, an extra room with the luxury of indoor plumbing—a brass tap over a shallow, glazed, biscuit-coloured sink and a built-in copper in the corner—was added at the back. The floor was of red brick and we called it the scullery.

The anticipated use of the front room as an office never actually worked out as Grand-dad found it more convenient to conduct his business in a small converted room in the corner of the store-room which was part of the farm out-buildings on the opposite side of the road. So in effect we had one more room than the other cottages and this was accepted as being all part of the perks of the bailiff's job.

The other three cottages in the row were also occupied by farmworkers as were another and slightly older row of four parallel with and just south of ours, all of which were hard on the road that ran northwards out of the village and over the hills to join the Brighton–Lewes road in a T-junction at Falmer, a little over four miles away. Our cottage, at the time it was being built, was the last dwelling out of the village and being, as it were, the end house became known as the 'end'us', 'us' being the local diminutive of 'house', as aplied to wood'us, ale'us, back'us, wash'us and other small outbuildings.

Our bedroom windows, particularly that in the garret, which was a dormer set in the sloping tiled roof, looked north and eastwards out over the wide expanse of open downland and southwards past the farm-buildings, over the clustered roof-tops of the village to the sea beyond. But though so close to the sea, there was never the slightest doubt that we were part of an agrarian community. Farm sights, farm sounds, farm smells, farm thoughts and farm language dominated every day and even at night, lying under the sloping ceilings of our bedrooms, our dreams of the farm were disturbed by the bronchial coughing of cows or the shifting and stomping of the great shire horses in the stables opposite and the noise of halters running through iron eye-bolts in the mangers, as they tossed their heads to be brought up short by the wooden ball threaded like a large bead on the other end.

When I was very young the store-room was my happy hunting ground where the live-long hours of boyhood passed peacefully and happily by in an atmosphere of calm and the blended scents of dried locust beans, cattle-cake, new wagon rope, stored potatoes and dry grain. Under a watchful eye from the inner sanctum of Grand-dad's office, where he spent much of his time perched at his desk on a tall stool scratching away with a steel-nibbed pen, I followed the idle and innocent pursuits of infancy in that brief period of indolence and dreaming just before the first yoke of responsi-bility, in the form of school days, has fallen into place.

I would probe the cracks between the floorboards with a straw in search of woodlice who would scamper off towards the nearest cover like miniature armadilloes or, if captured before gaining sanctuary, roll the protective armour of their scales into small balls that could be trundled about like marbles. I would play five-stones with black locust beans, that may have spilt from a holed sack, wondering if I would stumble upon the answer to the the eternal question, 'How many beans make five?' the answer to which, like the philosopher's stone, seemed, in some mysterious way, to offer untold wealth. For the highest compliment that could be paid to a successful man was, 'A-agh, 'e knows 'ow many beans makes five.'

On wet days, when the rain dribbled down incessantly in a series of tiny cataracts from a broken gutter overhead and fell across the open doorway like a glass-bead curtain, I would sit and watch the men slouch past with their hunched shoulders draped about with sacks, tucked in to form a kind of hood and cape combined. Rained off from their work on the hills they would make their way to the barns and cart-lodges to take up jobs in the dry while the carters, the flanks of their horses gleaming with wet and steaming like boulders on the beach after a summer shower, plodded disconsolately back to the comfort and warmth of the stables.

There was a kind of ante-room at the back of the store-room, the walls of which were lined with drums of sheep-dip, linseed oil, axle-grease and paint. There were no floor-boards and no windows, only brick-width ventilation slits in the flintwork. It was dark, damp and mysterious and seldom saw the true light of day. Only on summer evenings, just before the sun dropped behind the ridge of Beacon Hill, did it sometimes send its rapier beams thrusting through the gaps between the stacks of cattle-cake, the piles of empty cornsacks and bunches of new broomheads suspended from the beams in the main store to pierce the inky gloom in which, for the better part of the time, it was totally immersed.

Swarming with dust motes the horizontal shafts of sun would flood the dingy corners with unaccustomed light, startling the beetles and cockroaches and sending them scuttering across the cold, earth floor, dazzling the huge, fat spiders lurking in their webs and bewildering the slugs and warty toads in the dank, moss-grown corners while dry, black-parchment bats, hanging from the rafters, blinked reptilian eyes and stirred in their sleep.

It was a veritable lodging-house for all the fearsome creatures that favour dark and inaccessible places and abominate the brave light of day, and there was an eerie chillness and sense of ill-omen that struck into your bones as you stepped down in through the doorway. Unpleasant, uncanny and always to some extent unexplored, it held a strong fascination and even on the dullest day, when my eyes had grown accustomed to the lack of light, I would sometimes step cautiously in to probe its hidden secrets with every nerve-end in my body poking out like a snail's eye.

'YOU ALL RIGHT THERE, MAIRT?' The stentorian, grand-parental enquiry would come blasting through the heavy silence like a cannon, frightening me out of my skin, and with a pounding heart I would emerge and return to the work-a-day world and the welcome normality of the old man's presence.

Right opposite the store-room, lying well back from the road, was an open-sided cartlodge and a tarred, weather-boarded building with a roof of ancient red tile which was Dad's workshop. He was very much a working-bailiff by this time, about 1920, and on top of his normal duties, he worked as a tractor-driver and estate-carpenter.

I am speaking, of course, of the years immediately after the Great War, when the decline in farming, indeed the plight of the country as a whole, was beginning to make itself felt and the Rottingdean farms, in common with the nation-wide slide down into depression, had fallen far from the glory they had enjoyed about the turn of the century. There was a cutting back of stock and activity in general, and a consequent reduction in the number of men employed. We were moving inexorably towards the first farm sale in the village which in 1924 marked the beginning of the end of agriculture in the area on anything like its former scale.

The end of an era was approaching and the sale catalogue tells its own story. It speaks in the language of a century or even two centuries before. In fact some of the Lot details could be illustrated by the design that embellishes the Luttrell Psalter.

> Well grabs, 3 Dibbers and Pair Steelyards.
> Two scythes.
> Wimble, Hayknife, Seed-lip.
> Swaphook, 2 Turfing Irons, Pair ploughlines.
> Hand seed-barrow.
> Two wooden mangers.
> Shepherd's hut on wheels.
> Scuppet, Bushel and Shawl.
> Riddle.
> Milking pails, milking stools, Hurricane lantern.

As a young man, Dad had worked under David Turner

the wheelwright and Ben Hilton from whom, although not actually apprenticed, he had learnt a great deal about woodwork and farm carpentry, and his knowledge stood him in very good stead in the repair and maintenance of the equipment and implements that were still in daily use and which he had helped the older men to build some fifteen or twenty years before.

In David Turner's yard down on the clifftop overlooking the sea, all the local farm wagons, dung carts, ploughs, harrows, sheep-cribs, ladders, wheel-barrows and gates had been made. A wagon, it was reckoned, would cost £40. That was allowing £20 for the woodwork and £20 for the iron-work which was carried out at the blacksmith's shop and forge up near the pond. One such wagon, built for £40 in 1913, was sold at Rottingdean in 1928 for £25.5.0 and sold again at Standean in 1940 for £45.

Made of good solid oak and ash, they were practically indestructible and only became obsolete because horses were disappearing in favour of tractors. Even then some were modified and fitted with pneumatic-tyred wheels and suffered the final indignity of being towed behind the very tractors that had replaced the proud teams for which they were built. It was on a parallel with a gallant, square-rigged barque being dismasted and converted to steam.

Those old farm wagons, in whichever part of the country they were built and whatever small variations in detail the different districts introduced, were overall the perfect marriage between utility and aesthetics. The design, which no doubt evolved over a number of years, had to a great extent been dictated by necessity. The broad wheels and wide wheel-bases to ride the muddy, rutted lanes in the valleys or the uneven chalk tracks of downland, the waisted shape of the ribbed sides and the elegant lift towards the front to allow the forewheels to lock to a sharper angle, and the graceful curves of the shafts to accommodate the powerful flanks of the thill-horse, were all expedients introduced for specific purposes and yet the whole shape had developed under the keen eyes of generations of craftsmen with a good sense of artistry and the finished product was a joy to look upon.

This could be said of so many things in regular use on the farm in those days. The smooth, curving lines of the scythe in both sneath and blade, the sinuous strength in the helve of the axe and the ploughshare, curled like a breaking wave, were all planned to do a job but they were designed by men who also had a natural eye for beauty.

But, of course, the extended life of all this equipment was only made possible by continual maintenance, and the cart-lodge next to the workshop always housed the odd tip-cart or wagon in need of repair, new spokes or felloes for the wheels, or a new shaft, tail-board or axle-tree. And Dad always kept in stock pieces of well-seasoned timber suitable in size, shape, and grain, to be fashioned into the various replacements when the occasion arose.

Although not apprenticed and qualifying only for the local appellation of 'hedge-carpenter', Dad had a natural ability and inborn sympathy with the wood that elevated him to something very close to a first-class craftsman. To see him select a piece of oak and eye it first from this angle and then from that, noting where the sap-wood ended and where the hard heart of the wood began, smelling it to find out if it was well seasoned and sizing up the grain before he marked out the shape into which it would be sawn, planed and finally carved with a draw-shave, was to see the true country craftsman at work. He relied as much upon the accuracy of his eye as on the two-foot rule in the pocket of his apron.

The dimensions and details of all the implements and their different parts that were carried in his head would have filled a small book. The width of a gate, the diameter of different wheels, the height of the plough handles and the length of the beam were never arrived at by approximation but by precise measurements that were taken for granted. They were never committed to paper and seem to have been handed down from a great, common fund of knowledge shared by all country carpenters and accepted as naturally as we accept that there are twenty-four hours in a day. There was also a notable absence of the usual braggart attitude of the specialist. 'Height o' th' wheels of a waggin'? Why, four-foot for'ard an' five-foot 'indermost, o' course. Any fool knows that.'

His tools, the planes, draw-shaves, spoke-shaves, adzes, bowsaws, wooden-braces and gauges, many of them handed down from his mentors and bearing the initials 'D.T.' or 'B.H.', hung in neat rows above the long wooden bench. They were kept in meticulous condition and cared for with affection. A large 'grin'stun', some four feet across, mounted on a stout, but slightly lop-sided, oak frame out in the yard was in almost daily use and one of my earliest jobs was turning the handle and pouring water from a rusty tin on to the top of the stone to keep it moist as it revolved in a crazy fashion upon its worn spindle. Dad would hold the chisel, gauge, plane-iron or whatever tool he was sharpening steadily on the face of the stone, riding the eccentric gyrations with care so as to keep an even pressure on the cutting edge, while a steady stream of sandy water dribbled off the lowest point of the stone building up into a pryamid like a stalagmite. After the grinding came the slow, laborious rubbing down on an oil-stone on the bench inside and almost as much time seemed to be spent in the care of tools as in the using of them.

But of all the tools in any workshop, those that play the most important role, and without which all the others would hang idle in their racks, are the craftsman's hands. Dad had enormous hands with extremely broad fingers. He used to joke that he was unable to play the piano because it was impossible for him to strike one note at a time, and it was not so very far from the truth. Large, strong and capable, they were in fact, the living tools of his trade and were always to some extent bruised, scarred, scratched and battered from rough and heavy use.

In front of the workshop, between it and the road, was a piece of open ground which was a slurry of mud in winter and inches deep in dust in summer and this was always littered with a variety of objects needing repair. Sheep-cribs with broken staves, ladders with missing rounds, wattles wanting new heads, gates requiring new bars and a hundred and one other things waiting for attention.

It was here as I grew older that I spent many summer evenings, Saturdays and school holidays helping Dad with any of the jobs he thought I was 'man enough' to tackle. He used to reckon that another pair of hands, even if they were only a boy's, could cut the time spent on a job by more than half.

I seemed to spend many interminable hours 'dollying up'. When, for instance, a new plank had been fitted to the floor or side of a cart and nailed into position, all nails protruding on the inside or underneath would have to be clenched, that is bent over and hammered down flat. It was my job to hold a club hammer against the head of each nail in turn to take the thrust of Dad's hammer blows on the other side. Being on opposite sides of the work it was impossible to see exactly where the point of impact was to be and his instructions to correct any fault on my part were always most explicit.

'No, bugger, boy, you're not within a mile an it! Over t'ards the church a bit. Further! Whoa! Not over Saltdean Cuttin'! Back t'ards the mill a liddle. Steady. That'll do ye— 'old 'er there.'

I also had to paint the wagons and carts—bodywork blue, undercarriage red and all iron-work black—or, with a mallet and chisel, knock out the mortices Dad had drilled in wattle-heads, gate-bars or harrow-frames. 'Dun't watch th' end o' th' 'andle where you're 'ittin', boy,' he would say, 'kip y'eye on th' cuttin' edge o' the blade where th' works bein' done.' Or ' 'Old y' chisel this-a-way, look 'ee, then if the mallet wanders y' wun't 'it y' knuckle.'

The advice came in a steady stream. 'Always measure twice an' cut once.' 'Let the saw do th' work—dun't press on it.' I was frequently admonished for interrupting the job in hand to talk and this was never allowed, even to answer a question.

'Come on, boy, get on wi' it. You mus' learn t' whistle an' ride, y'know.' I could hear the words of David and Ben all the time and their ghosts were happy, for it was still their world. Although we were a good twenty years into the new century, here there was a marked reluctance to leave the old.

In that old workshop, where the inside of the door was daubed like an abstract masterpiece into a heavy pastiche of bright colour from years of cleaning brushes, where, although the bench was always kept clear and tidy, the floor was usually ankle deep in chippings and wood-shavings and there was always a smell of paint, linseed oil and the beery tang of fresh-cut, well-seasoned oak, the same old jobs were being done with the same old tools and the same old songs rattled round in the cobwebbed rafters. The teams still plodded past in the road and the wagoners still found time to wave a greeting and we still knocked off for dinner when the church clock struck one.

I have realized since that I was witnessing the last phase in a long, long chapter of human experience. The old ways of life in the country were still undoubtedly alive, but they were slowly and irretrievably dying.

The same old jobs were being done with the same old tools.

Chapter Seven

In a small square just off the High Street stood the village school. Built of flint with brick quoins and Gothic windows, it was identical with those that had sprung up all over the country in the 1870s and 80's as a result of the Education Act. All the heavy doors were fitted with noisy, iron lift-latches purposely designed, it seemed, to prevent any possibility of surreptitious entry by late arrivals, and there was a match-boarded, white-washed austerity about the place that constantly reminded you of the objective of your enforced presence.

To this seat of learning each weekday in term, fifty or sixty village children were summoned by a bell that hung in a small belfry under the apex of one of the gables. We shuffled obdurately into the confines of our respective class-rooms which were heavy with fug, an obnoxious blend of chalk-dust, ink, plasticene, camphorated oil, soiled jerseys and corduroy. In winter this was supplemented to no great advantage by the odour of wet clothes, boots and leather leggings drying round the fire, an Esse, slow-combustion, anthracite stove with mica windows.

Half a dozen or so families of children from outlying farms and the hamlet of Balsdean had distances of up to two and a half miles over open downland to walk each day before lessons began and frequently in winter their morning journey would be into the face of a south-wester blowing straight off the sea with driving, almost horizontal rainstorms. By the time they squelched into school, their shiny wet faces glowing from exertion, they were sodden to the skin and on

these occasions all their outer garments would be peeled off
and draped over chairs and forms near the fire around which
they, too, were allowed to sit, the smaller huddled up in
blankets from the headmaster's house. The smell was
unforgettable.

For the next five long hours, with three short breaks, we
would sit in fours at our desks, those academic anvils upon
which the teachers wrought, with such commendable
persistence, to hammer, twist and bend the crude iron of our
wills into something resembling culture.

We were a motley crowd with the prinked, be-ribboned,
combed and freshly-laundered and the tousle-headed, cut-
knee-ed, acne-ed, runny-nosed and seldom-washed all flung
together. But we formed together in small cliques between
which there was a good deal of rivalry and not a little
antagonism.

Daily we intoned the Lord's Prayer, the Creed, the
alphabet, multiplication tables, vowel sounds and parts of a
pound with ritualistic monotony until by sheer force of
repetition they were imprinted on our minds. Here we learnt
the simple rudiments of how to read, write and reckon, but
the long-suffering teachers had uphill work. They struggled
with dog-eared text-books, faded atlases and endless writings
on black-boards with squeaky chalk. But what chance had
William the Conqueror of holding our interest while Will
the poacher could be seen through the open doorway climbing the steep path up East Hill towards Lustrells Bushes with
his lurcher at heel and his bag of ferrets over his shoulder?
Who wanted to know about emus in Australia while seagulls
swooped across the small rectangular patch of blue sky
visible through the class-room window or hung poised
almost motionless on outstretched pinions like cut-out,
cardboard mobiles. There were so many distractions to
encourage mental absenteeism that I wonder even the basics
were absorbed.

Apart from the odd shaft of sluggish inspiration, I was
remarkably dull at school. On one notable occasion, however,

I soared to unaccustomed heights, I am told, in writing the following succinct, if not strictly accurate, definition of the difference between an island and a lake. 'An island is a piece of land with water all round it and a lake is a piece of land with water in it.' That, I think, must have been my finest hour, but for the better part I drifted along under a heavy, grey cloud of incomprehension. History was an insoluble mystery, arithmetic a series of impossible conundrums and geography as unintelligible as life itself.

Those academic anvils.

The contemporary scene, too, seemed to pass me by. The first I knew about the General Strike of 1926, for instance, was when the headmaster came into the class one afternoon and gravely announced it was all over.

Only during composition and drawing lessons, did I stir from my impenetrable desk-bound lethargy. Juggling with letters, words and sentences brought a faint but positive glimmer of response and when the dusty, wooden models of cones, domes, cylinders and cubes were taken down from the top of the cupboard, where they were usually kept, and arranged for us to draw on the class-room table in an unlikely group like the fallen ruins of some ancient temple. I really came to life. Struggling with a stub of H.B. pencil and an over-worked rubber or, with a camel-hair brush flirting amongst the crimson lake, scarlet, burnt umber, cobalt, Prussian blue and ochre of a paint-box, I became a model of tongue-biting scholastic concentration.

The fact that we somehow managed to pick up a rough and ready sort of education seems, in retrospect, to have been almost incidental. Probably the most important lessons of our schooldays came from meeting the different sorts of characters. The wan and the florid, the raw-boned and obese, the flippant and taciturn, from clench-fisted arrogance to pink-cheeked coquetry, from open-mouthed innocence to slit-eyed cunning.

Over half a century has not erased the pathos in seeing little Gus Hollands struggling to join in at football with the rest of us. Dragging a twisted and wasted leg encased in a heavy caliper, his small, pale face contorted with effort, he would be barged about and bowled over, but always managed the bravest attempts to smile as he picked himself up again. But his fighting spirit at games, like his indomitable spirit to live was, alas, in vain and by the time school-leaving day came round for the rest of us in that same age group, he lay under a small, green mound in the church-yard.

We could laugh, and did in fact, when a beautiful drive off the back foot by 'Tucker' Young sent a cricket ball soaring over the playground wall one day to knock the pipe clean out of old Tom Bennet's mouth as he shuffled quietly down the street.

Then came the time when girls ceased to be just ordinary playmates and were inclined to stand aside instead of joining in playground horseplay. There developed a hitherto un-dreamed of difference that erected barriers of modesty be-tween us and made almost anywhere you happened to grab hold of them seem slightly rude. Suddenly a tendril of hair curling round a delicate ear, a warm look from a pretty eye or an inferred affection from the wrinkling of a tiny nose would be enough to make the skies turn blue, to set the church-bells ringing.

Being part of a small community we also learnt to sink our personal differences in a common cause and take pride in striving for a single aim. When meeting other schools in friendly rivalry on the playing fields with what enthusiasm and zest did we sing,

> Rottingdean boys, Rottingdean boys,
> Eyes like diamonds, teeth like pearls,
> Laced up boots and corduroys,
> You cannot better those Rottingdean boys.

There was a stunted limetree growing in the school playground around which we used to play in those all too infrequent and brief periods of release from the stuffiness and confinement of class. Its blackened trunk provided a post upon which to tether one end of a skipping rope at Easter, a wicket for impromptu cricket in summer and, in partnership with the nearby wall, it became a goalpost for football in winter. Up into its branches at all seasons we climbed to impress the girls, beneath its shade we wooed them with flattery and fruit-gums.

It was gnarled with large, cankerous growths like warts on its trunk and limbs, and its upper branches were trimmed by the south-west wind into a clean-cut line that curved upwards so that most of its growth was on the north-east side and it looked like an inflated tam-o'-shanter worn well over to one side. Its roots erupted here and there through the tarmac which encirled the base of its trunk. It had been flourishing when our parents went to school and it stands there yet, although no longer in the school playground, for the school itself has gone. Each spring large heart-shaped leaves light up the dark tracery of its branches like bright, yellow-green lanterns and although so much that surrounds it and so many who have known it have changed or gone altogether, it lives on.

The fact that we played around the same tree as our fathers and mothers was quite characteristic of village life and the lime tree was not in fact the only feature that had endured since those earlier days. The headmaster Mr 'Joey' Carter had been a young, raven-haired junior teacher then, but in our days, still upright and dignified, he was crowned with an unruly mop of frizzy, white hair through which the light from the window behind, as he sat in semi-silhouette at his elevated headmaster's desk, shone like a luminous halo.

After more than forty years, his was the voice that stilled our wagging tongues in class, his the hand that wielded the corrective cane or administered pats of encouragement upon the heads of the diligent, but it was dismaying to be told, 'You'll never write such a good hand as your father did at your age.'

There were other reminders too. The fly-leaves of books as well as desk-tops bore the names and initials of scholars of our parents' generation and the sand-stone windows and door sills carried the marks where they had sharpened their pocket-knives and slate-pencils.

Nicknames, often handed down from one generation to the next, were almost universally used for boys and it was usually a sign of affection or at least acceptance into a gang. My cousin Charlie was known as Chaulker, which he had inherited from our uncle Charles. Cousin Ron was first Marzi, a contraction of marzipan, and later Wigan. My first nickname was Agony which was my reward for parodying a popular song of the time into 'The Sheik of Agony (Araby)' but afterwards, because of my well-covered frame, I became known as Plumpy. Later still as the puppy fat diminished this was modified to Plunky. Many other nicknames come to mind. Gager, Froggy, Winkie, Sprosser, Preacher, Cokin, Doctor, Goble, Shirt, Shaver, Lebby, Eggle, Skinner, Biddy, Bo and Bummer.

Cricket and football were, of course, the perennials of the playground calendar, but the lesser-known pastimes of our childhood had also changed little from those of forty years before. We whipped our mushroom-shaped 'window-breaker' tops along the deserted, traffic-free roads on our way to school, or played marbles along the gritty roadside verges.

We bowled our hoops with no more serious traffic hazards than the occasional horse-drawn farm wagon or carrier's cart.

Most of the manufactured toys available in shops in nearby Brighton were financially beyond our reach, it is true, but in any event we got quite half the fun from our home-made versions in the making or acquiring of them. Ernie Stenning, the local blacksmith, filled the heart of many a village lad with joy simply by allowing him to take from the heap of scrap-iron and worn-out horse-shoes at the back of the forge a discarded tyre from a plough-wheel to use as a hoop. This would be propelled by applying an even pressure with a stout wirehook on the lower half of the following edge. The friction of the 'slide', as it was called, polished the rim of the hoop to silver and elevated the proud owner to a king of the road with absolute sovereignty over the trundlers of mere wooden hoops.

We got more fun in searching the hedgerows for a growth of elder suitable for a whistle-pipe or pop-gun or a crutch of ash or hazel for a catapult strod than we would have from going to the best shop in town with a pound note. Not that I recall the choice ever having been offered, but I feel, had it come our way, that it would have been spurned out of hand by many of us. 'What th' 'ell d'y' want all that ol' shop tackle for?' we would have said, and I recall quite distinctly that the shop-bought 'cattys' made of cast aluminium and flaunted by one or two of the better-off down-streeters were considered very inferior to our home-made models.

Funnell's Hedge, just east of the village beyond the church, provided much of the raw material for our toys. A straight cut of elder some nine inches long and about three-quarters of an inch across, after the pith had been drawn, could be drilled at intervals along its length and cut obliquely at the thicker end to form a mouth-piece and became, in theory, a whistle-pipe. But usually the music that was eventually coaxed out of the finished instrument fell disappointingly short of Pan's 'native wood-notes wild', which we had had in mind.

On the other hand a similar piece of elder, hollowed but

not drilled, would make an excellent pea-shooter or, with a plunger of cork and cane inserted at one end and a cork in the other, a most effective pop-gun. Similarly any piece of metal tubing with a quarter to half inch bore could be made into a 'tater gun'. The gun was loaded by pressing the muzzle into a potato, swede or mangold and the pellet which remained inside could be ejected with great force by a hefty thrust on the plunger.

Key-guns were also great favourites and were made with a barrel-type key and a sawn-off nail that fitted comfortably inside the barrel. The heads of three or four safety matches would be crumbled from their sticks and loaded into the barrel and the nail inserted. When held by a string tied between the loop handle of the key and the nail-head and swung forcibly so that the head of the nail came into sudden contact with a wall, it would produce a most impressive detonation, sometimes enough to split the key.

After the ages of about seven or eight, we usually left the girls to keep alive the traditional ring-games and apart from one or two perfunctory performances during class-time, 'Sally-go-round-the-sun', 'Oranges and Lemons', 'Poor Mary sits a-weeping' and such were shunned by the boys in favour of ball games in which there was more opportunity to show their prowess.

One of the older of these games was 'Egg-in-the-hole'. A number of holes would be hollowed out of the ground about six inches apart at the base of a wall or fence and one hole would be allotted to each player. There was no limit to the number of players but five or six was the usual number. Then a rubber ball would be bowled from the base line, behind which all the players had to be standing before play commenced, and the player into whose hole the ball fell had to run forward and pick it up while all the others ran off in all directions until he had done so. The player with the ball would then call 'Stop', and the remainder would have to stand still on the spot while the player with the ball threw it with the object of hitting one of them. The player who was aimed at, usually the nearest—but personal likes and dislikes sometimes entered into the choice—would be allowed to take any evasive action with the exception of moving his feet. If he was hit by the ball or moved his feet he would be penalized or if, on the other hand, the thrower failed to hit anyone he was penalized. The forfeit in either case was a small pebble, or 'egg', placed in his hole.

The next stage of the game would be reached when any player had been penalized four times and consequently had four eggs in his hole. He would then be sentenced to stand against the wall and swing his leg while each of the other players in turn would throw the ball from the base line with as much force as he could muster with the professed object of hitting the swinging leg. But in effect the loser became a general Aunt Sally for the rest of the gang. It was a fate we all strove diligently to avoid.

Sometimes on the way to school, I used to pass a lone, dark-clad figure and, if I did, the dreamy, stone-kicking journey between the hedgerows would be touched with drama. He represented all the demon kings, the patch-eyed pirates and blind beggars that had ever come into my early fictional life. He was the embodiment of all the powers of darkness in the world.

The road was very lonely and often he would be the only person I would see. He was a road-mender and would perch on a huge pile of flints at the side of the road under a clump of fir trees, sitting on a folded sack and breaking the flints into more or less uniform sizes with a special hammer. He never gave any indication that he had noticed me passing and there was never the slightest pause in the monotonous beat of his hammer strokes. In all weathers he seemed to be there, sitting huddled over his work clad in a voluminous coat and a shape-less dark felt hat and wearing a pair of goggles with lenses of black, fine-meshed, wire gauze to protect his eyes from the flying shards. The mute, dejected, anonymous figure invoked intense curiosity mingled with fear. I always thought he was blind.

In those days, before the introduction of tar, all the roads in the countryside were macadamized. One day, usually in the back end of the year, the quiet normally deserted road leading from the village past our cottage would suddenly become a scene of bustle and activity. Men with large, bent-tined forks would be spreading the road with broken flints which were then watered by a two-wheeled water cart. This was drawn by a sagging, neglected-looking mare with the improbable name of 'Virgin'. There was a great deal of coming and going of men and horse-drawn tip-carts and cries of 'Whoa!' and 'Mind y' backs!' The ganger, in a shabby, well-weathered bowler, presided over the whole proceedings with all the dignity of a ring-master in top-hat and tails. But the pride of the entire circus was a lumbering iron monster of a steam-roller. Its pistons and all working parts were rustless and gleaming and the brass-work polished to burnished gold by the seldom-idle hands of the proud driver. In a well-washed boiler suit and his cap pulled well down over his fat, red face, he spent all his time, when not actually driving, fussing and cossetting his charge with a long-spouted oil-can and a handful of cotton waste. While a hissing, white, feathery plume above the safety valve proclaimed a 'full head of steam'.

Amid all the commotion and absolutely oblivious, it appeared, of all that was going on around him, sat the road-mender. As mute, as dejected as ever and breaking flints as if there was not another soul around for miles.

It was about this time that I acquired my first bike. It came from the scrap-heap and I could not believe my luck that someone had discarded what I considered to be such a treasure. It was rusty and it rattled. The inner tubes and tyres were perished beyond repair and it had no saddle. I wrapped a piece of corn-sack round the stem and tied it with binder twine, cut off the tyres and rode on the metal rims. At first I was forbidden from riding on the road and travelled only the foot-paths and cart-tracks close to home. The experience can never be forgotten. After a shuddering trip along the grassy lanes, negotiating cart-ruts and avoiding pot-holes, I dismounted quivering from head to foot.

Then came the day when I was first allowed to ride to school. The road surface was hard, rough and unyielding. I pedalled gamely on with the bell ringing constantly from the vibration. The noise of the metal rims running over the flint surface at ten miles an hour can scarcely be imagined. The rural peace was shattered. Horses and cattle shied away from the roadside hedges and dogs started barking three fields away. There were no mudguards and horse dung, with which at that time all roads were liberally scattered, adhered to the rims and was thrown by the back wheel on to the back of my jacket and by the front up into my face, impeding vision and presenting a constant hazard to road safety.

As I approached the road-mender I could see that his face was split into a wide grin and as I drew nearer he pushed his goggles up on to his forehead and slapped his knees with his hands. Then he threw back his head and exploded into wild, uncontrollable laughter. It was the full-blooded, unrestrained laugh of a Sussex workman and he continued to laugh until I was out of ear-shot.

Our relationship improved from that moment. He had become human and was no longer mute, dejected nor anonymous—and certainly not blind.

Chapter Eight

The exhortation carved deeply into the heavy oak lintel of the lychgate and under which we passed so frequently on our enforced visits to church was seldom seen, far less heeded, by us boys in the choir.

> Enter into His gates with thanksgiving
> And into His courts with praise.

We were far more observant of that which appeared under the clock in the Sussex-capped tower, 'Watch for ye know not the hour'.

The exhortation carved deeply into the heavy oak lintel
of the lychgate.

Nonetheless, on a similar principle to 'if you throw enough mud, some will stick', being so regularly bombarded with divine counsel and admonition had some kind of influence on even the most obdurate. None of us, I think, could claim that we were entirely unaffected by the four or five years which was the average term of a boy chorister's service before adolescence robbed him of that angelic treble which, more often that not, belied the thoughts and immediate aims of the singer.

Even during the service, while our nimble descants were dancing arabesques around the plodding old familiar hymn tunes and outstripping the turgid diapason of the organ, some of us at least were still beset with wickedness and trying on several of the seven deadly sins for size. Gluttonizing the wine-gums and pear-drops with which our pockets bulged, envying the freedom of our schoolmates seen through the latticed panes idling the summer morning away, suffering the agonies of confinement only for the pecuniary benefits it offered or entertaining the most un-cherubic thoughts concerning certain well-endowed young ladies in the congregation.

The romance that surrounds the church and its history was enough to capture the imagination of any boy. The very ground on which it stood bore living evidence of great age and the grass between the graves, in summer, wore bright clumps of yellow bird's-foot trefoil, purple patches of wild thyme, lamb's-tongue plantain and moon-daisies—all survivors of the original, indigenous herbage that clothed this little green eminence when the Saxon church, of which the present one mainly of Early English origins is a direct descendant, stood here.

The ancient fabric of the church, too, told its own tale and the reddish discolouration visible on the stone-work of some of the arches and windows inside was caused by the heat of the flames when the church, in which the villagers had taken refuge, was fired by a gang of French pirates in 1377.

The miscellany of ancient gravestones in the churchyard

were rich in drama and romance and we wove lurid tales around the sinister head-stone bearing a skull and cross-bones. What of the poor sailors who were cast up by the unrepentant waves, having perished when their ship foundered off the Isle of Wight in 1878? The fated vessel, H.M.S. *Eurydice*, sank to the sea-bed but the bodies of four of the crew were carried by wind and tide and deposited without ceremony on our foreshore. The ship in full sail is represented on the intricately carved stone erected by the Admiralty to commemorate their deaths. Here was a tale of the sea which rivalled any in our story books at home.

Beneath a flat-topped tomb of flint and sandstone lie the mortal remains of William Savage, 'vicar of this place' from 1569 to 1619, who, legend says, took his flock down to the cliff edge as the Spanish Armada was sailing past up-Channel and, looking out over the threatening waters, bade them fall to their knees and pray for their country's deliverance and the destruction of the foe. To which plea, as we know, there was a swift and effective response. Such tales sharpened our appreciation of history and a deep sense of belonging came from the fact that, according to records, the Rev. Savage had married our ancestors back in 1593.

Our organist and choirmaster, the talented and painstaking Mr Collins, travelled over to the village regularly by bus from Brighton where he kept a small sweet shop. He was, therefore, always well equipped to reward our diligence by dealing out handfuls of toffees to be shared amongst us. But he was not so well suited to admonishing our laxity or unpunctuality. He had a bad stammer which, when he was excited or bad-tempered, robbed him of any air of authority he might otherwise have had and instead of bringing shame and disgrace upon a late arrival his, 'Ah, th-there you are! What t-t-t-t-time d'you c-c-call this?' brought only a chorus of sniggering from the boys already there.

For special occasions like funerals and weddings we were paid an extra two shillings with a further shilling for any anthem we had to learn in addition to the standard hymns.

Once, for the funeral of a local dignitary, we had to learn, 'Crossing the Bar'.

> Sunset and evening star,
> And one clear call for me!
> And may there be no moaning of the bar,
> When I put out to sea . . .

The symbolism of the prospect of death was, of course, quite beyond us and the third line took us no further than someone complaining about the mild and bitter in one of the local pubs. So, to say the least, some of the significance and dignity of the anthem was lost on us.

But on practice night we struggled hard to master the rather difficult score and to help us with the rhythm Mr Collins had brought along a metronome, the like of which we had never in our lives encountered. He explained its use, put it on the seat beside him as he sat at the console, set it in motion and after the introductory chords we launched into the anthem. But the swinging action of the hand and pendulum and its loud 'tock-tock-tock-tock', like some crazy kitchen clock, dominated the scene. It was all too much for us and our singing collapsed into uncontrollable bouts of giggling. Poor Mr Collins was distraught, but his attempts to call us to order only made matters worse. 'B-boys, boys, b-boys,' he cried, 'you must remember that this is a s-s-sad occasion and you must all try to assume a s-s-sol-s-solemn aspect.'

Regular, compulsory church attendance tended to have a mind-dulling effect and the import of the services, however well conducted, was blunted by repetition. In the quiet, reflective pauses a dog barked up at Challenors or a cow could be heard coughing in the stalls that adjoined the churchyard wall. Through the clear glass in the choir window Mrs Marshall could be seen scrubbing the bricks in front of the dairy or scouring out the milk pails with water and silver sand.

The mind wandered and the murmured responses of the

congregation came and went into our deeply divided thoughts like the drowsy, intermittent droning of bees in a field of clover.

'. . . we have erred and strayed from Thy ways like lost sheep . . .'

Mrs Marshall was standing the pails upside down on a long wooden form.

'. . . we have left undone those things which we ought to have done . . .'

She was bringing the wooden butter-churn out into the yard.

'. . . restore Thou, them that are penitent . . .'

Hullo, Charlie Goddens was bringing his team out through the stable door to drink at the water trough.

'. . . that we may hereafter live a godly, righteous and sober . . .'

Here they come stomping and skidding down into the cobbled yard. Violet, Lion, Jim and Traveller.

This schizophrenic acceptance of the secular and sacred worlds and the alternate peeping into first one and then the other was brought to an end by the approach of the second hymn. If it was your turn to pump the organ you would creep as quietly as possible up the creaky-board stairs to where a well-worn wooden lever protruded through a slot in the side-panelling of the organ like a pump handle.

Presently Mr Collins, seated poised for action at the double-keyboard, though out of sight from the one upon whom his instrument depended for the breath of life, tapped smartly on the corner of the panelling with a thin cane which was the signal for the organ-blower to start filling the bellows with air. As this was being done, a wooden pointer on the top of the bellows was slowly raised until it was above a red mark on the wall, below which it must never be allowed to fall on pain of being held responsible for the collapse of the organist's efforts in a sad, sliding glissando of dying discord, calculated to undermine the dignity of the whole proceedings with humour which is as fatal to devotional activity as it is to romance.

Being practically out of sight at the back of the organ loft and protected, as it were, by the swelling strains of both organ and choir, offered an opportunity to indulge in a noisy, lip-smacking, apple-munching session and sometimes, during an interminable psalm or a particularly extended anthem, a crumpled copy of *Treasure Island* might be taken from the jacket pocket to pass the time. Diving headlong into some spine-chilling adventure and carried away to some distant and dangerous situation far removed from church on a Sunday morning, one would leave the pumping to a rather dilatory, subconscious action and this frequently led dangerously close to catastrophe.

Tap-tap-tap-tap-tap! The alarming tattoo of the cane on the corner, like the tapping of the blind man's stick, fetched one back to earth with a bump. The protracted double-fortes of the last verse and gloria had dissipated nearly all the reserves of air in the bellows and only by frantic, handle-rattling efforts with both hands, and with *Treasure Island* hastily discarded to the floor, would the pointer be restored to safety level and the situation—and with it the decorum of the whole service—be saved.

During the sermons many sound foundations for living were laid and much wisdom expounded while we from the elevated vantage-point of the choir gallery, and shamefully unappreciative of what was going on, looked down upon the backs of the congregation as they sat in the rows of wooden pews beneath us.

At Evensong in winter, the tops of their heads were illuminated by the pale yellow light of the sparse electric bulbs in the iron candelabras dangling on long chains from the roof-beams, and we could see all without being seen and were hidden even from the eyes of the parson in the pulpit by a blanket of gloom. As his voice droned on, I would watch the different ways in which some of the congregation beguiled the time. Behind one of the sturdy, Caen-stone pillars Mr Reid sniffed a crafty pinch of snuff, dusting off his cravat with a flick of his fingers and pinching his nostrils to prevent himself from sneezing. Even the demure and devout Miss Field, under cover of dabbing her nose with a white lace handkerchief, popped a surreptitious peppermint into her mouth and in the front pew, under the very nose of the parson himself, young Phillips, home on leave in his smart officer's uniform, held hands with the doctor's daughter behind the erect, black-coated back of her father who sat purposefully between them.

But in spite of all our sins of inattention, gradually, to a greater or lesser extent, the word got through. If a constant drip of water can wear away a stone what chance had our shrimp-shell defences of resisting the flood of oratory, poetry and music of the church and, above all, the great enduring truths it strove to express.

Of all the influences the church had, I think the most potent was the hymn-singing. In those simple, singable melodies I found the same joy that I had known at home in singing the old songs of my grandfather. The same familiarity of style and the same rolling bass harmonies. The manner of singing to which I had been brought up, ever since Grand-dad's deep notes had first rumbled into my heart, obviously owed a great deal to the influences of church music and this was where the church found my vulnerable spot.

Sometimes when torrents of rain lashed the southern windows of the aisle and the great roof-timbers overhead shuddered before the strength of the wind; when mighty seas thundered on to the shore only a few hundred yards away and our hymns for 'those in peril on the deep' were all but lost in the noise of the storm raging outside, I trembled with awe and was consumed with goose-pimpling guilt about my lack of attention to the service. Suddenly I would be aware that I, too, was being watched from on high by an omnipotent and all-seeing eye and hoped that my burst of enthusiasm in singing the last verse of the hymn would be duly noted.

> '. . . Thus ever more shall rise to Thee
> Glad hymns of praise from land and sea.'

The church seemed to be a great leveller between the well-to-do and the cottagers. Here for at least an hour a week all status was set aside and, as he removed his hat and lowered his head in the direction of the archangels Gabriel, Michael and Raphael in the stained-glass altar window, even the humblest parishioner found himself on a moral and spiritual par with his master. Everyone stepped off the ladder of social ascendancy and accepted as one the tonics and remedies for the good life prescribed and dispensed by that accomplished alchemist in the pulpit. There was that kind of unity that prevails at regimental dances or staff dinners when all rank is dropped—but only, of course, for the occasion.

The service over, we filed out to the up-lifting chords of the recessional sharing the same feelings of exhilaration and self-satisfaction that came from having fulfilled one's devotional duties for another week. Outside once again in the open air, our hats were put back on our heads, one by one we climbed back to our respective niches in the ladder and returned, rather thankfully, to normal.

Chapter Nine

Grand-dad had walked slowly and stiffly up the path at the end of the cottages, his heavy boots crunching and shuffling on the gravel and his legs sharing the laborious task with two stout ash walking-sticks which accompanied him wherever he went. Whether he was lying in bed, standing at the sawing horse cutting firewood or sitting down to a meal at table, they were always within arm's reach and not even the shortest walk was attempted without them. He called them his 'wooden legs' and if one of them fell to the floor from the corner of the hearth, where customarily they were propped while he sat in his chair at the fireside, and he was unable to retrieve it even with the crooked handle of its companion, he would holler, 'Come 'ere, master, an' 'and me up my wooden leg, will ye?'

Now he stood at the corner by the lilac bush, leaning slightly forward with his weight equally distributed between his 'wooden' and his natural legs. His trilby hat was set squarely on his head and his white whiskers fringed his chin like a foam of lather as if he had left home in a hurry in the middle of shaving. He wore a white celluloid collar fastened at the throat with a brass-headed stud with no tie, and his eyes, shaded by the brim of his hat, smiled down the garden to where Cousin Ron and I were playing steam ploughing.

We had upended a wooden wheel-barrow so that its legs stuck up in the air and its wheel turned freely. With two equal lengths of thin rope fastened to the hub, one on either side of the spokes and in such a manner that when one was completely wound around the axle, the other was unwound, we were giving a passable imitation of two steam engines pulling a plough back and forth across a field. I would walk backwards away from one side of the barrow, pulling my rope steadily so that the wheel revolved and wound up Ron's rope on the other side. When his rope was all wound, mine, of course, was unwound and then the procedure would be reversed with Ron backing off and me making towards the barrow. This was repeated endlessly turn and turn about with much shuffling of feet on the cinder path and a great deal of hissing and chuff-chuffing until our cheeks glowed red and an excess of moisture dribbled from our chins. Occasionally one of us would signal a halt with a shrill whistle and climb down from the cockpit of his imaginary engine amid clouds of steam to straighten the cable or clean the coulter of the non-existent plough from weeds and chalk. Then, with many shouts of, 'Whoa, there! Easy then, 'old on a bit. That'll do ye. Now then, let 'er 'ave it!' the ploughing would be resumed.

To heighten the illusion of steam, a thin wisp of stinking smoke trailed from a 'winter warmer' we had set on top of one of the barrow-legs. This was a device usually carried about in cold weather, made from an old cocoa-tin perforated to admit the air and suspended on a length of string to induce a draught. In it, a handful of old rags smouldered sullenly or glowed dimly when swung like an incense-burner. It stank to high heaven all the time, but when it was well heated, we held it to warm our hands.

Wise in the ways of country lads, Grand-dad could see instantly that we were steam-ploughing and entered into the spirit of the game at once. 'You cheps got much more to do on that cant?'

'One more went,' said Ron, 'then we can 'itch awf an' call it a day.'

'That's jest right, then,' said the old man, 'Miss Macintosh's got a job for a couple o' good men, if you goo along an' see 'er.' Miss Macintosh was a retired spinster and lived in one of the smart new bungalows.

Then he turned about and shuffled back along the path and we heard him out in the road shouting at Duke whom he had left harnessed to the heavy, farm tip-cart which was his means of transport. 'Git up out o' that, you ol' sod! You'll 'ave young Daisy out 'ere arter you drackly.' Then we saw him pull away seated side-fashion on the near-side shaft while Duke was still munching heartily with a bunch of snapdragons sticking through the bit-rings at the corner of his mouth. To hear Duke called an 'ol' sod' and mother referred to as being young made us laugh all the way along the road to Miss Macintosh's house.

'Please 'm, Gran'pap says you've got a job for us,' said Ron standing cap in hand at the open door.

'Yes,' said the august Miss Macintosh, 'my dear Tibbles has at last reached the age of feline senility and the time has come, I fear, for him to be put gently on the road to a catty heaven. I have asked Mr Kay to arrange for his demise, so will you please be good enough to take him down in this basket and bring his dear body back to be buried in the garden.' As we walked towards the gate she called, 'You will be sure to see that he has a peaceful end, won't you?'

We made our way down to the village, stopping only to skim a few flat flints into 'ducks and drakes' on the pond and throw a stick up into the branches of the tree outside The Plough to knock down one or two conkers, but by the time we reached the shop in the High Street the contents of the basket was mewing rather loudly and making other noises to the intense concern or amusement of passers-by depending on their natures.

While Ron went into the shop I waited outside passing the time by watching my reflection in the shop window and making my face turn different hues by moving it into the sunlight coming from the back of the shop and being reflected in coloured rays through the large, elegant, glass containers full of red, blue and green liquid which stood at the back of the window display. Ron reappeared, 'We've gotta take 'er round the coal-'ouse at the back,' he said.

Presently Mr Kay, peering intently through his rimless glasses as he tested the hypodermic syringe he carried before him to make sure it was fully charged, came smartly into the yard in an aura of brisk professionalism and smelling strongly of iodoform.

'Now, boys', he said, crossing the yard to the coal-house, 'come in here and, Ron, you take the càt out of the basket and hold him tight and you, Bob, shut that door and whatever you do don't open it.' There was no window and after I had carried out the first part of my instructions the only light came through a narrow gap at the top of the door and we were plunged into what at first seemed impenetrable blackness, 'Now, Ron, where are you?'

'Over 'ere,' came Ron's voice from the direction of where I had seen a huge heap of anthracite. I was aware of some fumbling activity going on and could hear Mr Kay breathing rather heavily and muttering to himself.

'Now, have you got him?'

'Yes,' said Ron rather uncertainly.

'Right.'

There was a spine-chilling screech and something flew past my head and landed with a thud on a pile of chopping wood in the opposite corner. 'Blast the boy. You've let him go. Now where is he?' As our eyes grew used to the light we could see Tibbles' bristling form crouching in the corner, his eyes wide with fright. 'Puss, puss, come here, puss,' cooed the would-be executioner stepping forward, tripping over the chopping block and dropping the syringe. 'Damn!' The cat, crazed with only half the lethal dose injected into his blood stream, set up the most blood-curdling screaming and Mr Kay grabbed a bass broom and advanced with it poised above his head ready to strike. 'Keep that door shut, Bob,' he called as he brought it down with a resounding thwack on the woodpile. But the cat had shot like a bullet across to the top of the anthracite and stood there petrified with an arched back and stiff, perpendicular tail, bristling like a bottle-brush.

Thwack! Screech! Thwack! 'Hold that door! Blast the cat! Look out!!'

The air was thick with cat's fur and clouds of coal-dust and something kept whizzing past my head, but whether it was the cat or the broomhead was difficult to say. After a nightmare which seemed to last for hours with the broomhead chasing a flying bundle of bristling fur and sharp claws which ricocheted from wall to wall letting out the most fearful noises, Mr Kay at last delivered the fatal blow. 'Got him,' he hissed through clenched teeth and the dust began to settle.

I opened the door gingerly letting in the daylight and could see the crumpled and inert form of Tibbles who, smothered in coal-dust, had been transformed from a pale marmalade to a smoky black. Mr Kay, too, had lost some of his professional manner and came out into the yard wiping the dust from his spectacles with a pocket handkerchief and blinking in the bright light of the afternoon. Sweat was trickling down his forehead, leaving little crooked trails in the thin film of dust with which his face and bald head were coated. One side of his starched collar had come unfastened at the neck and was sticking out at the side like a finger-post.

We wrapped the mangled corpse in an oil-skin winding-sheet and many layers of brown paper and tied it securely to make sure that the bereaved owner should not view it. Then we made our way, rather solemn and subdued, back up the dusty road with the lifeless parcel in the basket. We had been sworn to utter secrecy about the details of the means by which poor Tibbles had met his fate.

We handed the basket back to Miss Macintosh who took it sadly but serenely with a brave attempt to smile. 'He did have a peaceful end, didn't he?' she enquired.

'Yes, Miss Macintosh,' we carolled, and I fingered the shiny sixpence in my trouser pocket which was my share of the price of our silence. Soon four, large, brown pennies had joined it as the reward for carrying out the fateful errand so successfully and although we shared a dreadful guilty secret, we were rich and walked back home feeling like millionaires.

Chapter Ten

Mother was born and bred in the heart of London and I sometimes wondered what she thought of the simple, rustic life into which matrimony had led her. For, although her childhood and married homes shared the common denominator of poverty, there was a great deal of difference between being poor in town and being poor in the country. She was born, I believe, in Fulham, but later moved to Chelsea where her mother, Granny Clark, still lived when my sister and I were small.

On our infrequent visits to London as a family, Dad was always at pains to point out all the sights and wonders of the metropolis. He pointed out one day the Houses of Parliament and other landmarks of Parliament Square and I asked, 'Is this Miswenster, then, Dad?'

'Yes,' he replied, an' that,' indicating the world famous clock, 'is Miss Wenster's Benny.'

But no trip to town would have been complete without a visit to Granny Clark's. She occupied a ground-floor and basement apartment in Arthur Street, a narrow, grey street of terraced houses with street-doors of bewildering similarity which opened hard on to the pavement. Through the door of No. 101 you walked into a dimly-lit passage at the end of which a narrow staircase led down into the basement. As you entered, you were greeted with the homely scents of baking cakes and well-cooked cabbage and when Granny lifted you up towards her bristling chin to administer a welcoming kiss and clasp you to her ample and loving bosom, there was a curious smell of bread and butter and a distinct danger of being impaled on the pin of an immense silver brooch which fastened a black woollen shawl about her drooping shoulders.

Poor Granny didn't have far to lift us for she was permanently bent forward from the hips like a jack-knife due, we were told, to 'hard work, worry and old age' and she was condemned to go through her later life in a stooping position. She was a big woman but her features were small and even, and it was not difficult to see that she had once been a tall and very handsome woman. Her voice was low and rather cracked which was also, one imagined, the legacy of age but her disposition was gentle and kindly and her round face with its bright blue eyes, retroussé nose and smiling mouth could have been caricatured in a series of small circles enclosed in a larger one.

Down in the basement there was a heavy, cast-iron mangle with huge wooden rollers and a screw to adjust the pressure with a handle in the shape of a cross sitting on top of its rounded shoulders like a weather-vane. When not in use, it was draped with an old chenille table-cloth and its overall shape was not unlike the stooping figure of poor Granny viewed at boy-level from behind. There was also, standing

Down in the basement there was a heavy cast-iron mangle.

on a high shelf well out of reach, a much-coveted ornament of gilded brass, representing a bicycle the wheel-rims of which encompassed a clock and a barometer respectively and the handle-bars, mounted on a central pivot, were capable of being turned.

From an area at the back, three or four steps led up into a small garden hemmed in by a wall of soot-grimed bricks with a pallid lawn of debilitated grass not much bigger than a hearth rug. Over in one corner, by the outside privy with the saw-toothed ventilation holes in the top edge of the door, a stunted sumac, with true cockney determination, managed to suck enough nourishment from the exhausted loam to foliate its twisted, black branches and in rare moments, when the autumn sunshine pierced the smoke-pall overhead at just the right time of day and found its way down between the rooftops and chimney-stacks, the scarlet, crimson and orange leaves were touched with flame and turned into living fire.

But in spite of these rare moments of beauty and all the kindness and affection showered upon us at Granny's house, the impression of London as a whole was one of bewilderment and apprehension. It was all so claustrophobic, noisy and smelly and although Granny's stories of when she was young held us spellbound, they were seldom amusing. She told of the old women who used to meet each morning in the beer shops and sit 'doing the vegetables for dinner' in colanders or pudding basins on their laps while they sipped their glasses of porter. We heard of little girls 'with no shoes nor stockings to their feet' made to stand at street corners selling boxes of matches or bootlaces; of boys with flaming torches who, for a consideration, would guide the gentry to their homes through fogs 'as thick as a bowl of pea-soup that made you cough and spit up blood', also of crossing-sweepers who swept the horse-dung and bus-tickets from the paths of the well-to-do as they crossed the road and, most harrowing of all probably through pitying self-identification, of 'little shavers of boys who were forced to shin up inside the chimbleys of rich men's houses to fetch down the soot'.

Granny had graphic memories of Dickensian London but, alas, I realize their worth only now. I have since read about the literary cliques of the Chelsea of that time but if only I had listened more attentively I might have learnt a good deal more about the other side of the coin. While the Carlyles, Leigh Hunts and Rossettis were clip-clopping out in their broughams and the drawing rooms of Cheyne Row and Tite Street were loud with literary and artistic discussion, Granny was being brought up in the back streets, working in the basements and learning about life on the other side of the green baize door that separated a gentleman and his family from the servants.

But through her I learnt, at least, something of the indomitable spirit of the working-class women of those days who, with a scrubbing-brush in one hand and a Prayer Book in the other, struggled to keep their standards above that seamy side of life which was reported so luridly each week in *Lloyd's Weekly* and *Reynolds' Sunday News*. They were fiercely proud of their honesty and utterly scrupulous in money matters and cleanliness and, with the work-house doors always waiting to gobble up the failures, managed on a shoe-string to bring up their families honourably and to pass on the Londoner's heritage—an irrepressible sense of humour.

My grandfather on Mother's side had died before my arrival on the family scene but, if the snippets of talk picked up by the sharp ears of a little boy can be believed, he was something of an ogre who squandered an inventive genius and his considerable skills in the art of dyeing—to say nothing of the meagre family income—in bouts of drunkenness. Granny was therefore left pretty much alone to shoulder the burden of bringing up her family of four—two girls and two boys—and my mother, who was the eldest by several years, fell into the role of 'little mother' while Granny was out at work 'doing for' several ladies at different big houses and bringing home washing.

Mother could tell tear-inducing stories of having to nurse her younger sister and brothers when they were sick or of walking up to the butchers' shops in North End Road or at 'World's End' where, at ten o'clock on a Saturday night, they would be selling off meat cheap before closing down for the weekend. This was, of course, before the days of refrigerators and cold-rooms, when meat had to be sold cheaply rather than stored and here she would buy 'a scrag-end and three penn'orth o' pieces' which would have to see them through the week.

Her part of Chelsea was far removed from the elite colony of artists and writers near the Embankment and as far, also, from the fashion and bustle of King's Road. Few organ-grinders or German bands brought the joy of their music into the quiet back-waters of the poor and a trip to see the horse-buses trundling by briskly in the main streets or to stand at the bottom of the steps of Chelsea Town Hall to watch the ladies in all their finery, and their gentlemen escorts in toppers and tails, emerging from hansom cabs to attend a ball was like seeing something out of a fairy tale. They swished past in their long, colourful gowns, picture hats and feather boas, leaving on the air behind them a trail of exotic perfume, and as they went in through the swing doors and the dazzling lights from the chandeliers sparkled on their jewellery they little thought of the effect they were having on the eyes and heart of a small, pale-faced girl standing outside in the shadows.

From such a background at the age of about fourteen, Daisy, my mother, was sent out to work and, like so many girls of her class and generation, she was immediately swallowed up in the deep waters of discipline and drudgery in one of the big houses of the gentry. It seemed, as she was telling us, a story of unspeakable hardship commensurate almost with the middle ages. Here she received a nominal yearly wage of £9, regular meals and a clean bed in a garret shared with other girls. In return she was expected to scuttle about from one job to another from dawn until dusk. From cleaning out the ashes, laying and lighting fires before six in the morning, to washing and scouring greasy pots and pans after dinner at night. With only a short break in the afternoon, there was a never-ending succession of chores. Blacking grates, whitening hearth-stones, carrying coal from the cellar up the back stairs to fires on all floors, scrubbing, polishing and doing all the unpleasant jobs in a big house that were passed on down the ladder of seniority till at last they reached the one person who was not able to delegate. The 'tweeny' was a maid of all work and at the constant beck and call of each and every other member of the household staff. She stood at the toe of that unwieldy upturned triangle of organization which was the strictly observed hierarchy of life in domestic service.

Discipline was strict and leisure practically non-existent, but for an hour in the afternoon she would go to sit on the thin, straw mattress on the iron bedstead which was her only personal refuge. There she would reflect and compare the warm intimacy and laughter of life back in her poor home in Arthur Street with the regimented, insignificant role she played in this great opulent house. She would think of her young sister and brothers skipping and playing hop-scotch on the dusty pavements and could hear again the clanking of cog-wheels and the creaking strain of wooden rollers as she turned the handle of the old mangle for her mother down in the basement and recalled the warm, clean steam rising from the ironing-board and the smell of hot metal as the flat-irons were re-heated on the trivet in front of the kitchen range. Her life was one of unremitting drudgery, but unhappy and homesick as she was, she at least had the consolation of knowing she was self-supporting and no longer a drain on the home economy.

In the next few years, serving as kitchen-maid, parlour-maid and house-maid, and changing households whenever a chance of advancement offered itself, she worked in various parts of London, then went down to Ongar in Essex and finally, on the staff of Sir Thomas Leonard, she came to Woodingdean House, a mere mile away from the home of the lusty young carter who was eventually to become her spouse, and where she was to spend practically all the rest of her life.

Domestic service was the proving-ground for so many working-class girls in those days, and the disciplines to which they had been subjected remained with them in two forms. Firstly they applied them to their own homes and families and, in addition, they were themselves rigid self-disciplinarians to the unquestionable advantage of the whole household. Their trained knowledge in cooking, hygiene and house-management was the basis of many a well-run and happy home and I think that those who regret the lives now of the unliberated women of those times often overlook the fact that a great number of housewives and mothers were contented women and in fact proud to be the undisputed queens of their own domains.

The ameliorating influence of a good woman in the home was probably far stronger and perhaps more necessary then. Men working in conditions which today would be regarded as primitive tended to be coarser and rougher than their present day counterparts, and a woman played a very significant part in keeping up the level of moral and physical well-being. It was her hand that stirred the cooking-pot or soothed the fevered brow in sickness, for she was an encyclopaedia of simple remedies and cures and used to say, 'you are either your own physician or a fool at forty'. Mother it was who insisted on grace before meals and led the hymn-singing round the fire on Sunday evenings. She made the cottage into a home and consequently was given all the respect that her position commanded. It would be a mistake to think of her as down-trodden or under-privileged. The question of sex-equality never cropped up. Man and wife were complementary to each other and there was not the slightest suggestion of the competitive element that the aim for 'equality' implies.

Since that time there has been a revolution in the roles of the sexes. At the touch of a switch or the twist of a tap we can now obtain instantly those daily needs which once demanded the laborious hewing of wood or winding of well-handles. Slowly, insidiously, this elimination of manual effort has eroded our natural physical toughness and the gap between the sexes is gradually closing. But, whatever they may have gained, women have surrendered much of the dignity and respect they once commanded in the home.

Mother, then, was the hub of the home and even if there was a certain repetitive pattern in the weekly rote, the standards were meticulously maintained. At Northgate, each day brought its own jobs and, to a large extent, its own midday meal, and you could tell the day of the week by what you had for dinner. Sunday: Chop wood for week. Boiled sausages for breakfast. Roast for dinner. Monday: Washing day. Cold meat. Tuesday: Dry mangling and ironing. Various—probably rabbit. Wednesday: Clean downstairs rooms and windows. Hash. Thursday: Clean bedrooms and windows. Various—probably rabbit. Friday: Clean stairs and landing. Fish (or rabbit). Saturday: Scrub outside bricks, dunnikin and drains. Steak and kidney pudding. The evening meal for the children was invariably bread and cheese and cocoa.

This pattern was continued on broad lines for many years even after mother was crippled with arthritis and Dad, than whom no one less suited to housework could possibly be imagined, was obliged to give considerable help in the home. In a burst of man-to-man confidence, he once said to me, 'I dunno, boy, I'd rather build a wut (oat) stack or pitch a fold f' five 'unnerd ship (sheep) than do them bloody bedrooms out of a Thursday.' Then, fearful lest his loyalty should be thought in doubt, added, 'But dun't you let on, look.'

Chapter Eleven

A great deal of the charm and beauty of the English land-scape stems from the fact that it is so unnatural. The rural scene, of which many of us get but a blurred and fleeting vision as we spin along in our tiny, shiny metal boxes insulated from the wind and rain, the scent of the honeysuckle and the wild cry of the birds, is almost as far removed from nature as we are ourselves.

The orderliness and discipline of well-farmed land is in direct contrast with what nature intended and what we have come to accept as the normal countryside is really the result of man's continued efforts to bend the stubborn will of the land to serve his own purposes.

The waving fields of East Anglia, the broad, flat areas of rich loam in the fenlands, the deep, lush pastures of the home counties and the bare, sheep-cropped slopes on the chalk downs of the south have all changed beyond recognition since the third day of Creation. As man has striven to do as he was bid on the sixth day 'to replenish the earth and subdue it', they have been claimed, after centuries of careful planning and hard work, from the wildernesses of rank grass and scrub, the stinking marshes and overgrown forests which prevailed when nature had all her own way.

This little island has been so intensively cultivated for so long that we are apt to think that it always has been so. But the old country gardener was probably wiser than he realized when approached by the parson who, looking over his garden wall one day, said, 'You and the good Lord have made a capital job of your garden this year, George.'

'Ya-as,' replied the old man, 'You ought to 'a' sin it when 'e 'ad it to 'issalf.'

There is a deep-seated sense of satisfaction in looking at an area of land producing rich crops or supporting a high concentration of sheep or cattle as the direct result of centuries of good husbandry. It is the satisfaction of achievement and of having reached at least a working agreement with nature who, perversely, serves only those who are her slaves.

In the Rottingdean area, the farmer, in addition to all the usual hazards, has had to cope with difficulties peculiar to the district. The land is generally poor, and the shallowness of the mantle of soil can be seen from the foreshore to which the sheer, white cliffs plunge from heights of up to a hundred feet. Topping the solid calcareous mass is a mere foot or so of soil which, together with erosion from the sea, has posed considerable problems for the farmers of many centuries.

In 1340 the inhabitants, appealing against a tax, stated that since 1292 fifty acres of arable land in the parish had been destroyed by the sea; a further 240 acres were lying idle 'by reason of the poor quality of the land and the inability of those who used to cultivate it'.

Until the more general use of artificial fertilizers, farming in an area such as this was unthinkable without sheep. 'Fallow, fold and plough' was the creed by which the farmer lived and this system of rotation was known locally as 'the four-course shift'. I am indebted to Mr David Thompson for the following notes which he took down as Dad explained the manner in which it worked.

1st year   Fallow—bare—oat stubble. Rough it up with plough—left all winter. Start stirring in April opposite way. Then do him cornerways. Four times in all. Dress with goanna and ground bone. Then in May to end of June sow RAPE. In September/October fold it off for flocks. A flock of 450 sheep will eat one acre in four nights. Fold it off as they eat it in cants (strips). Follow up with plough and sow WHEAT as the sheep move on. In period from 2 weeks before Christmas and four weeks after, no sowing—So flocks would be 6 weeks ahead of us by February.

2nd year   WHEAT CROP—lay fallow all winter.

3rd year   April sow clover, trefoil and crop grass for haystacks and 'grattens' for sheep feed. Cut clover 1st crop. Second crop, let sheep on it. Plough it up in autumn, press and leave till Valentines Day and start OAT sowing.

4th year   OAT CROP.
(Now I've seen wheat 3 years running and they seem to get rather more than we did. I've thrashed it. It must be the artificials.)
Notes made 1951.

That, of course, was the rotation of crops for one field and it was necessary to have at least four fields with the system staggered at yearly intervals to maintain a continuous cycle. At Rottingdean there were a thousand acres of arable land divided into fields, or laines as they are called in Sussex, and to keep this system in constant operation in addition to root crops for cattle, green meat for horses and the like meant that Dad spent a lot of his time on the hills watching the results of past experiments, supervising work in hand and planning for seasons yet to come.

During the war the Government had requisitioned nine of the farm's thirty horses including the cob on which Dad had ridden on his daily rounds. This left him with no option but to go on 'Walker's wagon', so stout boots and a stick were essential parts of his work-a-day equipment.

Part of each day, regardless of weather, was spent walking round, deciding when to dress this field with lime, when to plough that, when and where to fold the sheep and when to put the binders in to cut the corn. As I got older, I was taken along as a very junior assistant, and as he strode along I trailed along behind him like a dog. Struggling over the deep, cledgy furrows of a new-turned field, swishing through the early dew-wet grasses till my toes squelched inside my socks or leaning into the wind with the rain dripping off nose and chin and glad when he paused in the 'lew' of a hedge or haystack to light a cigarette.

I said, like a dog. In fact some of the jobs I had to do involved detours of up to half a mile and I could have used another pair of legs. 'Nip over there and close that gate, boy'—'Goo an' see if that stop-cock is workin' in that drinking trough. It got 'ung up laas' wik an' they went middlin' thirsty for a couple o' days'—'Take my jack-knife, look'ee, an' knock that gurt 'og-weed arse-over-'ead yonder, afore 'e runs t' seed.'

But I was not treated like a dog. Nearly all the time we walked Dad would be talking and, in many ways, he treated me as an equal. Sometimes, rather puzzlingly, even in age. 'You remember ol' 'Atchy Welfare, dun't ye, down th' White 'Oss? No? 'Ow old be ye now, then? Ten! Oh wal, o' course you wouldn't. Bugger, 'e died when I was still at school!'

In this way we spent a lot of time together and without knowing it were laying the firm foundations of a very fond and life-long friendship with a deep understanding which is precious between father and son.

In the middle of the night when I was twelve he fetched me out of bed to go with him to the cowsheds at Challenor's to hold the lantern while he assisted with a difficult breach delivery. With an oilskin over my pyjamas and bare feet inside unlaced, cold leather boots, I shuffled down the road at his side, head bent into the rain, swinging the lantern and watching the shadows of my legs growing from the roadway up and out into the great outer darkness like huge, tapering tree trunks. They went sliding behind us in a crazy, nightmare sequence that never seemed to get them anywhere and with sleep still very heavy upon me it was difficult to grasp the realities of the scene.

In the warm cattle shed, sweet with hay and that peculiar aroma inseparable from bovine stock, I watched him sweat and tug in the shifting orange light. Man and beast working together desperately. Sweating, grunting, struggling towards the same end—to assist nature and bring another life into the world. And presently when the new calf, wet and bedraggled, stood unsteadily on legs splayed out like broomsticks and blinked its large bewildered eyes at the lantern flame, the suspense, the wonder and awe of it all were suddenly flecked with humour and I thought of the playground definition of a cow, 'Two lookers, two pookers, four stand-stickers, four dilly-danglers and a swish-about'.

We have been together on Telscombe Tye standing in bright early morning sunlight while the valley beneath us was filled with a thick, white, ground-hugging mist which drifted slowly down and out to sea like cream being poured from a shallow bowl.

One late afternoon in October up at Shepherd's Acre, the gossamer lay so thick on the grass that it reflected the glow of the setting sun like water. A glittering, golden path of light led from our feet down across the hill to the cliff edge and was continued unbroken over the surface of the sea to the far western horizon behind which the sun was about to sink.

We have looked across the hills and seen in the far distance a vast flock of starlings swirling, swelling and contracting in a shapeless, volatile mass like an erratic storm cloud. We have watched a brazen December sun come creeping up out of a sea of glass and its top half slide behind a bar of solid black cloud so that as the bottom edge was poised on the horizon, it was cut in half and reflected in the mirror of the water like an hour-glass of gold.

Dad was never too busy or preoccupied with work to stop and point out the wonders of the downland he loved. He pointed the diaphanous, white-plumed moths that danced amid the tall grasses of summer like out-of-season snow-flakes. But he didn't tell me their name. Somebody once told me that they were 'pterophorus ptilodactylus' and I immediately tried hard to forget. What a ridiculously clumsy, earth-bound and complicated name for these delicate, ethereal creatures that for a fleeting hour or two in July make the meadows such a delight.

He told me why the horse-chestnut is so called and showed me the horseshoe, complete with nail-holes, that is left on the bark when the stalk of a leaf has been removed. He delved into the white froth of the 'cuckoo spit' clinging to the bents of tall grasses and showed me the pale, gleaming yellowy-green larvae of the frog-hopper which it protected.

He pointed out the serrated edges of the five sepals of the dog-rose and how two were ragged on each side, two were smooth and one was ragged on one side and smooth on the other. Dad used to quote:

> There once were brethren five,
> By two full beards were worn,
> Another two were hairless
> As the day that they were born.
>
> The fifth not wishing to offend
> His shorn or bearded brother
> Wore whiskers one side of his face
> And was shaven on the other.

He had the knack of driving home a point with a practical demonstration which ensured that it was never forgotten. 'What d'you think that is, then?' he asked one day as we passed a clump of 'keck'-like flowers on the bankside.

'Looks loike yaller keow-paarsley, t'me,' I said, for this was before the spanner of necessity had tightened up my vowels for job-hunting in London in the '30's.

'Pull a plant up an' bring it 'ere t' me.' He took his knife, topped and tailed the root, scraped it clean and passed it back. 'Taste that an' then you'll know what it is.'

'Tastes loike paarsnip,' I said.

'Yeah, would do—that's what it is, wild parsnip, an' don't let me 'ear y' call it "yaller keow-paarsley" n'more.'

He taught me that the corn-bunting was a 'cloddy-bird'

and the kestrel was a 'wind-hover'—to rhyme with plover—
where the carrion crows, peewits and barn owls nested,
where 'rams-horns' and bee-orchids grew, where mushrooms
could be gathered, how to set a hare or rabbit snare, catch
birds with bird-lime or clap-net, and also how to avoid being
caught poaching.

*　　*　　*

'Stay a bit!' Dad's arm shot abruptly across in front of me,
bringing me to such a sudden and unexpected halt that my
feet squelched up inside the toe-caps of my sodden boots and
the weight of the heavy sack on my shoulder almost pitched
me forward. There was something in his tone which spelt
emergency and his voice exploded like a rocket into the
gloomy mood of abstraction which had gradually settled
upon me as we had trudged the last two miles down towards
home.

Actually, since conversation lagged, my thoughts had been
progressively outstripping my legs and at that moment were
at least five minutes ahead of us sitting comfortably in the
snug warmth of the kitchen savouring the hot meal I knew
would be set before us when we arrived. But the interjection
snatched me back to reality with a jolt.

We had been rabbiting up in Pardale bushes since midday.
The fine, drizzling rain in which we had set off, and which
had settled on the top of Dad's cap and the shoulders of his
coarse, tweed jacket, as we used to say 'like fog on a dog-
turd', had stopped halfway through the afternoon. The wind
had veered to north-east, the sky had cleared and now, as the
sun slid down behind a Venetian blind of cloud-bars well out
to sea, there was a strong hint of hard frost. It was pretty
obviously going to 'turn round and freeze' and the edges of
some of the muddy puddles in the cart-ruts were already
beginning to solidify into a filigree of ice-film.

It had been a good day. The ferrets had worked hard, the
rabbits had bolted well and the nets had closed fast and tight,
and eight good dinners, plump and well-fed off the corn-

stubbles, were swinging on a short length of rope from Dad's shoulder. Curled up in the corner of the capacious inside pocket of his jacket which extended from the front-fastening to the vent at the back, the two ferrets were enjoying a well-earned rest and nibbling the crumbled biscuit he dropped in for them from time to time. I was carrying the nets in a sack and a small spade which was sometimes necessary to dig out a ferret that had 'laid up' in one of the 'buries' with a rabbit it had killed.

'Th' ol' dog's on t' summat, look.' Bingo had been trotting ahead wet and bedraggled, his legs and lower half stained brown and 'slubbed up' with soil. With his head erect, he had been wearing an expression which was as near to a human smile of satisfaction as the canine countenance can get. But he suddenly stopped in his tracks with his ears pricked forward and the rumbling suspicion of a growl in his throat. 'What is it, then, mairt?' asked Dad.

The answer came from an elder bush about two hundred yards ahead where the track we were on joined the road that led past the cottage and across which we would have to go to reach the garden gate. The daylight was fading, but vision at this point was assisted by a street lamp, the last one on the road out of the village, and Dad's keen eyes had seen a faint spiral of tobacco smoke curl up and go swirling away on the wind.

'That'll be ol' Tom Tunnel waitin' for us t' get on the main road. 'E can't touch us while we're still on farm land, look.'

Tom was the local constable and the anomalistic situation of Dad being exposed to the risk of being caught poaching on the land of which he was bailiff had arisen from the fact that 'the Guv'nor' had been so tormented by loafers and lay-abouts from nearby Brighton leaving gates open and tramp-ling crops in their search for rabbits, linnets, mushrooms, cornflowers, moss or anything which could earn them a sharp shilling, that he had clamped down hard on trespassers and stipulated that no game should be taken from his land by anyone at all, not even farm employees, and had notified the police to this effect.

This was a bitter blow to Dad whose chief form of relaxation was to be out on the hills with a dog, a couple of ferrets, a gun or various nets and snares in pursuit of 'flick or feather' as he put it. There never was a keener sportsman. Who else would have taken his brother on his honeymoon so that he would have a mate to join him when he went rabbiting?

We withdrew into the bushes at the side of the track, but we knew that Tom had seen us. He had probably been watching our progress down the curving, mile-long track all the way from High Barn. Now the tricky thing was that he had no power to stop us until we were on the highway. While we were on the track, he had no powers of search. We stowed the nets and spade under the hedge as Dad outlined our plan of action. I was to walk slowly down the track, across the road and into the garden, affecting complete oblivion of the presence of the constable. This would claim Tom's attention while Dad, hidden by the bushes, crept along in the field that ran down to the road right opposite our garden.

I walked on down and when I passed the camouflage from which I knew I was being so closely observed, I could feel Tom's eyes running over me and through me like gimlets. I pretended I was unaware of his presence and crossing the road walked in through the garden gate with as much composure as I could muster and took up my position for the second part of the plan.

Tom, hunched up in his little bush and enshrined like a Jack-in-the-green, waited patiently for Dad to appear. His vantage point was a good one for, whichever means Dad might use to reach the main road, he would be visible in the light of the street lamp as he crossed to go into the garden. Then Tom could pounce with all the weight of the law behind him. But Dad at that moment was in the field immediately opposite me and as well as being just outside the ring of light thrown by the lamp was also screened from Tom's view by a couple of bushes.

Presently I heard the prearranged signal, a soft, low whistle not unlike the mating call of the tawny owl, and knowing what it presaged, I waited expectantly looking up into the sky. Suddenly a rabbit came hurtling down through the air slightly over to my right. I made an energetic effort to catch it but it passed over my head and fell with a dull thud smack in the middle of the sprout patch.

Tom must have thought the owl was in a particularly amorous mood that night for at about ten-second intervals the remainder of the day's catch followed the first, each one preceded by the soft, low whistle which signalled take-off. As my eyes grew accustomed to the darkness and Dad's aim improved I caught each one as it came flying down out of the night sky.

I took them indoors and laid them in a row on the brick floor of the scullery while Bingo lay in front guarding them with proprietory zeal, his nose pressed to the floor between his front paws and his eyes watching intently whenever any-one approached. From now on, Dad would be the only person allowed to go near them.

Out of the front-room window a little later I watched Dad come down the track. He walked boldly into the lamp-light blatantly empty-handed and flaunting his righteousness like a guest at a vicarage tea-party. If I had never seen a happy man before, I saw one then. He was joyful, he was jubilant and he was also in full voice,

> Oh the echoing horn sounds well in the morn
> To call the brave sportsmen away . . .

As he emerged on to the main road, he turned his head towards the elder bush, 'Goodnight, Tom,' he called.

The bush replied, feebly, 'Goodnight, Jim.'

Chapter Twelve

For all that he was steeped in tradition and a great champion of the old times, the old timers and their ways of life—particularly their singing—it would be wrong to imagine that Dad had in any sense the stick-in-the-mud mentality so often attributed to the countryman by those who know no better. He was in many ways progressive, had a lively imagination and his practical approach to life was revealed by a keen and enquiring observation of everyday things to which most people would not give a second thought.

There is a narrow passage or twitten running parallel with the village High Street which separates the gardens and grounds of a long-established and well-known preparatory school from its playing-field. It is some two hundred yards long and flanked on one side by a flint wall about seven feet high and on the other by a euonymus hedge of the same height. Its original purpose is rather obscure, but it is undoubtedly a public right of way although used by only a small proportion of the local population.

I personally recall using it to any real advantage only when on the sick-list and drawing benefits from Slate and Tontine Clubs run by the various local pubs. The rules of these estimable societies stated that beneficiaries should be home in their places of residence not later than 8 p.m. and by running the gauntlet up the main street after that time one would be almost certain to invite a report on one's late night activities by some zealous committee-man which would result in a 'termination of benefits'. So the passage offered a covert means of walking from the main road at the southern part of the village to Northgate where we lived.

It was also used extensively by courting couples, particularly on dark winter evenings when their clandestine relationships blossomed in its dark, protective shadows. Furtive carriers of sacks containing articles of doubtful ownership, too, sometimes slunk up its narrow length rather than subject their suspicious burdens to the public scrutiny they would almost surely attract in the street and this last might conceivably account for the fact that Dad from years of habit preferred the passage to the more exposed route up the street. On the other hand perhaps it would be more charitable, as well as quite true, to say that being an objective man he preferred the expeditious walk up the passage to the gossip-interrupted journey through the centre of the village, stopping every few yards to pass the time of day with the many folk he would be bound to meet on the way.

Whatever the reason, however, he was on intimate terms with Backway, as we called it, and had walked it quite as many times if not more than he had the village street. As a boy he had watched the wall being built and the hedge laid. There were also several trees planted at the same time and he recalled that they had almost all perished, but the stakes to which they had been tied took root and grew into the trees we see today.

'The cheapest is prit'near always dearest in the long run,' he said one day as we walked along the narrow pathway. 'You'd better believe it, boy. I bet when ol' Stanford built this wall on this side, 'e thought 'e'd be savin' money by layin' a 'edge on t'other. Wal, it might 'a' saved 'im a bob or two in the fust place but it's cost someone a 'elluva lot o' money ever since—an' will do all the time it's there. Let's work it out.'

Then he went through a series of mental calculations voicing them aloud as we walked on. 'Now I reck'n one skilled man an' a labourer wouldn' 'ave no trouble buildin' this wall in three months an' say the brickl'er's money was seventeen bob a wik an' 'is labourer thirteen, that's thirty bob a wik all in f' twalve wiks. So that'd be eighteen f' labour. Material? Wal, youd'a got the flints off th' 'ill, the sand off the foreshore an' you'd 'ave t' pay ol' Ralph Cheal f' cartin' of it, an' all you'd 'ave t' buy was a bag or two o' lime. Then there 'd be beer f' the brickl'er an' his mate, say four quarts a day at fo'pence a quart, that's four pound sixteen shillings f' the twalve wiks.

'Let's see, 'ow far we got? That's eighteen pound f' labour, say two pounds f' lime, five pounds at the outside f' carterage, four pound sixteen shillin's f' beer—so, even if you give th' beer-boy a copper or two, you'd still get some change out o' thirty quid.

'Now the 'edge wouldn' a' cost anything to start with but it's in the trimmin' of it where the cost comes in. There's a good wik's work f' one man to trim this 'edge both sides with 'and shears, an' it would want doin' three times a year, so that's three wiks work every year. Now, f' the sake of an argument let's take the thirty years from 1900. Wages 'ave changed a lot in that time, o' course, so let's take it in ten year spans.

'From 1900 till 1910 'd be thirty wiks work at, say, fifteen bob a wik—that's twenty-two pound ten. 1910 to 1920 at thirty bob a wik is forty-five pound. 1920 to 1930 at two pun'ten a wik is seventy-five pound. See, you've already spent over £140 an' th' Lord above knows 'ow much more it will cost before y' finished.'

It was certainly food for thought. The hedge is still there and I think even Dad would be surprised to know that his theory shows the following trends since then.

1930–1940	30 weeks at	£3.10s. a week		£105
1940–1950	„	£7.0	„	£210
1950–1960	„	£12.0	„	£360
1960–1970	„	£15	„	£450
1970–1975	15 weeks	£20	„	£300
				£1,425

Add to this the £142.10s. up to 1930 and we find that the hedge has so far cost over £1,500 to maintain against the cost of the wall at less than £30.

These are the sorts of things that made a walk with Dad so interesting. There was always plenty to think about. Tales, legends, experiences and opinions illumined the way. He knew his native countryside so well that almost every stick and stone, every bush and bank held a memory for him.

'What's that clump of bushes over there?'

'Coombe Bottom. Yeah, that's where ol' Bung Dudeney fell asleep arter dinner one day when 'e was trussin' straw. Prit'near boozed 'e was, an' 'is clay pipe fell out o' 'is mouth an' set th' straw on light. Burnt the barn, the outbuildin's, the lot right down t' the ground, it did.'

When we were walking, it was almost as if the rhythmic motion of his feet set in motion a process of reflective thought. As soon as we had climbed the hill away from the cottage, left the last of the houses behind us and had settled down to the pace of his long, raking strides, he would start talking. His style was divertive and, although physically striding forward with great purpose, he would meander leisurely up the path of a story, turning aside frequently as the mention of a name or the sight of a bird or flower whisked him away on to another track of thought. Like this, we travelled through a maze of ramifications to reach the end of a tale which might sometimes have seemed hardly worth the journey had the digressions not been so entertaining.

'I see ol' "Steady's" bin busy cuttin' that fourteen-acre piece o' 'ay over there. If th' weather 'olds 'e'll 'ave enough there t'see 'im right through th' winter.' We were looking across the valley to where old Charlie Pettit farmed a small-holding of about sixty acres, living in a tiny flint cottage which was set in a sea of rolling downland. 'Did y' know 'ow 'is farm got th' name 'Arvey's Stone?'

'I thought it was Harvey's Cross.'

'So t'is, but it don't make a lot o' difference one way or t'other. They put a stone to mark where th' ol' fella fell off 'is 'orse then, some years later, 'rected a marble cross. So the older people calls it Stone and you youngsters calls it Cross.'

We trudged on in silence for a while and I was waiting for the story to continue when we put up a hare which leapt up almost at our feet and went bounding away like the wind, its feet touching the ground only about every five yards or so.

' 'E's makin' f' Garden Bushes,' said Dad. 'See that bank over there, jest past the bushes along side the shepherd's 'ut? Me an' ol' Teddy Sherfold dug three badgers out there one Sunday aft'noon when we was shepherd boys. You 'member ol' Teddy, dun't ye? 'E was a rare ol' sportsman, 'e was. Flick, feather or fin, boy, 'e didn't care what it was s'long as 'e 'ad a bit o' sport. I couldn't stick 'is missus though, she was a tartar. If she'd 'a' bin the only girl in the world an' I'd 'a' bin the only boy, like in the song, wal, that'd 'a' bin the end o' the 'uman race, I dun't mind tellin' ye.

'You know one night ol' Teddy 'ad a bit of a ding-dong down the Royal Oak an' 'e didn't get 'ome till about ar' past two in the morning. 'E undresses quiet like, so as not to wake 'er up, an' was standin' there in 'is shirt an' jest as 'e cocks one leg up an' sits on the edge o' the bed she turns over, opens one eye an' says, "Where-ever are you going to at this time of the morning, Ted?" Wal, ol' Teddy was pretty often up in middlin' time t' catch the tide for a bit o' fishing and 'e didn't want t' upset 'er, so 'e says, "Prawnin', dear." An' 'e puts 'is clothes back on, went out an' spent the rest o' the night in the shed at the bottom o' the garden. E' would 'a' gone prawnin', look, only 'e couldn't—the tide was in.'

'What about this chap who fell off his horse, then?' I asked.

'O yeah. That was back in 1819. The master o' foxhounds 'e was, John Harvey, a major or somethin' in the army. One day when they was 'untin' these grounds 'e 'ad a 'eart-attack an' dropped t' the ground dead, an' they put up a stone t' mark th' spot.'

A large, blue-black cloud like a bruise had been slowly coming up from the west and now a sudden gloom descended on us as it blotted out the sun. There was a flurry of wind and it turned noticeably cooler. 'Do you think it's going to rain?'

'Oh, I don't 'ope so. We en't got no coats.'

But a moment or two later great sploshy drops of rain came splattering down and pocked the dust in the path into tiny craters. We quickened our pace and headed for Slonks Hovel, a small, square, flint building in the corner of a cattle yard, and reached it, wrenching open the grass-grown door just as the cloud opened and the water deluged down. 'Lawks, boy, look, it's rainin' stair-rods,' he said.

Inside the floor was littered with straw and it smelt damp and earthy. 'There's a well forty foot deep over in that corner,' said Dad, 'an' a couple o' foxhounds fell down it one day. The 'unt 'ad jest drawn Longdown Bushes. They put up Maas Reynolds an' 'e come in 'ere t' try an' dodge 'em, but the leadin' pair were on to 'im. They was tearin' in to 'im when the trap-door over the well, bein' rotten, give way and down they all went like a bushel o' bricks—fox, 'ounds an' all. The 'untsman comes in an' 'e can 'ear 'em down there so 'e does n'more than put 'is foot in the well-bucket an' gets somebody to lower 'im down the shaft. I wouldn' 'a' gone down there f'r all the beer in Beard's brewery. The windlass, rope an' tackle was all as rotten as a pear—it 'adn't bin used f' forty year. Still 'e got both 'ounds up all right an' I 'member bein' sent over as a young chap to concrete the well over an' make it safe. You can still see th' dome I made—under this straw, look'ee.'

The rain stopped as suddenly as it had started, as if it had been turned off at the mains, and we set off again climbing the gentle incline towards Steady's farm. 'How did ol' Steady get his nick-name?' I asked.

'Ah that's a rum 'en, thet is. 'E used to come down Rotten'dean every Saturday to do 'is shoppin'.'

'He still does,' I interrupted, 'Chaulker and I borrow his pony and trap to ride home to tea sometimes.'

'Yeah, wal, if 'e 'ad 'is missus with 'im, 'e used t' get on back 'ome about tea-time, but if 'e 'adn't 'e'd take th' ol' mare out the shafts, tie 'er up t' the tail-board, give 'er a nose-bag an' leave 'er in School Opening till it was time to chuck out at the "Black 'En". Wal, one night 'e 'as a tidy ol' wet, a little drop more 'an usual, like, an' when t'was time t' go 'ome 'e was all over the road. One or two of 'em give 'im a 'and t' 'arness up th' ol' mare an' then they put 'im up in. Some'ow or other in the scuffle 'is bowler-'at falls off an' as they're puttin' it back on, it comes in two sunders an' awf 'e goes wearin' th' brim round 'is neck like a necklace, an' jest the black crown sittin' on top of 'is 'ead. 'E looked like some ol' bishop or somethin.'.

'Next mornin', bein'' Sunday, 'e comes down the village agin for a livener an' they arsts 'im 'ow 'e got on goin' 'ome the night before. "Oh," 'e says, "instead o' goin' round th' road, I takes th' ol' gal down Smuggler's Track—"' Dad pointed across to a chalk track running down the precipitous side-hill which, although it was the more direct route to the farm if you were on foot, was far too steep for wheeled traffic—' "That put a tidy ol' strain on the breechin's, I can tell ye," he says, "But I lays well back an' kips sayin' t' th' ol' mare, 'Steady! Steady! Steady, ol' gal, steady!'" An' ol' Charlie's been "Steady" ever since.'

By this time we had reached Steady's farm and Dad pointed out the memorial within a few yards of the cottage which marked the spot where Major Harvey had dropped dead. There was a white marble cross on a three-tiered plinth inscribed to that effect and a small sand-stone set in the ground marked 'J.H. 1819'. The area was enclosed by an iron-paling fence about five feet high and some eight feet square and a small jam jar containing a wilting bunch of cowslips sat at the base of the cross.

'They do say,' Dad went on, picking up the tenuous thread of the story, 'that Harvey's ghost 'as bin seen round 'ere several times over the years. 'E wears a long, waisted ridin' coat an' a Billy-cock 'at an' gallops past on a ghostly 'orse about 'ead 'igh, with 'is coat tails flyin'. Strong men, they say, 'ave blanched at th' sight. Dogs roll their eyes sit up an' 'owl

an' 'orses shudder from nose to croup, flare their nostrils an'
refuse t' budge.'

I jumped at the sound of a footfall and the crunching of
gravel behind us. But it was only old Steady coming out
with a broad grin and a couple of glasses of home-made wine.

There was a white marble cross on a three-tiered plinth.

Chapter Thirteen

Dad was a man of very regular habits and his nightly preparations for bedtime, for instance, were ritualistic. At twenty past nine each evening, he would put aside whatever job he had been doing, push his chair back from the table and roll a cigarette, teasing out the ragged ends of tobacco and returning them carefully to the kidney-shaped tin which he carried in the left-hand pocket of his waistcoat. The cigarette would be placed on the mantel-shelf, within easy reach as he sat in his chair, ready to be taken down and enjoyed with his early cup of tea next morning.

Then, peering over his pince-nez spectacles at the clock which hung on the kitchen wall, he would check the time with the large silver watch in the opposite waistcoat pocket and wind it with twenty-four turns of the well-worn brass winding knob—no more, no less.

In summer he would have to allow an hour for he would never alter his own watch to match the 'new-fangled summer-time' introduced during the first world war because he had the strongest objections to 'Pokin' th' clock about, jest so as some an 'em can play tennis in th' evenin's. The ol' cattle an' 'orses want muckin' out an' feedin' same time in th' mornin' whatever th' 'ands on y' clock says.'

After this, he would loosen his tie and, with much neck-stretching and fumbling with the brass-headed studs at the front and back of the neck-band of his shirt, remove his celluloid collar and hang it with the tie on a nail under the mantel-shelf, also within arm's reach.

Then after winding the clock on the wall by pulling on

the chain until, with a noisy clicking of ratchets, the heavy lead weight had been raised to its highest level, he would disappear briefly into the garden, perform a little perfunctory toilet activity at the sink in the gloom of the scullery, and reappear, timing his movements so that at precisely nine-thirty he would be standing with one foot on the bottom stair holding a small, lighted paraffin lamp in one hand and his other on the lift-latch of the match-boarded stair-case door ready to pull it closed behind him.

There he would stand and pose for a second or two like an unconscious parody of William Holman Hunt's painting, 'The Light of the World', a sepia print of which adorned the wall of the bedroom for which he was making. Then, with an air of finality that positively severed connections with the world and all its works until the following day, he would address those of us who had not preceded him, 'Wal! I shall bid y' goodnight.'

The heavy, marble eight-day clock in the front room was wound once a week. At noon on Sunday Dad would come in from the wood-shed where he had spent the previous hour preparing sufficient kindling for the kitchen range to last a week and enough rough wood to boil the washing in the copper on Monday morning, and disappear upstairs with a horse-bucket of hot water and a large block of red carbolic soap in the patent tin soap-saver clipped to the side. Over his arm he carried a clean towel, a freshly-laundered set of woollen under-clothes, a pair of socks and a shirt, and for the next half hour the muffled strains of songs from his vast repertoire would come drifting down the stairs, squeezing under the doors and wafting out through the open bedroom window like wisps of smoke—indistinct but identifiable.

His mood could usually be assessed by his choice of songs, which he sang methodically from start to finish with only occasional interruptions while he fumbled for the soap or when a particularly delicate operation called for extra con-centration. But even if he started in the heaviest of spirits with say,

What's the life of a man any more than the leaves
A man has his season so why should he grieve,
Although in this wide world we appear blithe and gay
Like the leaves we shall wither and all fade away . . .

his mood would gradually improve as time passed and he would almost invariably finish up with something lighter, like 'The Farmer in Cheshire'. Sometimes his thoughts would follow a historical theme and 'Lord Thomas' would be followed by songs with a military flavour, 'Bold General Wolfe', 'The Battle of Alma' or 'The Bold Dragoon'.[1]

At about a quarter to one he would reappear wearing his fancy waistcoat with the gold chain of his half-hunter draped across the front, looking spick and span and refreshed in every way. The singing seemed to have purged his mind of work-a-day cares as effectively as the soap and water had cleansed his body. With bright eyes and a broad grin he was ready—particularly after a good dinner and a snooze in his favourite chair, which were his immediate prospects—to face the trials and tribulations of another week.

The soapy water would be taken into the garden and, on the precept of nothing ever being wasted, slung on to the broad beans to discourage 'the pook' and after a few deft strokes on the back-door step to sharpen the carving knife he would return indoors and go to the front-room mantel-piece. With much ceremony he would then take the hand-cut key from its hook and, at exactly five to one, just before the minute hand had reached its zenith and obscured the key-hole in the dial, wind the clock.

The morning's and indeed the week's activities having thus been brought to such a satisfactory conclusion, he would sit back expansively in his chair in the kitchen sniffing and savouring the mouth-watering smells of roast lamb and mint-sauce, green peas, new potatoes and suet pudding as one by one the steaming dishes were brought in and placed on the table.

[1] *See* pp. 228, 231, 234, 236, 238.

Dad, then, was very much a creature of regular and methodical habit and if the daily or weekly rote was interrupted or changed in any particular, it was immediately noticed by the rest of the household. So if at dinner-time on a Saturday he sneaked in and surreptitiously wound the front-room clock it was quite obvious that something was afoot.

When this happened he always seemed to be in a particularly good-natured and frivolous frame of mind and full of quips and irrepressible high spirits, which really gave a clue to what he had in mind.

'Are you going to mend that broken sash-cord this week-end?' mother might ask from the steamy depths of the scullery.

'Oh, shut up you damned ol' bitch!' he would mutter, his eyes blazing in mock defiance.

'What was that?'

'Nothing, my dear,' he would syrup, 'not a word passed my lips. I was silent as the grave.'

'Oh,' mother would say, briefly accepting the explanation with reluctance and obvious disbelief.

At tea-time he would start sprucing up a bit and to the discerning the tea rose in the button-hole of his jacket and the angle of his cap would confirm what had really been obvious all the time.

'I think I'll doddle off down th' road an' 'ave a wet.' Then he would walk up the path with a spring in his step, a song on his lips, a thirst fit to drain a brewery and we wouldn't see him till about Wednesday.

For the greater part of the time Dad was the paragon of virtue. A much-loved and undisputed head of the home and a well-liked and respected foreman on the farm. His sovereignty in the cottage and at work was never in question. But at about three or four monthly intervals he would tumble off the throne. His crown would slip over one eye, he would trip over his robes and, at the bidding of John Barleycorn, sink the whole fleet of his hardships, real or imagined, in an ocean of ale.

If he was methodical and painstaking in his work, he was equally thorough and whole-hearted in his relaxation. There was nothing impetuous in his bouts of gallivanting; they were planned and organized down to the last detail. He would hand over written instructions to his second in command on the farm and nothing would be left to chance, even alternative work for the men if the weather changed. Similarly at home, clocks would be wound, firewood chopped and everything left in apple-pie order and when he was satisfied that his absence would not be to anyone's great disadvantage he would plunge into a good old-fashioned bender.

While he was on the run he would go to ground, holed up in his favourite pub and revelling in the company he found where the beer was on tap and sawdust lay on the floor. For a brief and happy interlude he would throw off the shackles of employment and laugh, hiccup and stagger and sing in the best traditions of the English drunk whose long line of ancestry goes back to that anonymous, under-sung genius who first discovered that the fermented juices of hedgerow berries made him want to laugh.

Where the beer was on tap and sawdust lay on the floor.

Apart from clothing and speech, the mixed and motley crowd to be found in the bar would have changed but little over the years and the eternal question of who should pay for the next round of drinks had changed not at all. That bibulous fourteenth-century crew who were entertained so well by Beton (Betty) the ale-wife in *Piers Plowman* found their way of solving the problem:

... Glutton entered to find Cissie the shoemaker sitting on the bench, and Wat the gamekeeper with his wife, and Tim the tinker with two of his apprentices, and Hick the hackneyman, and Hugh the haber-dasher and Clarice, the whore of Cock Lane, with the parish clerk, and Davy the ditcher, and Father Peter of Prie-Dieu Abbey, with Peacock the Flemish wench and a dozen others, not to mention a fiddler and a rat-catcher, and a Cheapside scavenger, a rope-maker and a trooper. Then there was Rose the pewterer, Godfrey of Garlick-hithe, Griffiths the Welshman and a crew of auctioneers. Well, there they all were, early in the morning, ready to give Glutton a good welcome and start him off with a pint of the best.

Then Clement the cobbler pulled off his cloak and flung it down for a game of handicap. So Hick the hackneyman threw down his hood and asked Bett the butcher to take his part, and they chose dealers to price the articles and decide on the odds.

Then the two dealers jumped up quickly, went off into a corner, and begun in whispers to value these rubbishy garments. But as they had no scruples about it and couldn't agree, they asked Robin the ropemaker to join them as umpire, and so they settled the business between the three of them.

As it turned out, Hick the hostler got the cloak, while Clement had to fill the cup and content himself with Hick's hood. And the first man to go back on his word was to do the honours and stand Glutton a gallon of ale.

Then there were scowls and roars of laughter and cries of 'Pass round the cup!' And so they sat shouting and singing till time for vespers.[1]

In Dad's day the question of who should pay was frequently resolved by 'twizzling'. On a beam in the ceiling a pointer would be mounted in such a way that it could be spun round with ease rather like the needle of a compass. The points of

---

[1] Translation by J. F. Goodridge (Penguin Classics).

the compass, as it were, were marked either in numbers or sometimes with the letters, 'M.Y.M.Y. etc' and wherever the pointer came to rest decided who should pay—'Y'=you, 'M'=me.

Another method was 'selling the pony'. The company would take turns at being the umpire whose task it was to select an alphabetical letter on a page of, say, a newspaper and mark it by drawing a ring round it. Then he would fold the paper so that it could not be seen and place it on the table in front of him. At this stage he must be the only person who knows what the ringed letter is. Then he calls at random upon any member of the company to start the game and this person is at liberty to call out any one of the letters of the alphabet. Then the person on his left must call out the next succeeding letter and so on round the company and round the alphabet until the marked letter is called. The person who calls out the ringed letter, which is, of course, presented for corroboration, has to buy the drinks.

'Toad-in-the-hole' was a favourite pub game in Sussex in those days. It was basically a game of pitching a metal disc from behind an eight-foot hockey or base line into a small hole in a flat bed elevated some 21 inches from the floor. The bed, which was made of lead and measured about 18 inches long, 13 inches wide and $\frac{3}{4}$ inch thick, had a hole in the centre 2 inches in diameter, and the coin was $1\frac{1}{2}$ inches in diameter and $\frac{1}{4}$ inch thick. The bed was mounted on a small table 23 inches high at the back and 21 inches in front which gave it a slight tilt towards the player.

Each player threw four coins and if one was lobbed into the hole or was subsequently nudged in by another coin two points went to the thrower's credit and he also counted one point for each coin that landed and remained on the bed itself. The coins must not be allowed to hit the back-board and rebound but fall flat on the bed where they landed. Those that entered the hole dropped down into a small drawer from which they could be recovered when the throw was complete. The score was totted up on a cribbage board,

61 points being required for a full game, or 31 for a shortened version.

The word 'coin' in referring to the metal discs is used advisedly, as it is said that this game originated at the latter end of the eighteenth century and was designed to be played with the large George the Third twopenny pieces minted in 1797. They weighed exactly two ounces. As they became rarer with the passing of time, brass discs of the same dimensions and weight were used. The game is still played in some parts of East Sussex.

Another game popular then but seldom seen in these days was 'Ring-the-Bull'. The head of a bull, often a calf's head, stuffed and mounted on a board with a hook inserted in the end of its nose, was hung on the wall so that the hook was about 5 feet 9 inches from the floor. Directly in front of and about 4 feet away from the bull's head, a bull's nose-ring, 2 inches inside diameter, was suspended from the ceiling on a string which just allowed it to fall on the hook in the bull's nose. The hook, in other words, was on the perimeter of the ring's range.

The object was to stand in any position on the floor and swing the ring so that, in its curving, elliptical flight on the end of the string, it fell on to the hook. This called for a great deal of skill and the more experienced hands all had their own individual methods and style of throwing.

Running the twine between finger and thumb to ensure that it was not twisted, to prevent the ring twisting in flight, one might stand at right angles to the bull and appear to aim at the corner of the bar, another might turn his back to the bull completely and send the ring curving up towards the top of the grandfather clock in the corner, yet, in whatever direction it was set off, somehow the ring would swing round in its orbit and, if not actually fall on the hook, at least come very close to it.

Sometimes a bull's horn was used as the hook or even a mere metal hook mounted on a wooden back-board. Three successful shots in a row used to earn the thrower a free pot of beer but, so frequently did this occur in some houses, that it was restricted to a player's first throw of the evening before he had got his 'eye in'.

That it was a very ancient and popular game was reflected in the fact that the bull's head in some pubs had ceased to resemble in any respect the animals from which they had been so ignominiously severed. Bereft of hair from years of use, completely mummified, stained brown with the smoke from generations of shag-smokers and even sometimes heavily varnished, they looked more like a pig's head glazed ready for a Lord Mayor's banquet at the Guildhall.

So in the cheery, beery brotherhood of the tap-room, Dad would roister with the best of them, sing more than most and play the time-honoured games of the inn. When funds ran low they resorted to the most ingenious, not to say sometimes slightly reprehensible, means of re-establishing solvency. They would sell items of doubtful ownership and, on at least one occasion, raffled a duck which the unfortunate winner found to his dismay was still swimming on the pond and would be his, and even then not legally, only if he could catch it.

Then there were Tom Mockett's chickens.

*   *   *

Dad had always hoped for an opportunity to get even with Tom Mockett ever since that day at school when Tom had slipped a handful of frog spawn down inside the back of his breeches in class. 'Ga-ugh! That wadn't half a dirty ol' trick,' he said, 't'was like sittin' down on a lot o' ol' 'snot-gobblers' (ripe yew-berries). The trouble was that, bein' in class, I couldn't do nothin' about it, y'see. I couldn't even say nothin'. An' when I got 'ome didn't I get a beltin' for muckin' up me pants an' shirt-tail.'

The opportunity to level the score was very slow in presenting itself and it came in a most unexpected way. But the countryman has an elephantine memory and, from the nature of his calling, he has infinite patience.

(above)
Jack and Mrs Goddens having tea in
the harvest field.

(below)
Bob on the shore.

(right)
Jim Copper.

(above)
The blacksmith's shop.

(left)
Bob Copper in the school photograph.

(below)
Steve Barrow with his dog and flock.

Grand-dad 'up in' with Bob.

(below)
The old-timers.

(above)
Mockford's greengrocery.

(left)
Uncle John Copper.

(above)
A steam threshing gang.

(below)
The High Street and Black Horse, Rottingdean.

(above)
Len Avery driving a pen of
lambs to the slaughter house.

(left)
We used to sit in the little
meadow and hold buttercups
under each other's chins.

(right)
'Up-streeters'.

(below)
Frank Mockford, with his
mother 'up in'.

(left)
Grandad was a man
of the soil.

(below)
Steve Barrow, shepherd,
Rottingdean.

Dad was harrowing up at Mill Laine. He had been holding on to the ploughlines and 'hopping the clods' behind Captain and Rodney since seven that morning and keeping his couch-grass and rubbish fires burning on the headlands. It was a Saturday and getting on for 'knocking off time' and on Saturday evenings when the week's work was behind him he liked to doddle off down the road to the village 'for a wet' with a few mates.

When he reached the headland on the next turn he called his horses to a halt, took what few coins there were from the front pocket of his corduroys and had a 'crumb up'. They were crumbs indeed. He looked at the coppers in the broad, calloused palm of his hand and counted them. He turned them over slowly and counted them again but he couldn't make the total sum amount to any more than fourpence. Two pennies, three ha'pennies and two farthings. 'Fo'pence,' he thought, 'that's jest enough for a pint for me own salf an' no more. At one time o' day that would 'a' bin a 'latch-lifter'. If you'd 'a' filled up a quart jug with 'fo'penny' (fourpence a quart) an' took it across an' topped up the pots o' y' mates sittin' at the table in the corner, you could 'a' 'ad a full pot y'salf an' been all set f' th' evenin'. Specially if you was a fair 'and at playin' quoits or could sing a good song.' But 'fo'pence' was a sorry financial state in which to find yourself facing Saturday evening even in the 1920's. His credit was stretched to its limits at the 'Black 'en' and the 'Oak' and you couldn't get 'tick' at the Plough so it looked like being a dry weekend.

He looked at his watch and decided it was time to 'start making tracks', so he hitched off, leaving the three heavy wooden harrows in the corner of the field to await his return on Monday morning, hung his jacket and grub-basket on the hames and jumped up on to Rodney's back to ride side-fashion down the track towards home. A little way along he fell in with Tom Mockett also heading for home but on foot. 'Wanna jump up, ol' mairt?' called Dad, ' 'twill save y' a few steps.' There was no animosity between them. Dad just felt there was an old score to settle one day, perhaps, if the chance cropped up. If not, well, it didn't really matter. The biggest criticism he had of his old comrade was that he was so tight-fisted. ' 'E used t' go up the stairs two at a time t' save th' stair-carpet,' he said.

There was still about a mile to go down to the village, so Tom accepted the offer of a lift. He scrambled up and transferred the weight from his own legs on to Captain's and the two men rode along in a plodding silence for a while. Then Tom, with lamb-like innocence, laid himself on the altar of sacrifice.

'You don't know where you can lay y' 'ands on a few pullets do y', Jim?' he said presently, knowing Dad's reputation for being able to turn up the right thing at the right time.

'I dunno. Mayhap I do,' said Dad warily, 'Why?'

'Wal, I've got a dozen nice young Rhode Island Reds jest on the point of lay an' I could do with, say, another six to kip 'em company.'

'Mm-mm, now you've said that,' said Dad thoughtfully, 'I think I do know where I could pick some up. They'd be the same as you say, Rhode Island Reds on the point o' lay.' He paused. 'They wun't justly be mine t'sell, d'y' understand,' he said with a sidelong glance.

'Oh, I dun't care a bugger 'oo they belong to,' said Tom, 'so long as they be the right price.'

'Wal, a shill'n' a head wouldn't 'urt ye, would it? I tell y' what I'll do. I'll throw in 'alf a dozen for a crown so long as there en't no questions arst.'

'Yeah, wal, that sounds all kif t' me,' said Tom, knowing full well that that was only about a quarter of the current market price, 'I'll see y' down th' Plough t'night, then.' And that was the way the matter was left.

After tea when Dad had shaved and spruced up and tied a colourful Paisley neckerchief neatly about his throat with the tail ends looped under his braces and fastened in a tight knot across the top of his chest, he set off down the road carrying an empty bran-poke. The jaunty angle of his cap and the saucy light in his eye spelt his mood and the nature of his intentions.

It was quite dark by now and as he passed the Plough the lamps were lit and he could see Tom standing at the bar so he knew his path was clear. He went up to Park Place where Tom had a garden allotment and kept his chickens in a tarred, corrugated-iron shed. Opening the shed door stealthily, all the time making clucking and cooing noises to soothe the occupants, he carefully lifted six of the roosting fowls from their perches one by one, almost as smoothly and quietly as you could pick bottles from a shelf, and dropped them into the sack. Then he tied the neck of the sack securely and headed back for the Plough where he ceremoniously dumped it on the floor in the corner of the bar.

'All right then, Jim?' said Tom with a knowing look.

'All right, Tom. They be all yours,' said Dad with mental relish and a crafty wink, at the same time taking the two half-crowns which Tom was pressing surreptitiously into his palm.

After a drink to clinch the deal Tom, well pleased with the transaction, took his leave of the company and carried the wriggling sack up to his allotment where he carefully shot the contents into the chicken house and shut the door. He was a man who loved a bargain and his homeward steps were light and gay and the song in his heart was almost, but not quite, on his lips. His meanness in all things extended even to his forms of self-expression and the song was withheld for he would not like anyone to know he was happy.

Next morning, with all the pride of a man who had extended and improved his stock, he went and opened up the shed and, with a smile of satisfaction, watched and counted the birds as they trod gingerly down the sloping plank into the run. '. . . 9–10–11–12 . . .?' 'Ah,' he thought, the new birds would be a bit reluctant to come out at first in their new surroundings. He banged on the side of the shed with his fist but there was no response. It was, he thought, ominously silent inside the shed. He banged again calling, 'Coop, coop,

coop come along,' as if he was calling in the cows from three fields back and tapped on the feeding bin with the toe of his boot. Slowly a dreadful doubt was beginning to creep into his mind. Had they, by some unthinkable chance, escaped?

He opened the door and at the sight of the empty perches his heart fell with a thud into the mud beneath his feet. He counted the birds in the run again. There were only twelve, the same number as there had been this time yesterday. Then gradually the light of a fearful realization dawned upon him and he recalled the words of the previous evening.

'They wun't justly be mine t' sell, d'y' understand . . .'

'Oh, I dun't care a bugger 'oo they belong to, so long as they be the right price . . .'

He walked home dejectedly with the fateful phrase repeating in his head like a groove-stuck record. The morning sun shed no warmth upon him and the church-bells held no joy.

'What's up wid you?' said his wife, as he slouched into the cottage. 'You look as if you've found a shillin' an' lost a golden guinea.'

'I've bin twisted,' said Tom, 'an I dun't like it. Twisted of a crown I've bin, an' the trouble is I can't do nothin' about it. I can't even say nothin' for, in a manner o' speakin', 'twas my idea in the fust place.'

'Oh well,' said his wife, 'never you mind, I 'spect you'll live to' get over it.'

'Ah, I know all about that,' said the disgruntled Tom, 'But 'ave you ever 'eard afore of a man buyin' 'is own chicken? I can take a bit o' bad luck but this is the bleddy limit. I dun't s' much mind 'em stickin' th' umbrella up me arse, but this time I reck'n they tried t' open it.'

*   *   *

After he had sung all the songs out of his system and the fire of frivolity was spent, Dad would come back home ready, in fact eager, to get back to normal. On his return there was nothing contrite about his behaviour. Mother was slightly ashamed of his absences but accepted them with remarkable tolerance. Without the slightest reference to his disappearance, which he assumed everyone had taken for granted, he would roll up his sleeves, bend his back and return to work with renewed vigour and these periodic lapses were so directly opposed to that side of his nature for which he is best remembered that they must be regarded as mere drops of piquant madness in a stock-pot of bone-broth sanity.

Chapter Fourteen

Although the local expression 'them as is big enough is old enough' was the criterion usually applied to young women being contemplated in terms of courtship, it was also used in assessing a young man's ability to work. It was generally accepted that as soon as he was able a boy should help on the farm on Saturdays and during school holidays. The yoke of labour fell readily and not too uncomfortably upon our shoulders. It was the manner of life to which we had been brought up and the idea of working for a living came as naturally into our lives as night following day. 'Going out to work', in fact, was an important milestone on the road to manhood and the source of some pride.

I well remember the feeling of self-importance as I stepped out of the cottage all fitted out for my first day's flint-picking on the hills. I was twelve. Pushing my well-dubbined, hob-nailed boots into unaccustomed strides in imitation of the men, I soon found that the new leather spats encasing my spindly legs kept twisting round until the swelling curves designed to accommodate the calves bulged out in the front of my shins and I had to keep stopping to restore them to the correct position. This played havoc with the illusion of being a grown-up working man, but I stomped on resolutely hoping no one would notice.

I was wearing an old black oilskin cape, as stiff as sail-cloth, which was also several sizes too large. It was a relic of the past, salvaged from who knows what stable or outhouse and Dad had re-proofed it with lamp-black and linseed oil which, although effectively repelling the heaviest rainstorm, remained obstinately tacky throughout the remainder of its existence and always left persistent and grimy evidence of its use on my neck and the backs of my wrists and hands. It had, too, a most distinctive odour reminiscent of old, well-oiled cricket bats, but its chief disadvantage was that whenever I bent down to leeward, the wind got under it and filled it out like a balloon, threatening to carry me off my feet. So when I stooped to pick up flints I had to be sure to keep my head into the wind.

There were two men and myself and our job was to clear the flints from a twenty-acre field known as 'Old Walls' and carry them in buckets to a long heap at the field's edge eventually to be carted away and used to metal the roadways and tracks which networked the hills. Bill Cave, who was senior in years and experience and therefore in charge, used an old galvanized-iron seed-lip with a supporting strap over one shoulder. The field had been ploughed in autumn and the rains of winter had eroded the soil until the flints stood out clearly, but it was heavy work. As the day wore on, my boots became heavier and harder, and the cape and leggings grew larger and stiffer, while I seemed to shrink inside my armour and grow correspondingly softer until, plodding up Smuggler's Track on the way home, I felt like a very small hermit-crab in a very large whelk-shell. But the sense of achievement when I reached home and Dad handed me a shilling—which I think was out of his own pocket by way of encouragement rather than an official entry on the farm wages sheet—made me swell with pride.

Apart from the perennial fetching and carrying, like the early-morning collection of milk from Mrs Marshall at the farm dairy, feeding the ducks and chickens and bringing home the eggs, and taking midday meals out to the men in the fields, all of which were either outside or fitted in between school hours, the boys'-jobs, on a farm at least, had a wide range of variety and changed with the seasons. Early in the year we would have to keep the spring-sown cornfields free from birds by walking round waving our arms, shouting and rattling pairs of home-made wooden clappers to simulate gun-fire to protect the newly-sown seed from marauding rooks. I used to try to combine this job with gathering 'hand-picked' sheep-droppings from a nearby run of turf, for I was privileged to have an outlet for this commodity at sixpence a bucket, particularly during the tomato-growing season.

The grattens, or old stubbles lying fallow, had to be rid of noxious weeds and Grand-dad would take my cousins and me, armed with swop-hooks to knock over the docks, thistles and burdocks before they ran to seed. We would pile into a tip-cart and rumble off behind Duke up the track to wherever we were going to work. When we reached the field, the old man would position the cart in the centre of an imaginary square and send us out to the four corners. Then, with the tail-board taken out of its slots and set across the top-rails as a seat and a folded corn-sack by way of a cushion, he would sit there watching our progress as we quartered the area in towards him clearing the ground as we went.

This job was well named 'thistle-dodging', for it entailed a lot of dodging about and sometimes there was a squabble over whether a bed of thistles was in your patch or the next chap's. But Grand-dad would step in as mediator, his great voice booming across the field like a fog-horn. His word was indisputably final. From his elevated seat he had an excellent view of the ground and if you missed one, he would wait until you reached the cart, then, pointing with the stem of his pipe, he would say, 'There's one dodged ye back there look'ee, mairt,' and you would have to retrace your steps, sometimes the best part of a quarter-mile, to fell the wretched weed while the others clambered up into the cart to ride on to the next piece. The unlucky one would, of course, have to walk, or more often run, for he had to be in position and ready to start again with the rest. This gentle form of punish-ment certainly increased our diligence.

On still days, we could hear men shouting down in the village over whose roof-tops we looked to a sea of glass. Duke, wearing a dejected expression like a Dover sole, would stand patiently in the shafts. From time to time, he would shift his weight from one quarter to the other or, with a rattle of harness, toss his head or quiver his flanks to deter the flies while Grand-dad sat motionless, embalmed, it would seem, in a cloud of blue tobacco smoke like a bee in amber.

If we came across a partridge's nest, we had to lift it bodily from its hiding-place and carry it, complete with eggs, and lay it carefully on the floor of the cart, for Mr Gorham, a neighbouring land-owner and farmer, would pay Grand-dad a shilling for a clutch of partridge's eggs to set under a broody hen.

By the middle of the twenties, the number of sheep on the hills had diminished sadly. I say sadly, because the downland farmers had always been so dependent upon sheep for efficient husbandry. The old farming methods like the 'four course shift' of fallow, fold and plough were all based on the principle of the plough and seed-drill following along behind the shepherd, sowing corn on land recently enriched by the sheep that had been folded in rape or roots or grazing on the grattens. To the farmers of those days farming in this district was impossible without sheep and they regretted to see the once sweet, close-bitten turf on the hills growing rank and scrubby. But it was all part of the general decline in farming fortunes.

The sheep-shearing crews, who earlier in the century had travelled round from farm to farm shearing the substantial flocks, were no longer needed. But on the Rottingdean farms, although the sheep population had been reduced to something considerably less than a thousand, sheep shearing was still a sizeable undertaking. The shearing was carried out on the home farm, Challenors, and the barn—still called 'Drummer's Barn' by the old-timers who remembered old Drummer Cowley spending most of his winters there threshing out oats with a flail—was where most of the shearing was done. The yard at the back would be crammed solid with sheep and the approach of further flocks being driven down the chalk tracks from the hills would be signalled by clouds of white dust that could be seen a mile or more away. These would be folded in the fields opposite the cottages at Northgate to await their turn for the shears. It was a time of hustle and hard work, with the shuffle and padding of many hooves passing by in the road, the shouting of men, the barking of dogs and always the inescapable smell of sheep with which every indrawn breath, both outdoors and in, was tinged.

My job at these times was tar-boy which was the name given to the lad whose job it was to dress the accidental cuts in a sheep's hide to stop the bleeding and repel the fly that produced the flesh-eating maggots which were the bane of a shepherd's life. The name had endured from the days when they had used tar for this purpose, although in our days we used powdered or 'worked-out' lime, and we always understood that this was the true origin of the saying, 'Don't spoil the ship (sheep) for a ha'porth of tar.'

The scene in the shear-barn had changed but little. The shearers, eight or nine of them at times, would be bent almost double to their task holding the sheep partly between their knees as it lolled on the barn floor in an attitude of total submission while the hand-shears, operated solely by strong wrists, snipped and clicked away endlessly. When my services were not required, I had to help the wool-winder. Kneeling on the floor, we wound the shorn fleeces into tight rolls and stacked them in the mow of the barn. But occasionally I would be summoned by a curt 'Tar boy!' and sometimes as I went forward, armed with a kettle of lime and an old paint brush, the shearer—particularly if he happened to be one of the younger men who were always out for a lark—would squeeze the swollen teat of a late-lambing ewe and drench me with a well-aimed jet of warm milk.

One day I made a simple mistake which I was never allowed to live down, at least during the lifetime of the older men. My kettle was empty of lime so I was sent to replenish it across to a disused loose-box which was used as a store for sacks of lime, bone-meal, guano and other top-soil dressings. Unfortunately my inexpert eye could not distinguish between lime and guano and when I got back to the barn and went to dress the next casualty, my mistake set off great gales of guffawing laughter which went echoing down the years and to some of them I went down in farm history as the tar-boy who didn't know the difference between lime and guano. 'Gaugh, bugger, boy! That en't loime—that's go-anna. That wun't stop no bleedin'.'

In harvest time we used to go 'stand-fasting'. The standing corn, having been cut and sheaved by the horse-drawn binders and stood up into shocks with the ears uppermost to dry in the sun and wind, had to be carted and stacked. Sometimes there would be as many as six wagons, each drawn by two horses, working in the same field, making their way across the bristling stubble between the lines of shocks, which were spaced a convenient distance apart so that the sheaves could be pitched up on to the wagon without too much walking for the loaders.

The stand-fast's job was to lead the trace-horse, stopping at regular intervals so that about three or four shocks, each consisting of eight to ten sheaves, could be loaded from either side. Then he would lead on for another fifteen or twenty yards and pull to another halt while further shocks were pitched up. As the load of sheaves grew higher between the corner poles and the wagon bucked and lurched over the rough ground, particularly if it was on a steep side-hill, the two men stacking the load had to hold tight and brace themselves in order to avoid being thrown overboard. To give them warning that the wagon was about to move off, the stand-fast, before urging his horses forward, had to call out 'Stand fast!'

When the wagon was fully loaded we were allowed to mount the trace-horse and ride in to the stack in the corner of the field. But in the first couple of days of harvest we would have a longer journey. Before the stacks were started, the various barns in the village had to be filled and, from at least one stand-fast's point of view, riding the lead horse up the High Street in front of a tall, lumbering wagon-load of sheaves was the proudest moment of the whole harvest. Though it was only a very watered-down version of the old-time 'hollerin' pots' when Grand-dad used to sit at the head of the very last wagon load and shout: 'We've ploughed, we've sowed, we've ripped, we've mowed, we've carr'd our last load and aren't overthrow'd,' and call for three cheers.

During winter, when threshing was in full swing, we boys were sent bond-winding. In Court Farm behind the church, the threshing machine would be drawn round and placed across the barn in between the two large double-doors, and the steam engine driven round to the yard at the back so it could drive the drum with a belt running through the door-way. The engine-driver at that time was old Bob Cherryman, a red-faced man with twinkling blue eyes and a bushy beard. 'Cherryman!' the 'Guv'nor' shouted angrily one day, riding up and looking him straight in the eye as he stood in the cock-pit of his engine, 'You're a bloody fool!'

'Yes, sir,' said old Bob gently, 'an' I could touch another 'en with a liddle short stick.'

The sheaves from the mow of the barn would be tossed on top of the drum where the bond-cutter and feeder kept the machine supplied with work. As the clean, spent straw tumbled out, it was pitched through the opposite door into the front yard where three or four trussers would truss it up by hand. They would gather it towards them with one arm raking it lengthwise into line with a short three- or four-tined comb and tie it with a straw bond which was made in the following fashion. Holding the truss down with one knee they would twist a short length of rope out of the straw litter at their feet and form it into a loop through which the boy who was bond-winder had to put the hook of his wimble. This was a cranked handle, rather like the starting handle of a car, with a hook at the end. The boy would then walk back-wards turning the wimble so that it twisted the straw into a rope, or bond, as the trusser paid it out through his hands. When the bond was some eight to ten feet long, the trusser would shout, 'Whoa! That'll do ye,' and on removing the hook from the end of the bond the boy had to be very careful not to let it go or it would unwind and be useless and the trusser's opinion of his clumsiness would be made eloquently explicit. Then the trusser, with the skill that comes only from long practice, would wind the bond round the truss, secure it into a knot with a deft twist of his wrists and tuck in the ends to leave it ready for carting. If the straw was to be sold, the trusses had to be weighed off at 36 lb. each and sometimes if one was a little proud a couple of handfuls had to be pulled out or alternatively, if short, tucked in under the bond to make it good. But the old fellows were remarkably good guessers.

One boy winding bonds for four trussers and going from one to another in endless succession certainly had no time to get into mischief. But even then it was preferable to the other boy's job at threshing-time—raking out the cavings. Cavings —from, as the scholars say, the Anglo-Saxon 'Caef' meaning chaff—was the dust and rubbish that was shaken down through the riddles of the machine which separated and cleaned the grain. It fell in an ever-growing heap on to the barn floor under the machine between the fore and hinder-most wheels. We toiled ceaselessly, raking and forking it out and carrying it away but the shuddering machine spewed out its waste as fast as we could shift it and we had a job to keep pace, far less make headway. It was like running up an escalator that was coming down and at the end of the day we were nearly as black as Granny Clark's 'chimbley-boys' and only the red rims of our eyes and the inside of our lips were free from dust. We looked like nigger-minstrels but we didn't feel much like singing. Raking the cavings was not our favourite job.

One day when I was about twelve and Dad was ring-rolling up at Vicarage Laine, I was allowed to drive the Titan, the newly introduced tractor. He strapped me into the seat with the belt of a macintosh, set her in motion and left me to it. 'It don't matter where y' goo, boy,' he said, 's'long as y' kip 'er on the field an' cover all the ground.' I zig-zagged, circled, cut figures of eight, criss-crossed and diagonalled the field like some crazy ice-skater and the job was never done more thoroughly. But unfortunately mother got to hear of this and thought it was too dangerous so my tractor-driving career was nipped in the bud.

The Titan had arrived in 1919 long before I had started work on the farm. Tump-tump-tumping up the High Street, it had rumbled into farm life with a noisy, bombastic dignity and was given the kind of grudging respect extended to the unknown. The carters were as apprehensive and suspicious of its arrival as their horses. There was, however, a certain familiarity about it. The wheels and under-carriage, apart from being of slightly lighter construction, were the same as a steam traction engine. It had a heavy cast-iron fly-wheel at the side and was operated by a steering-wheel with a handle; all this was familiar enough. But instead of a chimney stack and boiler, it had a cylindrical fuel tank mounted horizontally up above the front wheels and a short exhaust-pipe sticking up in the air, surmounted by a small baffle like a Chinese coolie's hat. After having been started on petrol, she ran on paraffin, but it was necessary to go over to petrol again before switching off, so that the carburettor was full of petrol ready for the next time you wanted to start her.

The driver sat on a pan-type metal seat perforated into a scrolled and foliar pattern so that it would not retain moisture in the form of rain, the same as those on the old one-horse mowing machines. She was painted red and blue like the wagons and on the side of the tank was written, 'Titan. International Harvester Corp. Milwaukee Works, U.S.A.' which gave it that exotic aura of progress we always associated with innovations from the New World.

But if anyone saw the Titan as an outrider heralding the approach of a new age of farm mechanization then he had a long time to wait before the main body of the procession arrived. In fact it never did arrive in this district, for by the time mechanization had really got under way and the farm stables were emptied practically all over the country, the local farms of Rottingdean had dwindled into comparative insignificance.

But in those early days she was the subject of much talk and speculation as to whether or not she would take the place of the horses and Dad, who was given sole charge, kept a detailed account of her first year's work:

Work done with Tractor and Cost from Oct. 23rd 1919 to Oct. 22nd 1920.

Compt	ploughing	8 acres	Bannings	cultivate & harrow	12 acres	
Bannings	,,	11 ,,	Bannings	,,	12 ,,	
Compt	,,	6 ,,	Compt	,,	5 ,,	
East Hill	,,	6 ,,	East Hill	,,	3 ,,	
Bannings	,,	10 ,,	Bannings	,,	6 ,,	
Bannings	,,	11 ,,	East Hill	,,	10 ,,	
East Hill	,,	5 ,,	Whiteway	,,	10 ,,	
Loose	,,	16 ,,	Bannings	,,	10 ,,	
Bannings	,,	6 ,,	Whiteway	,,	8 ,,	
Vicarage	plough & press	12 ,,				
Loose	,,	18 ,,			76 ,,	
Longdown	,,	13 ,,				
Bannings	,,	12 ,,	*Binder.*			
Loose	,,	14 ,,	Vicarage	oats	17 acres	
Bannings	,,	12 ,,	Bannings	wheat & oats	11 ,,	
			East Hill	barley	6 ,,	
		160 ,,				
					34 ,,	

Longdown	rolling	14 acres	*Thrashing.*
,,	,,	14 ,,	6 Wheat stacks.
,,	,,	14 ,,	3 Oat stacks.
,,	,,	16 ,,	Chaff cutting.
Loose	,,	19 ,,	2 Oat straw stacks.
,,	,,	17 ,,	
Vicarage	,,	17 ,,	
East Hill	,,	9 ,,	
Slonks	,,	9 ,,	
Bannings	,,	17 ,,	
,,	,,	4 ,,	
		150 ,,	

Paraffin Oil.

		£ s. d.
210 gallons @ 1/ 4d per gal.		£14. 0. 0.
180 ,, @ 1/ 6d ,, ,,		13.10. 0.
840 ,, @ 1/10d ,, ,,		77. 0. 0.
300 ,, @ 1/11d ,, ,,		28.15. 0.

£133. 5. 0.

Petrol.

		£ s. d.
2 gallons @ 2/11d per gal.		5.10.
10 ,, @ 3/ 0½ ,, ,,		1.10. 5.
12 ,, @ 3/ 4d ,, ,,		2. 0. 0.
4 ,, @ 3/11d ,, ,,		15. 8.

£4.11.11.

No. of days at work.

170 days @ 6/5d per day		£54.10.10d.
104 ,, @ 7/1d ,, ,,		33. 7. 4. (sic)
66 ,, @ 7/9d ,, ,,		25.11. 6.

Labour	£133. 9. 8.
Oil	133. 5. 0.
Petrol	4.11.11.
Total	£251. 6. 7.

Chapter Fifteen

If there was one single incident in the village's more recent history which marked the most significant change it had ever seen and which, practically overnight, transformed its entire character, it was when the farm was sold for the second time in 1928. I speak, of course, as one of the 'up-streeters' or agricultural community upon whom its effect was more dramatic than on the 'down-streeters' or tradespeople. But as Rottingdean had been predominantly agrarian for by far the greatest part of its existence, this sale was a most important milestone in its history and heralded startling changes in the living patterns of the majority of the old villagers.

Men who had spent all their lives on the farm and whose families for generations had got a living from the land, had to shake the soil from their boots and look elsewhere for a livelihood. Shepherds, cowmen, and carters found that the knowledge they had accumulated in a lifetime of experience was suddenly of no further use to them and that they had to turn their minds and their hands to the timber, bricks, and mortar of the building trade. For this was the new door which slowly opened after the old familiar barn doors had been shut and as the sickles, scythes, sheep-crooks, and shears were laid aside, first one and then another took up the hammer, trowel, and paintbrush to provide homes for the new arrivals who were beginning to appear.

But all this took a certain amount of time and before the financial benefits of this new development were felt, there was a period of deep depression and anxiety. When Dad first found himself out of work in 1928, he was glad of the opportunity to earn a few shillings delivering papers for Miss Tuppen, the newsagent in the High Street, and a good many other men had to swallow their pride and forget their skills in order to live. It was a period when rabbit and homegrown vegetables figured prominently on our daily menus with shrimps and prawns by way of variation sometimes in summer, but, thanks to the untiring efforts and clever management on the part of mother, it cannot be said that we ever went really hungry. And Dad was a born optimist. He fitted a piece of greaseproof paper into the bank-note compartment of his soft, leather wallet—which rarely contained anything else—and when things were at their blackest, he would produce the wallet and wiggle it between fingers and thumbs to produce the encouraging sound that bore false witness to his lie, 'Never you mind, my dear,' he would say to mother, 'Jim's still got a rustler, hark ye!'

However, as the invasion of newcomers gradually began to gather momentum, and the tide of bungalows and mock-Tudor houses crept up and over the bare, green shoulder of East Hill, there were more and more opportunities to 'earn an honest crust' and although, undeniably, there was some resentment shown towards the new residents, mostly retired people, it had to be admitted that their arrival provided a lot of much-needed work in addition to the actual building of their homes. There were gardens to be laid out and maintained, fences and gates to be erected and some of the bigger households required cleaners, cooks and nursemaids.

Dad fitted out a workshop in the garden behind the cottage which he was at pains to make look as presentable as possible. It had a small bay window and the outside was clad with strips of natural cork-bark, which had washed up on the beach at some time or another, and gave it the appearance of a log-cabin. With honey-suckle and roses trained round the door and window it was really quite picturesque and there he was usually to be found in his white apron with a two-foot rule and a handful of nails in the large, marsupial pocket and a carpenter's pencil stuck up in the side of his cap just in front of his ear. Here he carried on his skills in carpentry, but instead of making farm-gates and sheep-cribs he made garden gates, chicken sheds and wheelbarrows.

There was a small iron stove down at one end, so that even on the coldest day in winter he could carry on working in the warm and dry. On a nail just inside the door hung a catapult and on a shelf directly beneath a small box of 'chats'. These were those tiny potatoes not much bigger than marbles that were not big enough to eat nor even keep for seed but which, if left in the ground would have grown into self-set plants and spoiled the following year's crops. So they were meticulously lifted with the rest of the yield and provided excellent ammunition for the catapult with which he kept the cats and birds off his seed-beds.

His marksmanship was never in doubt. Was not the large lantern over the work bench a tribute—in an oblique sort of way—to that very accomplishment? On Armistice Night 1918, emerging from the Plough at midnight, having tasted to the full his share of the nationwide, daylong celebrations to mark the end of war, he was suddenly seized with an excess of patriotism and, with several well-aimed flints, extinguished and smashed the oil lantern which hung with arched dignity over the gateway into The Grange opposite, wherein lived a certain exalted personage who was an eminent lawyer to boot and said to be of German extraction. This partisan gesture was applauded by a few of his companions but frowned upon, of course, by authority. However, the matter was satisfactorily settled by payment of a golden sovereign, the cost of replacement, and the guilty party somehow contrived to get hold of the old one, which he now regarded to be his by rights. He fixed it where it would shed light on to his bench, where it remained for many years.

Another little piece of Rottingdean's past was nailed to a beam in the form of a noticeboard announcing, 'That man who brings a Pipe or Cigar Alight in Here, The Forfeit is a Pot of Beer. The Rules of this Stable 1814. Thos. Patching, White Horse, April 6 1814.' It had at that time been displayed in the stables of the White Horse Inn down on the cliff top and when gentlemen rode or drove out along the coast road from Brighton for an airing, they would often go into the stables to look at the horses—rather as the present-day driver casts his eye around the car park to see if there is any model there more exciting than his own—and if, unwittingly, he was smoking at the time his attention would be at once directed to the notice by one of the hostlers or grooms, and the penalty was enforced to their great satisfaction.

I had to help Dad as often as my attendance at school and, later, work at the barber's, would allow, but there was one job which required two pairs of hands and therefore had to be arranged during the times when I was available. He had mounted a heavy, iron hand-pump on a stout, wooden, trestle-type frame with two handles at each end by which it could be carried in the manner of a stretcher. To the pump were attached two lengths of four-inch, armoured, rubber hose, which some years before had been used for filling the water-tank of the steam traction engine on the farm, and with this contraption we used to empty cess-pits at five shillings a time.

He had mounted a heavy iron pump on a stout wooden
trestle-type frame.

As our methods were a little unorthodox—merely running the outlet pipe over the garden fence or through the hedge and pumping the effluent out on to the nearest piece of spare ground—we usually operated after dark. So as dusk fell on the village two rather furtive figures might sometimes have been seen trudging one behind the other up the steep hillside track carrying something rather heavy between them and pausing at intervals 'for a blow'. Although it was not exactly the sort of job that could be taken lightly or conducted in a spirit of fun, I recall that there was never the slightest sense of despondency and certainly none of shame. We were doing an honest job for an honest reward and, though perhaps not the kind of task you would have done from choice, there was no need to be gloomy about it. We laughed and joked and even sang a snatch of song which was singularly appropriate,

> My father's the old village muckman,
> He empties the dunnicks at night,
> And when he comes home in the morning
> He's covered all over with—
> Sweet violets, much sweeter than all the roses,
> Take them, my darling, I plucked them on purpose for you.

I remember once returning home over the hill carrying our foul-smelling burden between us with Dad in the leading shafts. It was a warm night with a clear, star-studded sky and the moon glittered in a silver path like a ribbon of stars fallen into the sea. "Old 'ard, a minute,' he said, 'I could do with a smoke.' We set the cumbersome equipment down on the soft, downland turf and sat on it, one on either side of the pump, both glad of the opportunity to rest.

Presently the smoke from a cigarette he had rolled with reeking fingers began to drift round us on the still night air smelling fragrant and wholesome. It was quiet and peaceful after the clanking and groaning of the pump for the last hour or so, and the thought that we were able to work together so amicably on such an unpleasant job made us realize that we had a really tremendous bond of affection between us. The mood was accentuated by the sheer beauty of the scene before us. 'Look at that, boy,' he said, 'the King of England wun't never see a better sight than that—not if 'e travels the wide world over.' Then he started to sing,

Although I'm not rich and although I'm not poor,
I'm as happy as those that's got thousands or more . . .

We sang the song right through to the glory of the moment with no one to scoff or sneer at its quaintness, which in those days was considered by most to be dull and old-fashioned. For us the joy of the song was in the singing of it and of being together and being able and willing to do so. 'Bugger, boy,' he said, when the song was ended, 'I wish you'da bin m' brother instead o' m' son—I'd 'a' known y' longer.'

Before we moved off, we sang a couple more songs that seemed to fit the prevailing mood, 'Old Adam' and 'Bold Princess Royal'. But Thousands or More was always a great favourite.[1] The words seemed so appropriate and Dad sang with such conviction that I could not help but feel their significance too. Speaking as one upon whom all our old songs have had more than a passing influence, it is easy to see how they could sometimes provide more than mere entertainment and enter into a man's heart.

In the same way as our present-day idiom is peppered with television's cast-off catch-phrases, lines from the old songs had a habit of popping up in everyday conversation. The morn was 'pleasant and delightful' or the night bad when 'tempests beat and torrents pour' and the world was likely to be populated with 'fair maids' and 'roving blades'. The phrases tripped off the tongue like a schoolboy's excuses for truancy and as 'the lark sang so melodious' and the moon shone on the 'salt sea waves', each day was touched with poetry in spite of the poverty and hardship.

There was not the slightest doubt that Dad was influenced by the songs, as witness the following lines in which he borrowed freely from the songs he loved to pay tribute to his native county.

[1] *See* pp. 241, 242, 244.

L et's visit the country for a while where
I can roam so free,
F or there is peace and quietude and
E njoyment from the breeze.

I love to hear the harmless birds sing in the branches there,
N ought can with them compare.

G lorious 'tis on a May morning
O n Sussex downs to view,
O 'er hill and dale, midst gorse and thorn
D amped by the early dew.

O h country life of joy
L oud praises let us sing
D own by the old mill stream.

S o let us keep our country charms
U nscathed and clean and pure,
S erene in all its beauties,
S ustained by nature's lure.
E nthralled o'er hill and dale we'll go—
X cept when it doth rain and blow.

In these days of sophistication and brittle human relationships it may come as a surprise to realize that many of the
men who worked so hard, often in the most appalling
weather conditions, and who were as tough as any in the
land, were not the dolts and boors they are so often portrayed
to be in popular fiction.

Dan Alce was a native of Piddinghoe, a tiny village on the
west bank of the river Ouse just over the hill from Rottingdean. He had been an old sheep-shearing mate of Dad's at
the turn of, and in the early part of, this century though a
little senior, I should say, in years. I knew him well in later
life. He was a peace-loving, slow-moving giant of a man
with the strength of an ox and could 'work, drink and swear

along with the best an 'em'. He was almost aggressively honest, straightforward and diligent and 'God 'elp anyone as stood in 'is path.'

But a chink in his stout, exterior armour was revealed when his small grand-daughter died tragically at the age of three-and-a-half years. He had seen her tiny grave dug in the churchyard, where so many of his ancestors lay, and the evening before the burial service, unbeknown to anyone, he walked out into the riverside meadows and gathered poppies, cornflowers, dog-daisies, flowers from the hedgerow and moss from shady banks and he lined the 'narrow cell' to which she was to be confined with the beauty and sweetness of the surrounding fields. For, as he said, 'I couldn't a-bear to think of my sweet li'l maid bein' lowered into that pit o' cold clay ground.'

Dan was a celebrated singer of the old songs and if there wasn't a song from which he drew inspiration for this delicate deed, then one should be written to honour it.

Chapter Sixteen

After the farm sale of 1924 we had to start paying rent. Although Dad carried on his job under the new farmer, the cottages had not changed hands with the farm and still belonged to 'the Guv'nor— J.P.' All his old employees, who had occupied cottages on the tied system were allowed to stay in them on payment of seven shillings a week, but ours at Northgate, having an extra room, was thought to be worth eight shillings and I seem to remember a certain amount of covert complaining going on about us 'being hard done by'.

Dad was appointed unofficial rent-collector, although in fact as our cottage had to be passed by all the other tenants on their way down to the village, they almost invariably brought it round to the back door sometime during the week—often on a Saturday evening. The rent books, which were always in our possession, for such was the easy-going and trusting nature of the way business was conducted in those days, were kept in a small, dark-oak cupboard with brass hinges which stood on a high shelf at the bottom of the narrow stairway and on Sunday evenings Dad would take them down and mark them up to date. It is significant, I think, that, difficult as times were, I never recall anyone getting in arrears. He would put the total amount into a buff, manilla envelope which he marked with a carpenter's pencil, in a clear, decisive hand, 'Cottage Rent'. I remember the elaborate and flourishing capitals and the long tail of the 'R' which curved gracefully down to underline the 'ent' and I was secretly proud of my father's excellent style of handwriting. I sometimes practised pot-hooks, loops and thicks and thins in a feeble attempt to emulate him, but failed wretchedly.

On Mondays one of my regular errands was to take the rent envelope over to Challenors, the big house where 'the Guv'nor' lived and the visit was always a peep into another world. I would crunch up the short gravel drive from the road, where in spring we used to gather Stars of Bethlehem from under the clipped euonymus hedges, and later in the year sit in the shoulder-high grass of the little meadow between the road and the garden, and hold buttercups under each other's chins to find out who liked butter or blow o'clock on seeded-dandelions. Opening the green, five-barred gate with caution, I would creep into the large square yard across which I must walk to reach the tradesmen's door. Both eyes and ears would be on the alert for Sandy, a rather short-tempered Scots terrier with a bedraggled moustache, whose lip curled back in the ugliest fashion as he growled that he was the house-dog there and, even though I was the bearer of revenue, he disapproved of intrusion from any outsider whatsoever, regardless of his mission.

Once assured of Sandy's absence, the distractions were many. On two of its sides the yard was enclosed by flint-walled stables and outhouses and through the open door of the saddle room, Mr Newman might be seen polishing the household riding boots with a dab of heel-ball, a little spit rubbed in with the heel of the hand and a vigorous fiddle-stringing with an old army puttee. On the wall outside, pipe-clayed girths and brow-bands would be hanging to dry on the tethering-rings and inside saddles, harness and bridles gleamed in the comparative gloom. Blue and red rosettes nailed to the rafters and in various stages of colour-fading and dust collection according to vintage, proclaimed past victories at horse-shows and gymkhanas. There was a smell of well-dressed leather and the bench under the window was littered with dandy-brushes, curry-combs, dock-sponges, and hoof-picks and a shelf overhead was lined with tins of Propert's saddle-soap and neat's-foot oil and various blue and green bottles of liniment and drenches for use in horse medication.

Out in the yard again, having wasted a good ten minutes watching, in mute, open-mouthed admiration, Mr Newman's deft and effective efforts on the toe-caps of the boots, which reflected with equal clarity the diminished doorway behind my head and the huge, bulbous nose that protruded before me, I might catch a glimpse of Mr Cowley through the open, arched doorway that led into the kitchen garden.

Mr Cowley was the gardener and would be dressing the asparagus bed with rotted sea-weed or disbudding chrysanthemums and tying them to stakes with strands of bass pulled from a skein hanging from the belt round his middle. The entire garden was enclosed by high, protective walls and the south-facing one supported two fan-trained peach trees, the fruits of which I coveted in vain. Although an apple or pear, usually disappointingly unripe, sometimes found its way into my pocket if Mr Cowley's attention was temporarily diverted during my presence.

The rectangular plots were neatly divided by gravel paths flanked by box hedges no more than a foot high and everything was well tended and organized from the rows of fat, earthenware sea-kale pots, looking like something out of Ali Baba, to the small, square nursery beds of rich, dark loam. Down in a corner under a yew tree was the potting-shed and boiler-house to heat the greenhouses. From the mossy joints in its sandstone walls, young fronds of hart's-tongue fern unfolded like shepherds' crooks and on sunny mornings the fitful buzzing of blue-bottles in the ivy on the roof sounded like the bleating of lambs in a distant fold. Alongside a cold-frame among the heaps of wood-ash, soot and leaf mould, stood an old wooden wheelbarrow and an ancient garden roller with a stone cylinder and scrolled iron handle, and scattered around in mild disorder were telescopes of flower pots, watering cans, seed boxes, rakes, hoes, trugs, trowels and all the sensible, soil-bound stuff of gardening.

Sometimes I would be asked to fill the stone water trough from an old iron pump which screeched like a cock pheasant every time I wrenched its arm. But, apart from the protesting pump, there was a quiet air of unhurried efficiency. There was something extremely restful in watching an old man potter about in the garden. The panama hat, the green baize apron, the pipe and the steady, methodical movement all contributed to make it into such a quiet occupation. The

All the sensible soil-bound stuff of gardening.

clink of a spade on a flint, the sound of a sharpening stone on swop-hook or scythe, the steady clicking of hand-shears were all that you would be likely to hear and, though his back might be ready to break and sweat cloud his eye, the gardener's heart was at peace. But now a garden is a 'noisome' thing, God wot, and in any built-up area the summer evenings are a whirring, phut-phutting nightmare. We spare our muscles at the expense of our nerves—to say nothing of those of our neighbours.

Sooner or later I would arrive at the tradesmen's door. To gain audience, let alone admittance into the sanctum of the big house, it was necessary to notify your arrival by pulling a brass knob, worn smooth with years of wear and daily polishings, which was set in the brick-work at the side of the door. Allowing time for the taking up of slack wires and the wobbly action of a series of ancient, elbow shaped levers screwed to the walls, this eventually caused a bell to ring faintly somewhere deep inside the house and after what seemed an interminable interval the sound of approaching footsteps on the flagstones of the passages would be heard on the other side of the door. The white-capped and aproned figure who opened it, probably one of the lower order in the domestic hierarchy, took the proffered envelope with disdain, carefully holding it between finger and thumb at the extreme edge and keeping her pale hand as far as possible, it seemed, away from mine, which was probably pretty grubby. Then without a word or look of acknowledgement the door would be shut in my face.

Frequently this impersonal procedure was cut short by Mrs Dudeney, the cook, who, spotting me from the kitchen, would open the window and call cheerily, 'All right, sonny, bring it here. I'll take it.' She would take the envelope and pat me on the cheek with a work-damp hand that smelt of onions, 'My word, how you do grow—wait a minute!' Presently she would come to the window and hand out a large wedge of cold, gooseberry tart. 'There you are, me boy,' she would say, 'that's the stuff to give the troops. That makes little boys into big boys and big boys into burglars.' Then, with her strong bare arms akimbo, she would throw back her head and laugh like a ploughman, setting her ample, table-jelly form all of a shiver.

On rare occasions my presence would be required in the drawing-room and, although I would instantly become heavy with guilt wondering which of my recent exploits I would be called upon to explain and trying desperately to swallow the golf ball that seemed to have suddenly lodged in my throat, it was usually for nothing more serious than being asked to take a message to Dad. The summons into the august presence was usually delivered in a lofty tone by the same maid who was used to my weekly visits and always looked at me as if she thought I should hastily be swept under the mat. I would follow her at a respectful distance spitting into the palm of my hand to try to get my hair under some sort of control and pulling up my socks which, despite garters like tourniquets, always seemed to succumb to the force of gravity and drape themselve about my ankles.

After threading our way through a bewildering maze of passages and hallways, I would suddenly find myself standing in front of 'the Guv'nor—J.P.', who stood framed in a large bay window which looked out across terraced lawns towards the hedge that marked the boundary of the Quakers' burial ground and to the church beyond. There I would stand, painfully conscious of my dirty knees and wringing my cap in both hands like mother did the socks on washing day.

He stood feet well apart on the wide oak floor-boards, in riding boots and breeches, with his hands clasped behind him, rocking gently backwards and forwards on heel and toe. He was wearing gold, wire-framed spectacles perched on the end of his nose and as I entered he lowered his head and peered at me over the small, oval lenses. He was in his shirt sleeves which were fastened at the cuffs with gold links and supported just above the elbows with expanding metal arm-bands also in gold. This metal was again in evidence in the form of a watch-chain across the front of his waistcoat, the lower four or five buttons of which were undone.

He looked less severe without his hat and more human than when I doffed my cap to him in the High Street or he called me summarily from some absorbing game with friends in School Opening to hold his horse while he dismounted and went into the Post Office or bank. As we stood face to face, an unusual situation, he had a kindlier look than I had ever imagined.

'Mm-mm, Bobby.' He spoke slowly and prefaced nearly all his remarks with a high-pitched hum of approval and a slight nodding of his head, as if he had given silent consideration in his mind to what he was about to say and was giving himself audible assent to utter it. 'Mm-mm, I want y' father, Jem, to—' and here he would fill in the details of some odd job for Dad on the following day, '—now you will be sure to tell him, won't you?'

Challenors had been the manor house since the sixteenth century and there is something about an old house which has witnessed so many centuries of human habitation that gives it an atmosphere all its own. It is as if, over the years, it has built up its own character from all the dramas and comedies of life that have been enacted beneath its roof. Every fireplace has its dreams, every stairway and bed-chamber door its stories to unfold.

The tastes and preferences of the contemporary household were revealed in the furnishings and decor. Sporting prints and horse portraits by Stubbs hung over the mantel while the flamboyant rose bowls over-flowed their beauty and were reflected in the lake-like surfaces of mahogany table-tops. The glass-fronted book-cases which lined the walls were probably treasuries of reading with Hazlitt, Emerson, Trollope, Surtees, Sir John Lubbock's Hundred and the Waverley novels, but I was not to know.

There were signs of gracious living, too, through the partly open door of the dining room. A crumbly, port-fed Stilton, turbaned in a white linen napkin sat on a flat wooden board on the sideboard like a fakir on a bed of penance. Cut glass decanters sat regally enthroned in silver coasters with hand-engraved labels round their necks, like chains of office, identifying the wearers, 'Brandy', 'Madeira', 'Port' and 'Sherry' and a bodyguard of rummers and tinted claret glasses stood by, feet uppermost.

My knowledge of 'how the other half lived' was broadened by regular visits to all the bigger properties in the village in the course of a delivery-boy's jobs for various tradespeople, which was the means by which most of us boys supplemented our incomes after farming on a big scale had stopped. I must have been very impressed with what I encountered, for many vignettes still remain clear in my memory. But whether of this house or that I cannot recall.

The impact of almost any impression on the mind is magnified ten-fold by its being unexpected. I remember once at the impossible hour of six-thirty one morning in summer, halfway through my daily milk round and walking past the knapped-flint frontage of an elegant Georgian house where wistaria wove its misty blue magic round the latticed windows, I was passing large, double glass-doors flung wide open to admit the early sunshine, when suddenly the silence was flooded with the spirited opening chords of the Poet and Peasant Overture on a grand piano standing just inside. I was as suddenly lifted out of my early-morning, pre-school torpor and whisked away on the wings of sound to hitherto undreamed-of realms of happiness and as I walked on down the drive under the elms, slower now, so that the joy of the moment should not be lost too soon, the mood and the music followed me. It has never really left me, for that stirring opening passage never fails to evoke the hope and promise associated with early morning.

Another scene of more serenity that has remained with me for over fifty years was in a high-walled garden on a hot afternoon. Seated on the grass in the piebald shadow of a Spanish chestnut tree was a young girl in a white dress wearing a straw hat with a little chaplet of imitation daisies, cornflowers, and poppies round the base of the crown. She was leaning back against one of the wheels of a basket-work bath-chair reading aloud in a clear, cultured voice, from an open book on her lap. The occupant of the chair, an elderly lady, sat under a cream-coloured parasol with a green lining which was tied to the handle of the chair behind her. Her head was inclined to one side and her eyes were closed with the shadow of a smile touching the corners of her mouth. They were both so totally engrossed in the book that neither of them noticed my passing down the drive. The golden light of the afternoon sun, the green glow of the leafy shade and the classic pose of youth and age in absolute sympathy painted an indelible picture on my mind and I trod as quietly as I could and crept away so as not to break the spell.

All these things added up to something a long way removed from the plain fare and the scrubbed boards and drugget of home. But, far from being envious, I found them warmly reassuring. Being conscious, at the same time, that when on Sundays we praised God from whom all blessings flowed, many of the blessings He saw fit to bestow upon us actually reached us by way of the big houses.

One of Grand-dad's favourite stories was of an irate farm-hand who, before turning his back on 'the Guv'nor' and walking out of his job, concluded his speech of resignation with '. . . an' I en't gotta 'old my bread under your kipper t' ketch the fat, nuther.' This sturdy declaration of independence never failed to win my admiration, partly for the colourful terms in which it was expressed and partly, I believe, because independence was not one of the family's strong points. We were always given very clearly to understand that 'the Guv'nor' was a just and generous man and looked after us very well and, when on occasions mother's spirit rebelled and she criticized Dad for 'kow-towing' so submissively, she was told not to interfere for there wasn't nothing wrong with 'the Guv'nor' and the Lord above knew where the hell we'd be without him.

In effect, I suppose, holding our bread under his kipper to catch the fat was precisely what we were in the habit of doing. From my weekly visits to the big house I occasionally returned with various items of largesse which, quite legitimately, had been handed through the kitchen window by the ebullient Mrs Dudeney. Never the drippings from a kipper exactly, but certainly a bowl of good beef dripping at the bottom of which would be an inch or so of delicious, brown jelly or sometimes the considerable remains of a joint of roast ribs or sirloin on the bone or half a saddle of local mutton. These were the off-cuts which had been sent back half-finished from the dining-room and were far too good to be committed to the hog-bin or even, for that matter, to the stock-pot, and it was left to the cook to find a good home for them.

Items of clothing discarded from expensive wardrobes, too, were often put to a further term of service in humbler circumstances and most of us children remember only too well the discomfort of wearing shoes that were stuffed with cotton-wool or newspaper in the toes or fitted with thick in-soles of felt to pack out the empty spaces left by feet of inadequate proportions to fill them. Girls were sometimes made to suffer the additional indignity of wearing once-chic footwear, far beyond their years, with the high heels sawn off which tilted the toes up in a cruel burlesque of the original fashion, and this was matched only by the embarrassment of a boy having to wear a coat or macintosh waisted and gusseted to fit the female form which fastened up on the wrong side.

Life in the big houses, then, was echoed in different ways in the lives of many of us. Most of our mothers had done their stint in domestic service and this was reflected in the general discipline and table-manners of cottage life—at least it was in ours. You *will* wash your hands before sitting down to a meal. You *will* sit still and not tilt your chair back on two legs. You *will not* lean your elbows on the table. You *will not* eat green peas off your knife (even if your father does). You *will not* leave the table without saying grace and asking per-mission, 'ThankGodformygooddinnerpleasemayIgetdown'. So in one way and another the influences on village life from the houses of the gentry were considerable, whether we realized it or not.

Chapter Seventeen

Another form of fall-out from the upper atmosphere of the big houses were glossy magazines like *The Tatler*, *The Field*, *Horse and Hound*, *Illustrated London News* and *Country Life* which, having up until then spent their time decorating the drawing-rooms and studies for which they were originally published, suddenly fell from grace and found themselves in less illustrious surroundings. They went on to see long service in remarkably rough stations.

After a week or two of lying around, a little incongruously, in the cottage, they would be taken down to the barber's shop to beguile the time for those awaiting the attentions of portly Mr Adkins the barber, of whom I shall have more to say later. Several months afterwards, by which time they were well-thumbed, dog-eared and lacking several pages of gardening hints and pictures of young ladies modelling Wolsey combinations which had held special appeal for certain readers, they were bundled up and dispatched by post to Mr Bob Lively, c/o National Bank, Santa Cruz, Patagonia, Argentina, South America. I remember the address well for by this time I was working on Saturdays and Sunday mornings at the barber's shop as lather boy and it was my job to pack and post the parcel.

Bob Lively, along with several other young men, had left the village in about 1905 to work on an outpost sheep station in Patagonia. This resulted from a recruitment scheme conducted in the villages throughout this part of the south, presumably on the assumption that young men who had been brought up in sheep-farming communities would be more interested and better equipped to take on such a venture. Dad, who was one of the same generation, had very much wanted to join them, but Grand-dad had had other plans for him on the home farm so he was not allowed to go.

From time to time, the other men who went came home on leave, but old Bob seldom managed to get as far as Rotting-dean. It was said that after travelling the two hundred miles down river to Santa Cruz from the isolation of the sheep station and then a further fifteen hundred miles or so up the coast to Buenos Aires, he always felt that he had gone far enough. So he spent his time and hard-earned money in the saloons and bars in that garish city which offered such a welcome contrast to the austere life on the station, staying there until it was time to return.

I often wondered what it was like out there and as I handed the parcel over the post office counter, I used to try to imagine where the magazines would actually finish up. In some little, old hut somewhere out on the windswept plains, perhaps, but no really clear ideas were formed. One of the penalties for day-dreaming during geography lessons was that it had left me very poorly informed about such distant places. I recalled some talk about the bolas with which the gauchos caught and hobbled their cattle and I connected it in a vague way, and quite incorrectly, with the type of sling David had used to slay Goliath in the scriptures, but it was a very confused and indistinct picture. My knowledge of Patagonia, however, was soon to be broadened in the most interesting manner.

'Ol' Bob Lively's back home, then.' The news ran round the village with the urgency of those seasonal headlines, 'the mack'rel are in' or 'they're cuttin' "roons" (mushrooms) up on the Tye' and the barber's shop, being one of the local news agencies, was soon buzzing with stop-press reports on the Lively story.

It was not long before the tall figure of the man himself appeared. Ducking his head under the low doorway of the tiny flint cottage that served as the shop, he stepped down into the company of his own folk again after an absence of over twenty years. He stood there with the crown of his wide-awake felt hat all but touching the ceiling, holding in his hand a huge plaited-straw fish basket that as nearly reached the floor. He looked around unemotionally, his eyes narrowed to slits as if they were used to looking into far distances—or it may have been that he was adjusting his sight to the gloom after the brilliance of the sunlight outside.

Any preconceived notions I may have had of what he looked like were instantly shattered and fell in fragments at his feet. Here was no sun-bronzed hero bouncing back into the world of his youth with the breezy confidence of the adventurer who had made good. He looked round benignly but unsmiling, no rip-snorting, gun-toting bull-of-the-pampas he. There he stood in a baggy, tweed suit and large black boots, once more amongst boyhood friends in his native village looking for all the world as if he had never left it. His appearance was undistinguished to say the least. True his dark moustaches drooping down on either side of a rather sardonic mouth looked more South American than English, but his long, loose-knit figure sagged a bit at the knees, his shoulders drooped like his moustaches and his eyes were hooded and rather sad. He didn't say much, in fact he didn't have to, his appearance had set off such a bout of talk and cross-talk that he would have had a job to make himself heard anyway. When he did speak he did so slowly, deliberately and quietly.

' 'Ow do, fellas, nice t' see y'all agin,' he said casually, and without much enthusiasm, 'I guess I'll hev a shave.'

He sat down in one of the chairs facing the wash-basins and wall-mirrors and I tucked a towel under his rugged, bristling chin and started to 'lather up' with a string-bound brush in a china shaving mug with a bunch of violets printed in colour on the side. He lay back in the chair with his head on the neck-rest and his eyes closed as if he was asleep, quite unaware, it seemed, of the gabble of tongues around him and about him. Presently one eye-lid lifted and a brown button eye looked directly into mine. 'Hark at 'em, son,' he said, through a mask of white soap-suds, 'they're jest like a Portuguese parli'ment, I guess, ever'buddy talkin' an' nobuddy a-listenin'.' The eye closed.

Having been brought up on the strict understanding that little boys should be seen and not heard I carried on with my job in silence. A little later the eye opened again. 'You dun't say a lot, me ol' buddy boy.'

'No, Mist' Lively.'

There was a considerable pause. 'That en't no vice,' he said, 'you always remember, son, that a good listener is better 'an a bad talker.'

Although at first I had been taken aback, even slightly dismayed, by his unprepossessing appearance, I began to see that there was after all something which made old Bob stand out from his fellows. Here he was, a villager amongst villagers, a sheep-man amongst sheep-men, but his years of rough life on the Patagonian plains and daily contact with all sorts and conditions of men had imparted a tolerance and worldly wisdom that can be only bought with a life-time of experience.

Bob's easy familiarity and good humour ensured that he soon settled down to village life. He grew a few vegetables on a garden allotment on the steep hillside under the wind-mill and went fishing in a small rowing-boat he kept on the foreshore, acting out the dreams he had had in exile on the other side of the world. When the weather was bad and the pubs were closed, he would sit in a lop-sided shed, one of four at the side of The Gap, which was the track that sloped down from the end of the High Street to beach level, mending holes in a trammel-net or making up a cork-line for a lobster-pot and taking frequent swigs from a bottle of whisky.

As he worked, he would keep up a desultory monologue touching on every subject under the sun from the benefits to be derived from splitting the atom to the folly of Tommy Burns fighting Jack Johnson. He spoke softly and contemplatively, almost as if he was thinking aloud, with long pauses which he filled with a few bars from some unidentifiable tune whistled through pouting lips, then he would return to his theme at the exact point at which he had left it.

His demeanour was restful and calming and his stories interminable, since his unhurried manner, coupled with the musical interludes, took no account of time nor of the listener's patience. Not that the second consideration ever applied when I was his audience. I would be content to sit on the doorstep of his shed during the entire length of a rainy day listening to his tales of travel and adventure. Schooltime, mealtime, even bedtime would all be forgotten in the spell of romance he breathed out with the whisky fumes. I think some of his most fascinating yarns were locked up in that whisky bottle until he released them by pulling the cork with his teeth and pressing the neck to his lips. But, no matter, they gave one small boy a lot to think about in bed that night—and, for that matter, ever since.

'It's a big ol' country, son. There's well over a hundred million head o' sheep in the Argentine, but you'd never know it. There's plenty o' room for more. We used to steam out o' Buenos Aires in a li'l ol' clickety-clackety coal-burner with the salt caked on her funnel and upperworks like icing on a Christmas cake and it used to take us best part of a week to punch on down that long ol' coast line right through the roarin' forties to Santa Cruz. If there happened to be a dirty ol' sou'easter blowin' straight up off the Falklands great, grizzle-bearded fortyfooters would come down at y' curlin', churnin' and tumblin' like a cavalry charge o' greys. There wasn't nothin' in the world that could stop 'em—and that li'l ol' tub used to ride 'em like a cow-hand. When she crested 'em, her screw would fly out the water and she'd scream like a banshee in a windy cave. Then she'd plunge down th' other side, yawing like,' he paused searching for the right simile, 'like a constipated camel. Sometimes when they hit amidships, she'd shudder fit to break her back an' you thought you'd never see God's good dry land again.'

He told me of one trip when a sea-sick man in the bunk above his kept on moaning and repeating the Lord's prayer over and over again because he thought his time had come and how, on another occasion, on the first day out, the mate slipped on a companion-way, hit his head on a bulk-head and lay there 'dead as a herrin' '. They lashed him to a ventilation trunk in a locker in the galley to keep him out the way till they made port and every time the ship rolled heavily the locker door would fly open and there he would be standing 'a-watchin' of y' with starin', sightless eyes'. But Bob used to spend most of the time in the skipper's cabin drinking tequila out the jar 'till it made y' head sing like a kittle on th' hob'.

At Santa Cruz they would leave the coaster and pack everything on to a bullock cart which would take them two hundred miles up river to the sheep station near the shores of Lake Argentina. There was no other way of getting there. There they would live in wooden huts with earth floors that had been built by earlier settlers at the end of the last century and were not so very different from what I had imagined. They ate mutton so regularly they 'used t' bleat instead o' talkin', son. But when you'd been out ridin' th' plains you got so durned hungry you could have ate eleven o' the apostles and given the twelfth a run for his money. I've been so hungry, my ol' son, I could have ate a whole skimp without any bread.'

'What's a skimp, Mist' Lively?'

'A skimp, ol' buddy boy, is a donkey's tail stuffed with winkles.'

The Indians still rode around in tribes living off the game they caught on the plains and sheep they could raid off the station. They fought like 'Kilkenny cats' against other tribes and also amongst themselves and a fight between two men was always to the death. He talked of purple swallows, rats as big as dogs and Patagonian hares which had short ears and could leap like kangaroos.

I asked him if he ever got the magazines, 'Yes,' he said, 'we

used to pick 'em when we went foodlin' off down to Cruz.
I reck'n they helped save our sanity and sometimes even our
lives. When men live rough away from the sweetening
influences of a good woman, son, they get edgey. They get
mean, ugly and greedy and all clamped down in the screw
o' their own vices. Little things get blown up into big things.
We used to play a lot o' cards and I've seen a man finish up
with a bullet-hole between his eyes jest for the sake of a
couple o' notches on a cribbage board.'

Old Bob could make my flesh creep with his yarns, but I
never tired of listening to him. The names of the tribes and
the trees and much of the detail of what he told me have been
forgotten, but I do remember that it all seemed a long, long
way from that little fisherman's hut where he would sit
braiding nets with tarred twine, a skinny, hand-rolled
cigarette dangling from his lower lip and his blood-shot eyes
growing ever more dreamy until at last his head would drop
forward and he would fall into a deep, stertorous sleep. Later
he would wake and look around, blinking, light the cigarette
which was still hanging from his lip and say, 'I'd give me two
eyes right now, son, for a plate o' cold cabbage.'

Chapter Eighteen

Dwelling as we did ' 'twixt downs and sea', we had, as it were, a foot in either camp and this added another dimension to life. Even the most shore-bound and uninterested of coast-dwellers must constantly be aware of that great whispering mass of water close at hand, but for the susceptible, once he has fallen under her spell, the sights, sounds, and smells of the sea are with him night and day. Her devotees are many and of all ages but when you are thirteen and there is someone like Old Bob always on hand to explain the mysteries and kindle your imagination with long-spun, salty yarns, a mere flirtation can grow into a consuming obsession.

The seashore has a flavour all its own and the capstans, boats, oars, anchors, lobster-pots and nets savour of brine and stockholm tar. Fishermen talk of thwarts, rowlocks, warps, sheets, bollards, cleats, and rope's-ends in a language quite incomprehensible to men of the soil. They 'cock their eye to wind'ard' for weather signs and presage a storm from a 'catspaw of breeze' and if it does 'get shucky' they will not turn round and go home, like you or me, but 'turn about and beat back' in the best of nautical traditions.

My first love affair was undoubtedly with the sea. Not the whole, wide rolling world of seas but just that small, inshore area of English Channel which lapped or scoured the Rottingdean beaches.

For the comparative few of us who at that time succumbed to her charms, the sea became an over-riding passion. We fished in her, swam in her, floated on her, boated on her, plundered her bed for edible delicacies and watched her shores for flotsam cast up on the tide-line. When the tide was in we fished for bass, flounders, and silver-eels from the wooden groins and beaches. When it was out, we picked winkles from the rocks, dug lug-worms for bait from the sand—three quick spits from blow-hole to cast, for they are rapid movers—or explored the rocky, weed-draped pools studying the habits of hermit crabs, miller's thumbs and all the weird and wonderful forms of cold-blooded life which are to be found therein. There were star-fish and stickle-backs, razor-shells and ragworms and the ever-present sea anemones, those fleshy flowers of the sea that burgeon in their native watery element, but are so shy and retiring when deserted by the tide. On hot summer days we splashed and swam in the delicious cool of her waters or built rafts out of oil-drums and made adventurous, drifting voyages along the coast. In winter we gathered driftwood for firing or went 'black-sanding' for coins and jewellery dropped on the beach by summertime visitors.

The foreshore, that strip of land which surrounds our island like a pelmet and lies between high- and low-water marks, can be described neither as proper under-water sea-bed nor good dry land. Instead it leads a Jekyll and Hyde existence posing first as one and then the other. Being inhabited by so many forms of sea-life which made welcome and appetizing additions to the larder, it attracted a certain number of part-time fishermen, particularly at weekends, and offered good hunting comparable with that on the downs, but with the additional advantage of not carrying penalties for poaching.

'More prawners than prawns today,' old Bob would say, as one by one the weekend fishermen trooped down the Gap to follow the ebbing tide out to their favourite spot, Every rock, every gully, every strip of sand was mentally charted with the precision of an ordnance survey map and the more distinctive features had names. The Dardanelles. The Point, The Flat Rock, Sandy Sou, The Benches and Dr Fawke were all favourite prawning locations. Dr Fawke was the wreck of an old wooden vessel of that name, the ribs of which were exposed only at the lowest ebb of a spring tide, but all the rest were rocks partly submerged in the pools left behind by the receding tide and under which nets could be laid to entice the wily prawn. The nets, known as lades, were spoon-shaped and baited with limpets and 'jack-avells' (shore-crabs) impaled on a piece of split cane like a kebab and placed across the mouth. A great deal of care had to be taken in inserting the net for at the first hint of impending danger the entire prawn population of the pool, with single flicks of their strong tails, would flash into the inaccessible recesses under the rock and live to swim in another tide.

Before they were fully grown, prawns were known as 'shiners' but it was the large, fully-roed females, or 'brooders', which were the real quarry and a fair bag would be six to eight dozen. In the event of the occasional glut, many more would be caught and sometimes, of course, the catch was considerably less. But the fisherman, walking back up The Gap with his bag stuffed full of sea-weed for the sake of appearances, always concealed his disappointment by saying he had 'got enough for Sunday tea'. 'Yep,' Bob would say, knowingly, 'I s'pose you can always make up with plenty o' bread an' butter an' cake.'

Shrimps were caught on the sandy stretches accessible at low tide in about two to four feet of water. A large, rectangular net some six to seven feet long and about three feet wide, was pushed forward so that the smooth wooden bar in front ploughed up the sand and scooped the shrimps back into the bag of the net. A satisfactory haul for one tide would be about a gallon and sometimes the shrimper took home a nice Dover sole or lobster that had found its way into the net along with the sea-horses, jelly-fish and, of course, the bane of his life, seaweed.

We used to lay long lines on the sand at low tide, covering each baited hook with a handful of sand to protect it from the seagulls until it was safely under the waves. They are voracious birds and would devour any fish you managed to hook, too, if you weren't there to collect it immediately the tide had left. Lobsters were normally caught in pots just beyond low water mark on a ridge of rocks known as the Bar which could be reached only by boat. But one year when a large number of octopuses invaded our coast they drove the lobsters into shallower waters where they could be found in gullies between the rocks and particularly in the well-known prawn holes. They had every reason to be terrified of the octopuses for the shells of some who had not managed to avoid the searching tentacles could be found discarded. They were perfectly normal on the outside, but on closer examination proved to be sucked completely clean like empty egg shells. An unusual method of lobstering during that summer, which has never to my knowledge been repeated, was to impale an octopus on a length of stiff wire and, having prodded him until he had exuded all his inky outpourings, thrust him under a rocky ledge, as you would a prawn lade, and simply wait for the lobsters to come flipping out at your feet having unwittingly surrendered themselves into the hands of the more cunning of the two predators. It was rather like ferreting for lobsters.

The variety of articles washed up on the beaches was endless and many had an aura of romance about them because of the mystery of their origins. Sections of coconut husk might well have drifted from the 'tropics and the palm green shores', a stripped banana stem may, of course, have been jettisoned from the galley of a passing liner, but it was interesting to think that it could have washed all the way from the Canary Islands. Lifebelts, wreckage, hatch-covers, fenders, almost everything that came ashore invited a dream. Over the years an astonishing and bizarre miscellany of flotsam has ended up on our shores. Bales of raw rubber, blocks of coconut butter, dead bullocks, barrels of wine and beer and bamboo canes have all turned up at some time or another in large quantities. For many years the village gardeners supported their runner beans with bamboos which washed ashore in about 1924. They were almost indestructible and I know that at least one is still in existence. After about forty successive years in the garden, it is now used as a walking stick.

Being on the coast somehow banished that feeling of insularity that prevailed in inland villages of a comparable size. It was, particularly in those days before air travel, rather like living at the edge of the highway from London to everywhere and, in their passing, the liners and tankers on their way to or returning from distant ports, trailed a little of the romance of far-away places. Old Bob used to study the shipping news and knew the docking and embarkation times at the Port of London, East India Docks, and Tilbury, so we watched from the top of the cliffs for the vessels which would sail past out in the shipping lanes. When visibility was good, they could clearly be seen with a good telescope. 'I had a very fine glass once,' he quipped, 'but I strained it trying to look too far through it.'

At fairly regular intervals the entire village would be almost blasted out of bed in the middle of the night by several rafter-shaking blasts from a great foghorn no more than a quarter of a mile away. 'That'll be old Bert Roberts,' we would all think before pulling the bedclothes up over our heads and attempting to sink into sleep once again. Bert was the captain of a cargo ship plying between certain continental and Mediterranean ports and home, and if he was due to tie up at Newhaven or Shoreham he would sail close inshore opposite the village and give three or four sharp blasts on the ship's siren to let his mother know that he would be arriving home some time on the following day. The fact that everyone else in the village knew as well and that his name was imprinted, rather unpopularly, in the minds of all those who remained sleepless for the rest of the night seemed not to worry him in the slightest.

To me the sovereign attraction of the sea was to be out on it, but I had frequent disappointments and the preparations, mostly verbal, to row out and lift the lobster pots or go hooking seemed endless and out of all proportion to the number of trips we actually made. A considerable part of a longshoreman's day seemed to be spent leaning on the wall looking out over the water. Physical movement was languid, in fact almost imperceptible, the conversation fragmented and what it was we were actually looking for always escaped me. We would watch the tide go out leaving the sands to dry in the sun, then, if the rain kept off and the daylight held, we could watch it come back in and cover the sands again.

The reasons why anyone should put to sea were nearly always heavily outnumbered by the reasons why he should not. The porpoises were 'runnin' east'ard' which meant it was going to blow, or she was 'showin' 'er teeth' which meant the waves were breaking on the Bar and it was already blowing. Neap tides were no good for this type of fishing, spring tides no good for that. The west wind stirred her up till she was 'like pea-soup' and she was 'clear as gin' when the wind went east, both of which conditions were considered unfit for something or other. It sometimes seemed that the launching of a boat was a course to be adopted only as a very last resort and when it could not possibly be avoided.

But there was plenty of talk, most of it as idle as the hour and as unproductive. The topics were mostly grey and mundane but through it all, like a golden thread in a dish-cloth, ran old Bob's inimitable wit and wisdom. Len, one of our gang whose approach to life was strictly biological, was boasting as usual of his sexual prowess and giving highly exaggerated accounts of an illicit episode in his supposedly crowded love-life when Bob called him to order. 'It's a pity, young fella . . . you don't try t' raise your mind . . . above the level of y' hips once in a while,' he said, using his whistling pauses to great effect. 'Anyways, before you go creepin' up another fella's back-stairs . . . you want t' think hard an' tread soft . . . you might be a-tramplin' on his dreams . . . an' dreams, son, is the only thing that lifts us above th' animals.'

After a long silence during which most of us were a little subdued or at least mystified, he rambled on, 'Living is a very tricky ol' business . . . an' you want to take it very careful for it ain't no trouble t' upset the apple-cart . . . in fact, I sometimes reck'n that ol' apple-cart is like a wheel-barrow with only one leg, it don' take a lot t' upset 'im. . . . When y' hear that ol' preacher man spoutin' the Holy Scriptures . . . he'll keep all on about the wages o' sin an' the paths o' righteousness an' this that an' th'other . . . but he's jest talkin' . . . an' talkin' ain't nothin' but blowin' hot air out over y' vocal chords . . . so that's just a lot o' ol' gas. Believe me, any man worth twopenn'orth o' cold gin knows, without all that yappin', what's good an' what's bad . . . an' all he's gotta do is make his mind up. It's jest as simple as that.' He made it all sound very easy.

Sometimes the waves wrote tragedy on the sands. One golden morning, some five days after a cargo ship had foundered off the Isle of Wight in a raging south-west gale, we were faced with the grave spectacle of the sea giving up her dead. In the storm the brave captain, struggling to save his vessel, had been washed overboard off the bridge. The lifebelts, vainly thrown to his assistance, had already come ashore and for half a mile of its length the foreshore was strewn with a cargo of timber which had broken adrift from the deck of the doomed ship. The longshoremen, wise in the ways of weather, wind and tides, shook their heads, 'The ol' man'll turn up 'ere in a day or two,' they said.

The wind had died away and the sea dropped down to a sullen calm with flat discs of foam the size of dinner plates floating on the surface as placidly as lily-pads on a horse-pond when the morning tide left his broken body, still wearing reefer and slacks of navy blue, lying face downwards on the sand. It had a desolate, discarded look like a doll dropped on the nursery floor by a child who has tired of play.

Later in a grim-faced procession we trailed behind two policemen who carried their sad, crumpled burden on a stretcher, covered with a blanket. At one end two black boots dangled at impossible angles and the wind slapped the flag-staff halyard at the top of the Gap in a steady, melancholy tattoo.

'Poor fella,' said Bob, then filled a long pause with his characteristic whistling. 'Life y'know, ol' son, is a very funny thing. . . . It's jest like suckin' honey . . . suckin' honey off a sprig o' fuzz-bush.'

★　　★　　★

We were fetching up Channel whiting as long as your arm three at a time. The wind, which had backed to south'ard, was freshening noticeably every minute and the dinghy, tethered at the bow by her anchor cable, was bucking and rearing like a fractious pony fighting against the halter. Each time her clinker-built hull smacked down on the surface of the water, a cloud of spray blew inboard and drenched us. We were soaked to the skin and blue with the cold, but we were happy because we were catching fish. But it was a race against time—at least, against the tide which is synonymous. With the sea getting up as it was and having to return eventually to a leeshore, we would have to get back while the tide was still flowing across the sands, for once it started to climb the shelving beaches we should never get ashore without being swamped. But it was tempting to stay until the very last moment all the time the fish were coming up like that.

We raised a sail far down to the east'ard beating up against the wind towards us and as it grew nearer, we could see she was a barge loaded right down to the gun'ales. She came up and went past just outside us with the waves slapping on her bluff bow and the creak of straining blocks and stays. She was 'laying well over' with only about six inches of free-board on her leeside which was towards us and was so close we could see the features of the man at the helm, a short, stocky figure wearing a blue guernsey under a rough tweed coat with a short, briar pipe clenched firmly in the vice of his jaws. He had, I should have said with my newly-acquired professional knowledge, about ten days' growth of whiskers.

Just as she was on our beam, the galley chimney belched out a great cloud of foul, black smoke which blew down all round us and when it had cleared, the face of the person responsible, a boy of about my own age who had just stoked up, appeared in the galley doorway with a wide cheeky grin. I shall always think he did it on purpose. As the wind was getting stronger all the time she was carrying a little too much sail for comfort so the boy was sent to take in a bit of canvas and as she drew away from us we could see him struggling for'ard clinging on to the weather shrouds. By the time she had become a diminishing dot to the west'ard the waves were beginning to snarl and turn over with growing anger. We had shipped a fair amount of water, the bait tin had fallen over, the box holding our catch was spilling over with fish and some of the sleek-sided whiting, who had so recently been flashing about in the watery world beneath us, were swilling around ignominiously in bilge-water amongst a writhing mass of obscene-looking lug-worms which had been the cause of their downfall in the first place.

'Best up-hook an' head for home,' said old Bob, and with aching fingers all wrinkled with salt water, I unfastened the cable and hauled the anchor aboard. Then, taking the oars, I pulled towards the shore, running in before the wind. The cold had got right into my bones and even the exertion of rowing could not stop my teeth from chattering. We were followed all the way by a group of gulls who swooped down repeatedly over our heads yapping like pomeranians. Having come ashore, we dragged the boat across the sand and up the beach above high-water mark and carried the catch and the gear—oars, rowlocks, anchor and cable—up the green-weeded, slipway steps to Bob's hut. It was nice to get in out of the wind.

Bob slumped down on an old lobster-pot, fumbled in his fish-basket for the whisky bottle and took a long swig. 'Aa-agh! The life o' man,' he sighed, licking the brine from his lips. 'Why, you got the shakes, me ol' buddy boy,' he said directly, 'you must be half dead with cold. Here y'are, work some o' that into y'.' He handed the bottle across to me. I drew the cork, gingerly pressed the neck to my lips and was about to take a sip when he reached over and tipped up the bottom of the bottle and I gulped down a great mouthful of the neat spirit. A firecracker exploded in my throat and the top of my head flew open like a jack-in-the-box. As the sparks slowly settled and I floated back down to ground level, I could feel the warmth returning to me right to the tips of my fingers and toes. I stopped shivering and sat down on a coil of rope just inside the door watching the colour come back into Bob's face, and the tip of his nose fade gradually from blue to red as he continued with the dosage.

'What sort o' boat was that went past us this morning?' I asked presently.

'That was a Thames sailing barge, son, laden with Flemish bricks f' the buildin' trade makin' f' Shoreham . . . out of Amsterdam, I should reck'n.' This obviously gave him a train of thought which shunted around in his head for a while before he gave it utterance. 'Did I ever tell y' about that ol' buddy o' mine who became a one-man international situation overnight? . . . I don't think I did . . . It's a true story, son . . . as true as I'm sittin' here a-ridin' this horse.'

My head was quite distant with the whisky and felt as if it was severed from my shoulders and hovering like a ping-pong ball in a shooting gallery and Bob's face, as ever, being quite devoid of expression it was some while before I realized he was being facetious. But he had this disconcerting way of introducing into an otherwise perfectly serious story some dead-pan imbecility which tended to discredit the tale as a whole and yet most of his yarns, I believe, were founded on truth.

'When the war broke out, this fella was running a small-time engineering firm down in East London somewhere . . . makin' tin-eyeballs f' wooden rockin' horses or some durned thing or other. Wal, the Gover'ment took him over an' put him on t' makin' munitions, an' though he had to work hard an' long hours he also made a lot o' 'spondulicks'. Come Armistice he sold out and having a few thousand quid he thought he'd take his wife on a trip round the world.

'So he went to a sale of ex-naval vessels down at Pompey and had a good look around. There were pinnaces, Admirals' barges, jolly boats an' all manner o' craft, but he settled for a strange ol' lady. She was an ol' sloop about hundred an' fifty foot in the keel an' just over a thousand ton displacement. She was both steam an' sail, three masted with a single screw an' had been stripped of her guns some years before, an' to compensate for the loss of weight she had pigs o' ballast stowed around in the ol' gun-mountin's to keep her trimmed up. Nobody else bid for her an' he got her for a hundred and twenty-five quid. He sailed her down to Bristol for a refit, converting her into something with a little more comfort in the way of cabins an' bunks . . . an' changing sail-lockers into wardrobes, fittin' mirrors on the bulkhead doors an' all that sort o' thing on account of his wife's gonna be aboard. Eventually they signed on a couple o' hands and set off on a circum-navigational cruise . . . or round-the-world trip to you . . . an' the world was their oyster.'

'What's that mean, Mist' Lively?'

'Wal, son, the world . . . was theirs f' the takin'.'

'But they couldn't eat it, could they, Mist' Lively?'

'No, son, o' course not, but . . . wal, it's jest a sayin', y'see.'

'Why can't you say "the world was their scallop"?'

'Aw, I dunno, son, . . . I s'pose it's got somethin' to do with the pearl in the oyster or somethin' . . . Anyway, off they go. They looked in at Shannon t' load up with 'taters an several cases o' Irish whiskey . . . that's the tackle, son . . . puts muscles in y' eye-lashes . . . tastes a li'l like peat, sorta smokey.' This was the cue for a further application of the tonic from the bottle at his side and he certainly seemed to be responding to treatment.

'Then right out an' away they goes, striking right across the north Atlantic to the Banks of Newfoundland. The fishermen there are so tough they cuts up li'l fellas like you f' cod-bait. Then they follow all on down the coast an' run up into Baltimore and see Yankee clippers stood so thick in the harbour their masts look like a larch forest. All down along through the islands they go callin' in f' fresh water an' provender an' explorin' the water-front saloons where sailormen wear big straw hats an' play guitars an' hockerinas. That's a sort o' hollered-out sweet-potato, son, an' sounds like a li'l ol' fella sittin' inside an empty beer-barrel playin' a tin whistle-pipe. In to Jamiaca they go an' across the Caribbean to Panama, an' out on the west coast they make their way right down to Valparaiso where the dagoes wear sombrairy hats an' grin at y' like a row o' gravestones . . . but they'd stick a knife between y' shoulder blades as soon as look at y'.

'They ain't seen nothin' yet, though. Out into the Pacific they steam with dolphins playin' about their bow-wave, flyin' fish perchin' on the rat-lines an' singing like nightingales . . . an' jelly-fish floatin' past in the clear, blue water like the dreams of a drunken man. They saw coconut islands and atolls, blue lagoons an' scarlet coral reefs . . . an' silver, sandy shores where the natives put to sea in canoes made o' bamboo canes an' the skins o' rice-puddens all sowed together with shark's-teeth needles. They came out an' laid-to under the rail selling pineapples, pomegranates, mangoes an' bread-fruit from the ban-yan trees . . . an' when they went on shore they see ladies there a-dancin' without any vests on an' shakin' their bellies enough t' make y' toe-nails curl.

'They lay becalmed under the tropical stars and they weathered hell-fire electric storms with li'l blue flames run-nin' along the rail like snakes. Then they battered their way down through the roarin' forties to New Zealand . . . which is the place where all the people went when Old Zealand was swamped by a tidal wave an' never come up no more. Right up across to Singapore an' Malaya they go, an' India too, goin' in all the ol' bazaars where for a few red cents an' the smell of an oil rag you could get parakeets, cockatoos, marmozets an' chimps from li'l ol' men with wizened faces . . . who looked like one o' their own monkeys dressed up.

'Wal, money was runnin' short. One of their hands had jumped ship in Auckland an' they thought it was about time they was headin' f' home. So they ran up through the Suez, got buffeted black an' blue in the Bay o' Biscay an' finally ties up in a thick pea-souper opposite Deptford Stairs. They paid off the remainin' hand an' spent their time in li'l quay-side ale-houses . . . listenin' to land-bound sailors singin' Henry Martin and Shenandoah to the tune o' wheezy concertinas . . . an' fiddles that sounded as if their cat-gut had never been taken out o' the cat. And, o' course, they had plenty o' tales t' tell o' their own adventures.

'One night a storm gets up an' it blows seven different colours of hell out o' the nor'east . . . an' they start draggin' their anchor an' were in danger of runnin' aground. So they want somethin' heavy to lower down-along the anchor cable to put a bit o' slack in it . . . so the drag won't be direct on the anchor . . . to act, as you might say, as a shock-absorber. Then they remember these pigs o' ballast in the gun-mountin's. They were all about the same size, just over a foot high, shaped like a pear with a ring-bolt where the stalk is, an' coated thick with tar . . . any God's amount of 'em there was . . . so they took two or three an' slid 'em down the cable an' rides out the gale.

'Next mornin', they fetches the pigs back aboard an' he goes off ashore alone t' start lookin' for a job 'cause they hadn't got any money. When he comes back at tea-time, his wife says, "What d'you reck'n those things o' ballast would be made of?"

'So he says, "Cast iron, probably, but they might be lead. Why?"

' "Only when I was straightenin' things up on deck this mornin'," she says, "I noticed that some of the tar had been rubbed off those we used last night an' it looked to me like brass."

' "Brass!" he says, "If it is, we're rich. It's fetchin' any price y'like right now on account of the shortages."

'So next day he saws a chunk off one of the pigs an' takes it in to a metallurgist friend of his who worked in the city . . . that's a man who specializes in metal, son. Wal, the chap takes it out into his back room an' when he comes back he

looks as if his mother-in-law has just died an left a fortune . . .
only she'd scratched his name out o' the will. "How much of
this metal have you got?" he asked.

' "Oh, I dunno," said my ol' buddy, trying to work out
the price of a ton o' brass in his head, "about fifty or sixty ton,
I shouldn't wonder."

' "Then," said the metal-man, sitting down all of a
heap an' wipin' his forehead with the back of his hand, "if
that is so, we have a serious situation on our hands . . . it's
gold!"

'They went to the boat, scraped the tar off the pigs an'
weighed 'em all up an' found they'd got seventy-four tons
eight hundred-weight . . . but, o' course, that included the
ring-bolts. My ol' buddy tots it up quick on the back of a
packet o' Woodbines an' he reckons that, give or take a bob
or two, it's worth twelve million quid.

'When they reported it at the local police station, that put
the cat right in amongst the pigeons . . . the Home Office,
the Board o' Trade, the Admiralty, the Coastguards, the
Police an Rotten'dean Girl Guides an' God-all-knows-who
was dashing about making enquiries, takin' statements,
swearin' affidavits an' ringin' up the Pope an' what all. And
then, o' course, it bein' Treasure Trove, the Coroner had to
hold an Inquest on it.

'They found out that the sloop had been found in the
Channel by a Naval patrol during the war. She was luffin'
an' wallowin' about like a hippo in a mud-bath an' when
they hailed her there was no reply. They boarded her an'
found no one there but a couple o' fishermen with German
papers . . . an' they were both dead. The cabin was a
shambles an' there'd been the father an' mother of a scrap . . .
but there was nothin' in the log or anythin' to explain why
all that gold was on board.

'This had happened at a time when the war was startin' to
go very bad f' the Kaiser . . . an' it was reck'ned to be a
scheme to smuggle the gold out o' Germany t' some neutral
country like South America. But that was only a theory,

mind . . . and why the fishermen on board had fought each other to the death is anybody's guess.

'Anyway, my ol' buddy's share o' the spoils was enough t' set him up like a duke. He's got a flat in Mayfair, a 3,000 acre estate an' manor house down the New Forest way, two or three yachts on the Solent, Bentleys an' Rolls Royces layin' about all over the place . . . an' he's laughin' an' splashin' about in champagne an' brandy an' livin' the life o' Reilly.'

He raised the bottle to his lips and tilted it till it was perpendicular and the last drop of whisky trickled down his throat. 'Some folks get all the luck, don't they, son?' He whistled a few bars of something which sounded rather like an old song 'All that glitters isn't gold'. 'Still,' he concluded, 'we got a nice lot o' silver fish, ol' buddy boy, didn't we?'

Chapter Nineteen

'Ah, the sweet smell of new-mown hair,' said old Bob, stepping down into the barber's shop and shaking the rain off his sou'wester and oilskins like a terrier fresh out the village pond. It was one of those grey, gusty days of incessant rain which get November such a bad name. He stamped his feet on the door mat, sniffed hard and looked around the crowded little room with an expression of extreme distaste. "S enough to choke a bleddy Spaniard,' he said.

The pungency which had prompted his wit came from several different sources. Brilliantine, shampoo, bay rum and soap powder were putting up a barrage of perfume against the broadsides of stench from sooted-up clays, briars, and hand-rolled cigarettes but the great, puffing clouds of British Oak and Nigger's Head shag smashed the slender defences of verbena, parma violets, and old English lavender and the result was almost suffocating. To add to the humidity already created by too many people in a confined space wearing wet clothes, there were two separate sources from which steam was rising in steady streams. A tin kettle on a gas-ring in the corner, which supplied hot water for the shaving mugs, and a shaggy, rain-soaked sheepdog curled up in front of the fire over whom we had to step each time we stropped our razors. 'You could fire a Lewis gun down that ol' street this mornin' and you wouldn't hit a durned thing,' said Bob, 'not even ol' Corny Solomon's cat . . . even he's holed up somewheres.'

A disproportionate number of the male population of the village were 'holed up' at that moment there in the barber's shop. The wind and rain had driven the longshoremen off the shore, the fieldsmen off the fields and the shepherds off the hills, the street was deserted and in that tiny room there must have been the highest concentration of humanity for miles around. The forms and chairs ranged round the wall were fully occupied, a game of pontoon with the players standing in a group was going on in the corner by the gas-ring, there were two shaves and a haircut in progress and another two or three men standing just inside the door. Many of them were what we called 'barbermongers' who merely came in to while away an hour or so in the dry without spending any money, for the barber's shop was one of the most popular social centres in the village, particularly in bad weather.

I had by this time left school and at the age of fourteen become a full-time lather-boy and had graduated to shaving a few brave faces, the owners of which selflessly volunteered to risk their blood in order that my inexpert hand should gain experience. Mr Adkins, the boss, as his nickname 'Porky' implied, was in appearance inclined towards the porcine and my initial job each morning was to shave him with my very first razor (a Crown and Sword, $\frac{5}{8}''$ hollow-ground blade, double-shouldered with a file-cut tang) of which I was in-ordinately proud. It cost half-a-crown and was being paid for by weekly deductions of sixpence from my five shillings weekly wage.

The fact that his cheeks and chins were bland and rotund made the task so much simpler than negotiating the angular mandibles, sunken cheeks, cleft chins and wrinkled necks of customers who favoured the lean and hungry look, and during the operation he also went through a series of the most amazing facial contortions, pushing his chin first to this side and then to that and pulling his top lip down over his upper teeth like a roller blind to ensure that my trembling blade had a smooth and wrinkle-free passage. He was the perfect guinea-pig. He always demanded the full treatment with hot towels and face massage, first with an astringent followed by a good pummelling with Madame Tomfrey's skin food, a pink concoction kept in a large glass jar with a rusty tin lid, after which he felt ready to meet the world with a face that was flushed and whisker-free and glowing with the bloom of a Victoria plum.

He was a very good hairdresser and knew his trade well and had opened his shop a few years earlier, replacing the services of old Mr Blaber who had, up to that time, looked after the two extremities of human needs. He had kept the villagers dry shod and, the men and boys at least, neat and trim about the head, for he had combined the trades of snob and barber to great effect for many years. That his hands were always black from the nature of his other calling was accepted but there was one slight criticism of his hair cutting methods. He always removed the hair-clippings from his client's neck and ears by blowing hard through pursed lips and, as he was an 'old chow-bacca', there was a tendency for the current of air thus expelled to pick up a certain amount of moisture as it filtered through his moustache and proceed in the form of a fine spray which he would, with great consideration, wipe away with the sleeve of his shirt. But otherwise he managed to keep Rottingdean satisfactorily 'topped and tailed'.

The new shop had been set up in one of two downstairs rooms of a tiny flint cottage called 'The Nest', which stood in the corner of School Opening just off the High Street and, as if to preserve the Blaber tradition at least in a small degree and not to separate customers too widely from the smell of leather and waxed thread and the thump of a hammer on the last while they waited to be shorn, the other room was occupied by Bill Avis the cobbler. The establishment was graced with the title 'Saloon', announced in bold letters over the door, and there was an emphasis on efficiency and hygiene neither of which, I imagine, had figured too prominently in the claims of previous village exponents of the trade. The nature of the business was also proclaimed by a barber's pole outside painted in spiral bands of red and white representing, we were told, the blood and bandages of barbers' shops of old when barbers were also surgeons of sorts. I didn't much care for this 'blood and bandages' theme and in those early days of apprenticeship, when the responsibility of wielding such a dangerous blade upon such vulnerable necks weighed heavily on the mind, the connotation was an ever-present nightmare.

The inside of the saloon was fitted with large porcelain basins with marble surrounds and backshelves which looked as if they had once adorned much grander premises. They were surmounted by wall mirrors and the room was further equipped with reclining-backed chairs with adjustable neck-rests. It really left little to be desired and was a stride along the path of progress which was entirely in step with the times.

The inside of the saloon was fitted with large porcelain
basins, with marble surrounds.

We were now in the thirties and change and improvement were the order of the day. Horses were rapidly giving way to petrol, on the roads if not on the farms, oil-lamps were being condemned to lumber rooms in favour of electric light which was generated in a tin-shed at the back of the school by a dynamo driven by a gas-engine which kept up a relent-less, tanky, 'T-thomp, t-thomp, t-thomp', throbbing away the long hours of learning. Telephones were becoming more numerous, but were still capable of striking fear into the hearts of the unsophisticated and I well recall the pathetic, petrified, inarticulate creature to which I was reduced by an overwhelming attack of nerves when called across to the post office one day to receive my first telephone message in the absence of the Boss.

There was a new, forward-looking way of thinking, the old order was indeed changing and it was an interesting age in which to be growing up. This, of course, was not realized at the time and it is only in retrospect that one can see that the people with whom one had daily contact had been brought up in three successive reigns during which immense changes had been, and were still being, made. They represented three entirely different modes of life. There were the old timers steeped in tradition and the unchanging ways of mid-Victorian times, then the generation of men who had been so mercilessly pitch-forked into the upheaval, horror, and suffering of the Great War and, finally, my own contemporaries who were emerging into a fast-developing world of petrol-driven and electrical power, mass-production and the insidious but strong social influences from America. From these widely separated sources we absorbed a little of each to emerge as an unlikely amalgam of all three. We were, as the old chaps would have said, 'Neither fish nor fowl nor good red meat." From the hob-nails and corduroy of earlier days, we were being converted to more fashion-conscious clothes. The open vowels and gentle accents of local dialect were being infected by wireless and 'talkie'-borne germs from afar and the indigenous and familiar sayings were being replaced by foreign and strange-sounding terms. 'My maid', became 'Baby', 'All kiff' became 'O.K.' and the old traditional songs and even those of the Edwardian music hall were being ousted by importations from across the Atlantic. It was a transitional period, during which the old established standards and the beginnings of a new way of life were both strongly represented, living side by side but in constant conflict.

The other member of the barber's staff was my cousin Chaulker, six years older than me, an adept manipulator of the scissors, comb, and razor and towards whom, in more ways than merely hairdressing, I directed my youthful aspirations. He was a stylish dresser with his colourful Fairisle, V-necked pullover, 24-inch bottomed Oxford bags in silver-grey flannel and his 'winkle-picker' brown brogues with side panels of white buckskin. His hair was combed straight back and plastered down with Anzora Viola till it shone like the flanks of a well-groomed horse. He knew all the words as well as the tunes of the latest songs, 'Carolina Moon', 'Glad Rag Doll', 'All by yourself in the Moonlight' and on Saturday nights, after the shop closed at nine o'clock, he went 'stepping the light fantastic' at The Masthead Tea Rooms, a large, wooden, ex-Army hut on the cliff-top. I would join the smaller fry gathered outside the doorway and, leaning on my rusty bike, would gaze open-mouthed as the flappers of the village arrived in twos and threes and emerged from the obscurity of macintoshes and rain-coats dressed in gorgeous, home-made creations of colourful sateen like butterflies bursting out of their chrysalises.

Chaulker was a flamboyant and dashing character, as flippant as a jackdaw and with a keen sense of humour. He was popular with the men and never short of girl friends and epitomized the new-found spirit of bounce, brashness and overt confidence which we were seeing for the first time in the early 'talkie' films. His influence on his callow relative was incalculable.

It was through his enterprise that I was introduced to a variety of simple gambling games almost invariably involving the loss of twopences and threepences by one or another of those barber-mongers who were misguided enough to fall in with his suggestions. There was the car-number game in which each participant chose two numbers from 0 to 9 and every time a car went up the High Street, which on an average was once in ten minutes, the number was noted and those players whose numbers were represented were given one penny from each of the others whose numbers were not in evidence. Chaulker and I would be sure to choose 3, 4, 6 and 8 between us and, of course, it was not a coincidence that the small private bus that plied at regular intervals bore the number A.P. 8448 and the T-type Ford van which made deliveries of provisions from the grocery stores just round the corner was C.D. 6333. This ensured a steady flow of pennies in our direction and either built up our winnings or compensated for the losses suffered in the vagaries of pure chance.

There was also the 'lottery' for a packet of cigarettes. One other person in addition to Chaulker and me would invest two-pence towards the cost of a packet of Players, at 6d. for ten, and the object was to guess the number of the cigarette card which was in the sealed packet. With a great display of courtesy the victim was invited to make his guess first and we would then 'box him in' by choosing numbers on either side of his, varying the size of the box according to how many times he had won. If, for instance, he chose the number 12, by choosing 11 and 13 we would have reduced his chance of winning to one in twenty-five or fifty, depending on the number in the set. But this was mostly avoided because it would have made the system too obvious. There seemed to be nothing terribly wrong or dishonest in these little games, they were always played in the lightest of spirits and we felt we were merely bending the rules a little in our favour. But it was certainly a side of life I had never met before.

To supplement the slender returns from trade at sixpence for a haircut and threepence for a shave, we also sold plants and seeds in spring and summer, and in winter made nets of various sizes for rabbiting, shrimping and prawning to sell to local sportsmen. We spent about ten hours a day together in that small shop but we were a happy company. The Boss, in moments of what he would have called felicitation, was given to rendering in a nasal and rather strained baritone, songs of his earlier days like 'Moya My Girl', 'My Ain Folk' and 'I passed by your Window' to which I would add an extemporary and pretty ineffectual harmony while Chaulker provided a totally unsuitable rhythmic background with an otherwise quite impressive tap-dance. These performances were, of course, confined to periods when the shop was empty of clients and we were busy with our netting needles.

The Boss had a flair for words and although his literary output was restricted to cross-word puzzles and competitions, his eloquence was part of his stock-in-trade. He spurned small talk and gossip and entertained his often bewildered clients with non-stop dissertations on matters of political, historical, or religious interest and although much of his knowledge came from *Answers* and *Tit Bits* or *Everybody's Weekly*, his grasp of things was really quite extensive and certainly quite beyond the rest of us for, as he used to say, 'In the land of the blind the man with one eye is king.' His head was a storehouse of proverbs, slogans, and rhymes from which he would frequently quote either to make a point in conversation or sometimes, seemingly, just for the pleasure of doing so. He would, for instance, for no apparent reason, repeat the drill for the assembly and firing of a Lewis gun, which went something like this.

Place magazine on magazine post spring catch to the right painted portion to the rear. Shake down gently clear of poles. Rotate in a feed direction until resistance is felt. The gun is now loaded. On pressing the trigger the gun will fire and continue to fire until the pan is empty.

The wisdom of one of his little rhymes impressed me greatly.

> I'd rather be a 'could be'
> If I could not be an 'are',
> For a 'could be' is a 'may be'
> With a chance of reaching par.
> I'd rather be a 'has been'
> Than a 'might have been' by far,
> For a 'might have been' has never been,
> But a 'has' was once an 'are'.

Proverbs and quotations fell in plenty from the cornucopia of his mind. 'Nothing succeeds like success', 'The strength of a chain is its weakest link', 'Grab opportunity by the forelock, for he hasn't got a tail' and, an odd choice in a barber's shop, 'Vanity, vanity, all is vanity'. He seemed even to think in epigrams and once when someone was praising the skill of our cobbler neighbour he summarized the wisdom of being well-shod with 'Wet feet—cold feet; dry feet—warm feet'.

Words flowed from his lips in a steady stream as if they were bustling and jostling in his mind striving to get out. Long words, short words, words we had never heard before, words we were seldom to hear again. There is no doubt that he sometimes became—as he would have said—'intoxicated with the exuberance of his own verbosity.' But how I admired his fluency.

If the mosaic of one's character is made up of tiny pieces of influence picked up over the years from various sources, and to a great extent I believe this to be true, then between them Porky and Chaulker have a lot to answer for.

Chapter Twenty

If, through my own lack of attention, my primary education had been sadly neglected, the barber's shop was to prove an excellent finishing school and provide a crammer's course in many aspects of life I had never before encountered. Having taken to heart old Bob's advice that 'a good listener is better than a bad talker', I was all eyes and ears and soaked up like a sponge the worldly knowledge that was expounded in that little room in the course of everyday conversation. My vocabulary was rapidly extended, particularly in the vernacular which was not always, I fear, within the bounds of propriety, but I also met characters and heard yarns that seemed to belong to a world far removed from that I had known hitherto. Yet sometimes, when the older men were talking, I could hear echoes of Grand-dad in their sayings and expressions and I felt that fingers from the past were plucking strange but familiar chords of recognition within me.

They always seemed to be talking about the old days and it was like listening to an audible scrap-book of village history. To hear them talk you would never have known how hard and long they had to work for so little money nor in what tiny, squalid homes they had settled down to married life and brought up such huge families on penny-pinching budgets. The years had drawn a veil across the past and only the highlights of happiness shone through. Nostalgia is not the prerogative of contemporary youth. These men spoke with great affection for the old days and resented the changes that the Great War seemed to have brought about. The summers were never so hot as when they had been young, nor the harvests so bountiful. The winters were never so cold, nor the snow and the ice on the pond so thick. The mushrooms were never so big, the prawns so plentiful, nor the rabbits so numerous. The beer was never so strong, nor the laughter so loud and hearty. The girls were plump and pretty, the grass was green and life, in retrospect, had been good.

There was a much-used opening phrase which prefaced many a sentimental journey back into days gone by. 'A-agh! That was the day . . .', they would say and follow with some favourite story like, '. . . when ol' Ben the shepherd went up to the forge and arst ol' Ernie Stenning for a coach-bolt fower an' fower-eighths inches long'.

'Yeah, wal,' Ernie had said, 'that'll be four an' a 'alf, wunnit, Ben?'

'No 'twun't,' rejoined Ben adamantly. 'Fower an' fower-eighths it was—I measured av it on de ruler—an' fower an' fower-eighths I warnts.'

Old Ben had also had a quick and easy solution to the problems facing our military leaders on the battle-fronts of France in the Great War. 'Dere's only one way to deal wid dem 'ere Germans, Maas' Copper,' he said to Grand-dad one day. 'What dey warnts t' do is let goo a swarm o' bees, dat 'ud purty soon roust 'em out av it. No emeney could face dey.'

Jokes, like everything else in those days, were made to last and they could never depend on a surprise ending for appreciation because they had been told so many times before. Old Jim Murrell used to come in for a shave every Saturday morning stepping stiffly down into the shop and breathing heavily from the effort of walking down from his cottage by the forge. He would be blowing sibilantly through his lips like the sound of a railway engine. 'Here comes the Great Northern,' Chaulker would say out of the side of his mouth. Jim was never very long in the shop for his jaw was framed in a Newgate Fringe and only a small clearing on his top lip and chin had to be shaved. With the job done he would say his farewells and make his laborious way up the step and out of the doorway. If the weather was fair, someone would be sure to shout, 'Leave the door, Jim,' and with unfailing dependability, he would turn slowly round and say, 'Why, you dun't think I wuz gunna take 'im along wid me, do ye?'

Every fourth Saturday, Jim would have a haircut and beard-trim and in preparation would remove his jacket and his collar and tie so that we could clip as far as possible the snowy white whiskers which grew on his throat and neck and down to a point of mystery somewhere below the level of his neckband. When the operation was complete he would start to dress again and fixing the stiff, celluloid collar on to brass studs at back and front was managed only at the expense of a great deal of concentrated effort and red-faced exasperation. At last he would be ready for his jacket which he was unable to put on without assistance and it was my job to help him.

In the twenty years or so since Jim had bought the jacket, he had thickened up considerably in girth and we always found it a bit of a tussle. But by our joint efforts, Jim thrusting his arms down into the sleeves and me hoisting the jacket up by the neck, we slowly made headway. After several minutes, he would call for a halt. 'Whoa! 'old 'ard a minute,' he would gasp and stand there like a trussed chicken with his arms halfway into the sleeves and locked behind his back. 'A-agh, 'tis as the monkey said t' the cat, y'know boy.' At this point it was my monthly duty to enquire, 'Oh, what was that then, Mus' Murrell?' ' 'Tis a tight fit, poor puss,' he would chuckle.

Jack Stiles was an unattached, wild sort of man, a restless and rootless creature who lodged at various homes in the village when he could find the rent but otherwise, particularly in summer, was perfectly happy to sleep rough under a hedgerow or on the beach in the 'lew' of a wooden groin. He was a raw-boned man of rather more than average height with sharp features and a very red complexion bespattered with big freckles like flakes of bran. Seeing this mottled pattern also on his wrists and the backs of his hands, one wondered if he was freckled all over his body. His eyebrows and the lashes of his pig-like eyes were bleached to the colour of oat-straw as were the whiskers on his cheeks and chin which, with a few strokes of my trusty blade, I removed regularly on his weekly visits to the shop.

He had a lively and energetic manner, although he was noticeably furtive and even when indoors repeatedly cast wary glances over first this shoulder and then that; his bright blue eyes were never still from a lifetime habit of keeping a sharp lookout for water-bailiffs and game-keepers. He wore whip-cord knee breeches and a pepper-and-salt tweed jacket the pockets of which always bulged with rabbit-nets, snares, fishing lines, floats and other gear revealing his sporting tendencies, and from a large pocket on the inside of his jacket the pink nose of a white ferret would sometimes muzzle up under the lapels of his waistcoat and under his chin.

He had but one pair of boots and when the time came round for them to be mended he would take them off and leave them with Bill Avis next door to be cobbled while he came into the shop and waited in his stockinged feet. The term stocking is a euphemism for they were practically footless and resembled knitted leggings with but a few woollen strands to anchor them down to his feet. The ' 'taters' in the heels extended beyond his ankles on either side and most of his toes were unencumbered and open to the day.

Jack's origins were something of a mystery but he wasn't a ' 'Deaner'. He hailed from up country somewhere and was regarded as a 'furriner'. From his talk, it was obvious he was a stranger to the sea-coast, to the bare downland, the wind-shorn gorse, and stunted blackthorn and would have been more at home in the lush, inland water-meadows where towering oaks and elms raised their classic friezes against the sky and reed-fringed rivers flowed slowly seaward above the reach of the tides. But, for one brought up to tickling trout, snaring pike, and taking roosting pheasants from low branches, he adapted quickly to our local forms of sport. It wasn't long before he could lay a long line for bass or set an eel-pot with the best of the villagers and, when required, he could be relied upon to produce a brace or two of partridges or rabbits or a nice hare.

He was an impetuous man in word and deed. He spoke in short sharp bursts of rapid patter matching his words with impulsive action which contrasted sharply with the peaceful, slow-moving characteristics of the local men. He came up to me on the beach one day as I stood looking at a dead porpoise stranded above the water-line. 'That's what they call a "sea-hog", y'know,' he said briskly. 'See them four marks,' he went on, pointing out four smudges of darker pigment on the creature's pale underside. 'That's where his legs used to be.' Then with no further ado he took out his jack-knife and, making a neat incision down the length of the belly, performed an expert autopsy pointing out that the porpoise was a mammal, not a fish, and retained all the rudimentary organs of a pig. As he talked he illustrated the point by holding up in turn the heart, lungs, liver and kidneys while the blood dripped from his fingers and stained the beach at his feet. 'They do say,' he concluded, 'they are the Gadarene swine that went mad and run into the sea.' He rinsed his hands in a rocky pool, shook off the drips and wiped them dry on the seat of his breeches while I stood by, rendered quite speechless by his knowledge and the adept use of the knife, and Jack was at once added to my list of boyhood heroes.

But his most unconventional escapade took place before he had made an appearance in Rottingdean. A farmer out shooting one day had the misfortune to shoot himself accidentally in the foot, and was carried on a hurdle to the nearest cottage and taken straight to hospital where he remained for a week or more. He lived all alone in an outlying and lonely farmstead and in the excitement the fact that he had left his dog chained up at home was completely overlooked.

When eventually someone went up to untether the dog, they found that it was crazed with hunger and thirst and lunged at the end of its chain snapping and snarling at whoever went near with spine-chilling ferocity. No one could get near enough to untie it and it was suggested that the only answer, though sad, was to shoot the dog to put it out of its misery. But Jack, who was one of the few onlookers, would have none of this. 'Look,' he said, 'it's a shame to kill a good dog like that. If we can get him off the chain and let him run round till he's tired hisself out, he'll soon settle down after a good meal and a drink.'

'But who's going to undo the chain?' they said.

'I will,' said Jack, 'but I'll have to do it my way.'

He walked up to within a yard or so of where the dog, literally at the end of its tether, fought with every ounce of strength to get at him and tear him to shreds. Its eyes were bulging and blood-shot and its drooling lips curled back to reveal a frightening array of treacherous fangs. Jack stood steady looking straight into its eyes, meanwhile undoing the buttons of his braces and unfastening the brass buckle on his belt. Then turning completely round so that his back was towards the dog, he suddenly dropped his trousers to his ankles, bent down, flipped up the tail of his shirt and stared at the dog between his legs.

Being suddenly confronted with this unusual aspect of God's noblest creation—freckles, perhaps, and all—the poor animal was completely nonplussed and froze into immobility. 'Caw, he'd never seen anything like it afore in his life,' said Jack. And when he started to shuffle backwards towards it uttering the most blood-curling, 'Ee-eek along, long, long, long, long, long, lo-ooong!'—a cry he had picked up in the hunting field somewhere—the dog went back on its haunches as if mesmerized. As this strange apparition slowly advanced howling and screaming like a thousand devils, the wretched animal gradually decided to give it best and slunk off into the corner of the wall quivering all over and whimpering like a puppy.

As soon as Jack was within reach he turned smartly round and grabbed it by the collar and released the chain. Then he restored his dignity by pulling up his trousers and tucking in his shirt and having, as it were, risked his all in a good cause, strode away the hero of the hour.

*　　*　　*

On Sunday mornings we opened at ten o'clock and for the first hour or so, with the kettle murmuring on the gas-ring and ready for instant action, usually stood around idly in our starch-crisp, white coats straight out of the laundry basket and as clean and unsullied as the week that lay ahead. There was little trade to start with. An occasional piece of wreckage from Saturday night's alcoholic storms would wash ashore, all bleary-eyed and splintered on the rocks of the morning after, and come shuffling into the shop in carpet-slippers and braces, seeking a remedial shave and a packet of fags, but otherwise all was quiet. Porky and Chaulker would read the Sunday newspapers making unenthusiastic comments on items of national disaster or exclaiming wildly at unexpected football results while I, rubbing the steam from the inside of the small, square window-panes, looked out across School Opening at the village going about its lawful, Sabbath occasions.

It seemed to have precious few Sabbath occasions to go about, lawful or otherwise. A family group walked briskly churchwards in their Sunday-best with polished shoes and beaming faces, eagerly answering the bell in the church-tower. A disconsolate shrimper who had overslept and missed the tide slouched homeward again in dry sea-boots, his net still furled and an empty bag hanging at his side. A couple of Sunday-morning gardeners, in a drifting cloud of tobacco smoke, headed for the allotments in the Hog Platt carrying their tools across their shoulders. But apart from these occasional signs of life, the street was deserted and after they had passed the stillness and silence flooded back with increased intensity.

Sometimes a gardener would pop in for a packet of vegetable or flower seeds, for at weekends the horticultural side of the business came to life—or at least drew a few tentative breaths. Stored in air-tight tins on the top shelf above the cigarettes and tobacco were quarter and half ounces of Rousham Park Hero, Ailsa Craig, and Bedfordshire Champion onion seeds, James' Intermediate and Scarlet Horn carrot, Crimson Globe beetroot and pints and half pints of Peter Pan peas, Canadian Wonder French beans, and Painted Lady and Long-as-your-arm scarlet runners. We had packeted them in manila envelopes on which I had spent many quiet hours inscribing in minute hand-writing with a mapping-pen the high-sounding declaration that the law demanded and which, with tongues in cheeks and fingers crossed, we believed, or at least hoped, to be true. It is engraved on my mind like a prayer.

These seeds have been tested in accordance with the Seeds Act, 1920. The germination and purity thereof are not less than the percentages prescribed by the Seed Regulations. Packeted . . .

Here the current year had to be inserted and this made for a lot of extra work. Soon after Christmas each year all those seeds remaining unsold were taken out and repacketed in envelopes bearing the new date couched in the same long-winded rigmarole and, of course, it fell to me to do the writing. I was very pleased when, as business improved, we were able to invest in a rubber stamp.

On a smoke-stained sheet of paper tucked into the frame of one of the fly-dotted wall-mirrors, beside the cards of styptic pencils and small, round boxes of Union Jack corn cure, was a notice, 'Haircut 6d. Shave 3d.' and in smaller letters underneath, 'Sundays 8d. & 4d.' and this to a great extent, coupled with the fact that many men considered a shave every other day to be sufficient for their needs, accounted for the lack of ordinary cash trade on the Sabbath. We only saw those who, for one reason or another, had

missed the opportunity for a shave on Saturday or those one
or two who seemed to use a Sunday shave as a symbol of
affluence and were flaunting the fact that a mere penny was
of little or no consequence to them.

But we ran a Barber's Club and for a monthly subscription
of four shillings members were entitled to a haircut every
fortnight and a daily shave and for the last hour, as the
Sunday-morning gardeners came in on their way home, the
shop would be crammed with 'club shavers' determined to
have their money's worth before we closed. Outside in the
yard, forks, spades, rakes and hoes would be left leaning
against the wall with trugs of new potatoes, young carrots,
'pickin's o' peas' and other seasonal vegetables and, usually,
a colourful nose-gay of sweet williams, canterbury bells or
other flowers for 'mother'.

Inside the talk would be exclusively gardening and although many of the technical terms were only approxima-
tions, there was lots of good sound knowledge to be picked
up.

'My green-stuff's lookin' a li'l ornery this year.'

'You wanna wop some o' that 'ere "cider noter" (nitrate of
soda) into 'em. That'll make 'em sit up.'

And humour was never very far away.

''Ow's y' lettuces comin' along?'

'Bleddy slugs en't arf givin' 'em socks.'

'You wants t' sprinkle some o' that ol' "Slug-dead" along
the rows.'

'No, bugger, if they can't eat 'em without that, then let
'em bleddy well goo without.'

While all this was going on, the three of us would be
shaving against the clock and, although we closed the door
at 12-45 p.m., we had to race to get the shop clear by one
o'clock and sometimes we came very close to producing
beads of that rare phenomenon, jokingly said to have been
known to kill rats and be worth a guinea an ounce—'barber's
sweat'.

*   *   *

As my skills as a barber improved, I was sent out to what we used to call 'outside work' to shave or trim the heads of men who, for one reason or another, were unable to come to the saloon. By going into people's homes in this manner, one became a link with the outside world and was often in a position to be of help by posting letters, delivering messages and being a life-line, as it were, between the house-bound and the particular form of business or recreation from which they found themselves forcibly severed.

Sometimes the experience was, to say the least, eye-opening. The most devout of church-goers, whom one would never have associated with the sporting world and who had probably never even heard of Lord Rosebery, have on occasions surprised me by surreptitiously sliding a betting-slip into my hand with explicit whispered instructions. 'Tell him (the bookie) that I have four shillings to come from a non-runner last Friday and if there's any to come from today's investment would he please put it all to win on the favourite for the two-thirty at Ripon tomorrow.' The most abstemious in appearance and overt behaviour, too, have at times revealed a remarkable addiction to the pleasures of the bottle by asking for secret deliveries of their favourite tipple on my next visit.

One customer in the upper income bracket, who was permanently confined to his big house which stood in its own grounds, was a roaring—and the word is chosen with care—alcoholic and suffered from the most distressing bouts of delirium tremens. An obsequious manservant by the name of Wickham was constantly in attendance gliding about in a morning coat and striped trousers without uttering a word. His master, on the other hand, unless he was sunk in torpor, scarcely ever stopped talking, or sometimes screaming, and shaving him was a nerve-racking experience for all concerned. From a stertorous slumber while I had been lathering his face, he would sometimes suddenly awake to see me stropping the razor and fly into a panic-stricken rage. 'Wickham! Wickham! Where the hell are you? He's goin'' to cut me bloody throat. Come here at once. HELP!'

In quieter moments he would try to inveigle me into smuggling in a bottle of brandy or press a note into my hand which read in minute, spidery hand-writing, 'S.O.S.! S.O.S.! Get a bottle of brandy from Richardson's Stores and put it in the peony bush under my window. Tell them to put it on the account.' All this, of course, was unbeknown to madam whose majestic and overbearing presence was seldom witnessed. On the few occasions I had seen her, strutting about like a Leghorn cockerel draped in voluminous and flamboyant satin dresses and wearing necklaces of pearls like pigeon's eggs with pendant and matching-ear-rings which were so heavy that they had stretched the lobes of her ears to unbelievable proportions, she had terrified me. I was so scared of her, even when she was in a good mood, that, however much I had been tempted, I would certainly never have done anything to incur her wrath.

Once a week on a Saturday morning, I had to go to Stanley House in the High Street to shave Jack Reed, the retired game-keeper. The old fellow would be sitting huddled in a chair by the kitchen range, his span of useful life long since over like that of his old muzzle-loader shot-gun which stood in the corner of the room and had not been fired for years. Age had brought him at last to a passive domesticity and gone were the days when he strode his master's lands with an aggressive authority that brooked no question. The voice which had struck fear into the hearts of birds'-nesting boys and doubt into the minds of midnight poachers, had diminished to a childish treble and on my arrival he would struggle to his feet and shuffle across the room to a chair by the window. His progress was painfully slow with frequent pauses while he leaned heavily on the table blowing and wheezing like a pair of outworn bellows.

With him seated at last in the light of the window I would get to work with brush and razor. The skin on his neck, like his celluloid collar, was now several sizes too big for him and was puckered and pleated like the neck of a corn sack. This made the task all the more difficult and, to add to the hazards of shaving him without mishap, he always tried to talk, punctuating my razor strokes with a few mumbled, scarcely coherent words in a laborious effort to make himself understood.

My appearance always seemed to remind him of some escapade he had shared with my grandfather when they had been boys together in the 1850's, and spark off a long, rambling account of the adventure. But though his themes were difficult to follow and the recounting of his stories desultory and not altogether intelligible, I always felt that he enjoyed my weekly visits and I, too, found in his company a living link with old village days.

This close contact with the older men of the village accounts for my interest in their ways of life, and I seemed to build up a strong affinity with them. Many of them still wore those extraordinary beard styles favoured in Victorian times with clumps of whiskers dotted about here and there in the most unlikely places, and which seem once again to have come into vogue. The point which most of the hirsute men of the present day seem to miss is that the original beard shapes were more often than not born of necessity, or at least convenience, and not from vanity. Before the introduction of safety razors, many men found shaving themselves with an open blade a tedious, if not downright dangerous, operation. So if a man invariably cut himself when trying to negotiate the angle of his left jawbone, for instance, he would steer round it and allow the whiskers to grow, doing the same on the other side in the interests of symmetry. These evasive measures were also taken to avoid repeatedly cutting the head off a prominent mole or to dodge an area of thin skin which was prone to 'razor rash' and, to a great extent, this in the first place accounted for the Newgate fringes, mutton-chop whiskers and Chiswick beards which are enjoying such a widespread revival at the present time.

One of the regular outside jobs I did was to shave 'Buck' Alce every Friday morning. 'Buck' was an old farm hand

and had been a bit of a reprobate in days gone by, but the years had overtaken him and he was now confined to his bed in a small cottage in West Street where he lodged with the Collins family. Every Friday morning at ten o'clock would see me walking briskly down the High Street carrying the small leather attaché case containing my tools and white coat with a certain exaggerated sense of self-importance instilled, in part, by Mr Adkins' repeated assurances of the worthiness of our calling but stemming, also, from the natural exuberance and innocence of youth.

One particular morning, Mrs Collins answered my imperious knock on the door and admitted me into her parlour. 'Oh, come in,' she said, 'I'll put the kattle on. Would y' like a cup o' tea while we're waitin' for it t' bile?' Having filled the kettle at the kitchen sink she returned in a moment or two, set it on the open fire and poured a cup of black, stewed tea from a chipped enamel teapot which had been simmering on the trivet.

'I'm glad you come t'day,' she went on, 'it'll tidy the ol' chep up a bit. The relatives come down t'morrer.' There was a pause while we sipped our cups. 'The funeral's on Tuesday.'

The kettle was beginning to sing and wisps of steam started to curl lazily from its spout. 'The funeral?' I asked. The conversation had taken an unexpected turn and I hadn't the slightest notion what she was talking about. She drained her teacup and put it in the saucer on the table. 'Yes,' she said picking tea leaves from the tip of her tongue, 'he died yest'dy aft'noon.'

The kettle burst into spluttering life, the tin lid rattled like a kettle-drum and water spewed out on to the embers sending clouds of steam up the chimney and billowing out into the room.

'Died?' I said, as she took the kettle and stood it in the hearth, and my voice sounded faint and far away, as if it was coming through a long tunnel and the blood began to pound like a hammer in my temples.

'Yes,' she said in a matter of fact tone, collecting the

empty teacups, 'a very peaceful end. Your water's ready, look.'

I took the handle with the kettle-holder and filled my shaving mug. I seemed to have lost control of the situation and was being carried away on a tidal wave of events with no power to stop it. Surely she didn't expect me to shave . . .

'Ah well, I'll leave you to it then,' she said, going out of the back door into the yard. The wave was beginning to curl and the surf crashed about my head. There was no going back now.

'You'd better take a candle,' she called, 'I've pulled the bedroom blind down and you mustn't let it up agin out o' respect f' the dead. He has bin laid out.'

I delayed the lighting of the candle for as long as I could, but my fumbling fingers found difficulty in striking the match anyway. What could I do? Apart from moving as slowly as possible to put off the dreadful moment, I could see no way of averting my fate. I remembered having read somewhere that an old negress with commendable philosophy once said, 'Some troubles is so little that you can step over 'em. Some a little bigger you can usually step round. But some is so durned big all you can do is duck your head and go wadin' right on into 'em'. And so it seemed with me at that moment.

I donned my white coat and, taking the case and the shaving mug in one hand and the candle-stick in the other, walked with leaden feet up the narrow, creaking stairway. The stair-carpet was worn into harp-strings at the edges of the treads and the brass stair-rods reflected the orange light of the candle. My heart bumped slowly up behind me—stair by stair. Up on the landing, I stood for a moment before lifting the latch on his bedroom door and going in.

Pulling the white sheet back from his head I saw the old familiar face fixed in the horrifying, waxwork mask of death. I went about my task mechanically while my mind flitted about among the crowded memories I had of old 'Buck' in life. The puckish humour, the glint of school-boy mischief in his eyes which now stared sightlessly at the ceiling. The beer-sodden jokes when he had staggered into the saloon one day, carrying a potted plant describing it as 'a spiraea or lemmin plaant' and not knowing whether he wanted 'a sh—, shave or shampoo.' I recalled his cryptic comment on the edge of my razor once in reply to the customary enquiry, 'Wal, bwoy,' he had said, 'if I kin kip from cryin', that bugger'll stop me from laughin'.'

Now I was thinking sadly that, even if the razor did pull, poor Buck wouldn't feel it and wondering why the pressure of my finger-tip on his cold cheek left a depression that was slow to fill and whether or not he would bleed if I cut him. It was a traumatic moment, macabre and pathetic, and I was torn between repugnance and sympathy. When I had finished, I pulled the sheet back over his head with a slight shudder and went downstairs in a dream.

I walked slowly up the street and back to the saloon like a person possessed. The bounce had gone out of my step, my bubble of self-assurance had been pricked and I had aged by at least five years in the previous half hour.

Chapter Twenty-one

The civilized practice of tipping the barber never really found its way down to Rottingdean and had very few adherents amongst our regular clientele, but we were ever hopeful. We did our best to play the perfect valets, brushing off the shoulders of their jackets, helping them on with their overcoats and handing them their sticks or umbrellas with the utmost courtesy, and sometimes a gentleman from one of the big houses or a summer-time visitor would respond by slipping a couple of extra coppers into our anxious palms. But more frequently our efforts were rejected summarily. 'Dun't you come round 'ere fiddle-fartin' about with that thing. Th' ol' coat en't bin brushed since my ol' daddy's funeral—an' that wuz ten year agoo.' And the idea of gratuities was dismissed with characteristic logic. 'Bugger, you've bin paid for what y' done, en't ye? I dun't see the sense in given anybuddy more an' what they arsts for.'

But on the first Christmas I was at the shop, I was allowed to put up a collection box to receive contributions from those who, in the spirit of the season, might find themselves overcome with feelings of goodwill and generosity, and to prod the consciences of the more obdurate, I wrote a notice illuminated with robins, snowflakes, and sprigs of holly to help engender the Christmas spirit.

> Christmas comes and Christmas goes
> But only one a year,
> And on most Christmas cards it says
> It brings about good cheer.

On Christmas Eve in hope of gifts,
The kids put up their socks,
The lather-boy, instead of this,
Puts up his Christmas Box.

So appreciative customers
Can show their satisfaction
By putting something in the box,
Be it only just a fraction.

And so, good folks, this Christmas-tide
May your luck be of the best.
These greetings I will give to all
From the barber's at 'The Nest'.

We also ran a raffle, putting in as prizes sticks of shaving soap, bottles of bay rum and brilliantine which had stood so long on the shelf that their labels had become fly-soiled and yellow with smoke, but as a further inducement we added a few packets of cigars, cigarettes and tobacco. Old Arch Holder came in on Christmas Eve for a trim up for the holiday and when he took out his leather purse to settle up he said to Chaulker, still talking as if he had been round the village picking up the 'h's' all the rest of us had dropped and was determined they shouldn't be wasted, 'Ho, Charles, Hi'll 'ave a hounce hof British Hoak, if you don't mind.'

'I see you've been lucky in our raffle, Mist' Holder,' said Chaulker, reaching up for the packets of tobacco, 'you've won twenty-five Manikins.'

'Ho, 'ave I?' said Arch, 'Hin that case, Hi'll honly 'ave 'alf an hounce hof British Hoak.'

That night when we closed at nine-thirty and all the customers had gone, Chaulker opened the collection-box and spilt the contents out on to a newspaper spread on the seat of one of the chairs. It was indeed a brave show. Apart from a few foreign coins, trouser buttons and unsigned I.O.U.s, we counted out fourteen shillings and seven-pence ha'penny. It represented nearly three weeks wages and when Porky made it up to a pound so that, with my wages, I went home with twenty-five shillings in my pocket, I really felt Christmas had arrived.

At home Christmas was still celebrated as whole-heartedly as it always had been in spite of the fact that Grand-dad had died in 1924. There was a very special feel about Christmas morning and right from the moment you woke up and even before you got out of bed you would hear Dad downstairs singing carols as he raked the ashes from the kitchen range. By the time you got downstairs, he would be lighting the fire in the front room and this was a sure sign that it was a very important day.

The job of taking the Christmas dinner down to the bake-house at the back of the Black Horse had been passed down a generation to Ron and me, and at about half-past seven we would set off with our precious load. We still had a huge round of beef every year, although it was no longer a present from the farmer as it had been in Grand-dad's day, and for the convenience of carrying this and the large turkey, to-gether with an enamel dinner-can with a tight-fitting lid in which to bring home the dripping, Dad had made a wooden carrier like a stretcher about six feet long with two handles at each end. The bird and the joint, thickly daubed with dripping, would be covered with grease-proof paper, then with several layers of clean corn sacks to keep in the heat on the return journey and finally draped with a white linen table cloth.

As we walked down to the village and turned into the almost deserted High Street, the funereal appearance of our burden would prompt suitable quips from the one or two men we did see. 'Let's 'ave a look at the ol' man afore y' screws 'im down'—'You've come too far, en't ye? You've passed the grave-yard' or 'It's a shame, I say, t' lose a loved one at a time like Christmas.'

After breakfast, we would help Dad decorate the front room. He obviously loved every minute of Christmas and went joyfully about the task of slinging paper-chains from

the corners of the room to the electric light rose in the centre
of the ceiling, sticking holly behind the pictures on the wall
and entwining runners of ivy round the turned columns of
the elaborate mahogany over-mantel. Coloured glass
baubles, carefully saved from year to year, were hung
amongst the greenery and a blue and silver blown-glass
peacock with a long tail of silken plumage occupied the
centre of the room clipped to a carpenter's pencil stuck into
the side of the light-fitting.

As he climbed each chair in turn reaching up to fasten a
paper bell to the ceiling with a drawing pin or tuck another
spray of yew behind the curtain rail, he would sing an
appropriate snatch of song:

> The mistletoe hung in the castle hall,
> The holly branch hung on the old oak wall,
> The Baron's retainers were blithe and gay
> All keeping their Christmas holiday . . .[1]

His mood was infectious and we joined in with both the
decorating and the singing with enthusiasm. Practically
everything seemed to be a cue for a song. A cold wintry day
would prompt:

> Crying, Father, I pray, let me in,
> Oh, come down and open the door,
> Or the child that I hold at my bosom will die,
> As the wind blows across the wild moor.

A fine, sunny morning would invite

The morn was fair the sky was clear, no breath came over the sea,
When Mary left her highland cot and wandered forth with me. . . .[1]

This festive mood seemed to winkle out little fragments of
song we seldom heard at other times and which never found
their way into his song book because he didn't know all the
words. Songs like 'Seventeen Come Sunday' and 'The Lawyer Bold' and 'No John No'[1], all of which had been old Steady

<hr>

[1] See pp. 246, 248, 250, 254, 256.

Pettit's songs.[1] After singing as much as he knew, he would reminisce on the old singers, as if he was thinking aloud.

After a couple of verses of Lord Thomas he would add, 'Ol' Stevie Barrow's song—shepherd along with my brother Johnny—audacious ol' fella—could jump a five-bar gate when 'e wuz seventy (so 'e said)—used t' wear a mole-skin cap.' Or after a fragment of Dick Turpin he would say, 'Ah, that wuz ol' Fred Tearle—dirty ol' sod—used t' live down Golden Square.' 'I Wandered by the Brookside' had been Will Wales' song, 'A kind-hearted ol' chap—a straw trusser and flail thresher.' 'My ol' daddy used t' sing The Bailiff's Daughter of Islington, but I don't think even he knew all the words.'

It was, incidentally, not until 1954, shortly before his death, that we were able to hear him sing the fragments as complete songs. I had come across a copy of 'Folk Songs of the Upper Thames' by Alfred Williams and I lent it to him to read. He lapped it up recognizing many of the songs printed in it and he wrote a supplementary index, giving the song title, page number and the name of the village man who used to sing it. Fortunately he was well enough to sing them over softly to me and so, with the help of the words from Mr Williams' book, we were able to salvage more of the songs that used to be sung in Rottingdean.

By twelve o'clock on Christmas morning the front room was bedecked and burgeoning like a green forest glade. The sideboard was laden with bottles of port wine and sherry, bowls of tangerines and nuts and boxes of dried figs, dates and crystallized fruits, while a fire crackled merrily in the hearth. Mother and two or three odd aunties were busy in the scullery cooking vegetables and preparing sauces and all the attendant etceteras without which the main ingredient— gently browning in Mr Hilder's oven—would not be fully appreciated, and steam from the Christmas pudding, as it bubbled gently in a large iron saucepan at the back of the hob, filled every nook and corner of the cottage with spicy, ambrosial aroma.

[1] *See* pp. 231, 238, 261, 262.

The company, mostly relatives, was beginning to assemble with everyone in a jovial mood and on their best behaviour, showing off the ties, socks, handkerchiefs, and pairs of gloves they had received as presents that morning and as the glasses of wine were handed round, a vibrant sense of warmth and good fellowship prevailed. There was an air of excitement and the women-folk were becoming intensely concerned with laying the three tables, one in the front room, one in the kitchen and another in the scullery (for the children) which were necessary to get everyone seated. They scuttled in and out with plates, glasses, cutlery, and cruets, arranging and re-arranging fussily until the spread met their critical approval. The men, in an expansive mood, talked of Christmases gone by with the seats of their trousers to the fire and handling their unaccustomed cigars like cows with muskets, while we, the small fry, were left pretty much to our own devices.

One year our devices included surreptitiously filling our glasses with sherry instead of ginger wine and the holiday spirit suddenly slipped into top gear. Life put on a great big smile and Ron and I laughed and skylarked all the way down to the bakehouse to fetch the turkey and joint of beef. On the journey home with our succulent load swinging between us I had an inspiration. There had been a pretty sharp frost that morning and the pond was frozen over. One or two small children had been tentatively testing the strength of the ice but the chances of it bearing any substantial weight were slim. 'Ron,' I said, all valiant with sherry, 'we've never took the ol' bird across the pond before. Let's give 'er a try, shall us?' Ron mumbled dissenting noises behind me but as I was in the leading shafts he had no option but to follow me.

Gingerly easing one shiny, brown shoe in front of the other I edged forward on to the yielding ice. Ron kept up a rumble of protest at the back but I pushed on over the undulating surface. 'The more she bends the more she bears,' I cried. I was feeling buoyantly confident and we were already more than halfway across. 'Come on, we're goin' t' make 'istory t' day, ol' kiddy,' I said. 'Yeah,' was the sardonic reply, 'we'll make 'istory all right, if we drop the bloody lot in the pond.'

Just then there was a fusillade of sound like rifle fire and I dropped through the ice and stood knee-deep in freezing water. The stretcher tilted dangerously and the two dishes started to slide forward and were only saved from a watery grave by Ron slowly sinking down behind me till he stood in the mud on the same level as I, restoring the stretcher to an even keel. It was a fearful moment. We took stock and, ignoring the state of our clothes, were thankful enough that the dinner was still intact.

With the crisis over, we sploshed ashore and on to the bank where, with handfuls of grass, we wiped off the worst of the creamy, grey mud with which our best shoes and the trouser legs of our Sunday suits were plastered. 'I told y' it wouldn't bear,' said Ron as we squelched up the road leaving a sad, dripping trail behind us.

Back in the cottage the state of our clothes passed unnoticed in the excitement and bustle of dishing up what was generally considered to be the meal of the year. It was an unqualified success and, as we looked round at the happy faces munching away ecstatically at the loaded plates before them, we observed a diplomatic silence about how narrowly their dinner had avoided finishing up at the bottom of the duck-pond. Ron gave me a knowing wink and we tucked another guilty secret under our belts alongside the stolen gooseberries and Miss Macintosh's cat.

The evening was dedicated to singing with perhaps a perfunctory game of whist going on between the ladies in the corner. With Dad and Uncle John in the seats of honour on each side of the fireplace—the positions once occupied by Grand-dad and great Uncle Tom—we sang the carols and Christmas hymns with a zest and enthusiasm undiminished over the years. All the old rules were still strictly observed including 'every song a drink' but 'no spirits on the table till half past nine' by which time the carols and hymns had all been sung and we began to branch out into all the old favourites, usually starting with 'The Twelve Days of Christmas'.[1] I sat by Uncle John modelling my singing on his while Ron was over with Dad, his mentor, providing the bass section or 'heavy brigade'.

The songs flowed like a river and as Christmas night developed into Boxing morning and we curled up on the sofa, in the narrow space not occupied by avuncular backsides, and drifted close to sleep, the old familiar and melodious sounds went on. By sheer weight of numbers, as well as an inborn affection, these old songs were being driven into the very marrow of our bones.

Chaulker, who was the oldest of our generation, was not quite so devoted to the old ways. He kept one eye on the clock waiting for the slightest opportunity to slip out for a drink with his mates or to meet a girl friend and when, one Christmas night, he absconded out of the back door to a dance, it was frowned upon as downright sacrilegious—but not so much a sin against the church as being contrary to the sanctity of family tradition.

Aware of the changes that time was bringing, Dad one year called Ron and me up and made us stand together in front of him and sing any one of the old songs of our choice. We chose 'Sweep, Chimney Sweep'[1] and the old man sat listening with a critical ear. When we had finished, he smiled his approval. The cogs of continuity were turning to his satisfaction and the old songs, he thought, would be going on for a few more years yet.

[1] *See* pp. 265, 266.

Chapter Twenty-two

Every summer the village used to be visited by a small number of holiday makers, mostly from London, and it was then that the differences in our backgrounds became apparent. In those days the same families came down year after year and we got to know the visiting children quite well. They were smarter in dress, slicker in talk and wit, and their funds of superficial information left us speechless. Amongst other things, the details of the public transport systems which patterned their paved and many-chimneyed world were known to them like a creed. 'I believe that if you catch the No. 11 bus to Charing Cross, then take the Underground to Walham Green and get a number something tram to somewhere or other—you will save both time and money spent in fares.' They fairly bristled with knowledge about current West End shows. They sang songs from 'White Horse Inn' and 'The King of Jazz' and were always right up-to-date and on easy and familiar terms with the contemporary social scene and the latest catch-phrases and sayings. But of wind and weather, tides and seasons, broody hens, swarming bees or when to sow cabbage seed for next year's cropping, they were remarkably ignorant.

In verbal battles we, the locals, almost invariably came off second best but there were always opportunities to level the score. Any country child knew the wisdom of avoiding the patch of lush growth which in those days usually appeared in the copse or behind the hedge at the end of a row of cottages for the obvious reason that that was where the muck-buckets were emptied. But to 'townies', brought up in the luxury of porcelain pans and complicated plumbing systems, our more primitive methods of waste disposal were a complete mystery. We used to take an unfair advantage of this sometimes when playing chasing games and when hotly pursued, would skirt the danger area where the grass and burdock grew tallest knowing that our summer-time friends, in order to gain a yard or two, would run straight across only to plunge ankle-deep or more into a morass of stinking, unspeakable 'mud'.

Having since childhood witnessed without wonder the uninhibited behaviour of the denizens of farmyard and field we were, I think, more inclined than children brought up in the glass-house of urban life to accept as inevitable and natural the roles of the two genders of the animal kingdom. Our education in these matters was both practical and demonstrative and the happenings which constituted our lessons were accepted as part of everyday life. This is not necessarily to say that we found it any easier to cross the difficult frontiers that lie between infancy and adolescence.

True we had sniggered at the spiral, anatomical peculiarities of the boar, giggled at the size and virility of the bull and laughed outright at the penial form of the common stink horn, which lurked in the long grass under the hedgerow and made putrid the early morning airs of September. Both boys and girls had romped and rolled in the summer fields or the haylofts in winter playing those innocent, exploratory games of childhood like Mothers and Fathers, Doctors and Nurses and a local variant known as Mr Murrell's Pigs, during which many closely guarded physiological secrets were mutually revealed. But on the whole, our approach to the problems of growing up was characterized more by laughter than real lust.

When summer dusk descended, we would go to some deserted beach and drink cider from the flagon which was passed from lip to lip as indiscriminately as our puppy-love kisses. We would dance on the sands to the tinny tones of a portable gramophone which tinkled out popular melodies till the sentimental lyrics, poignant with meaning, had us close to thinking we were in love. We would shed our clothes and run naked into the surf, swimming right out into the golden pathway to the moon, laughing and singing those haunting tunes which we found almost as intoxicating as the cider.

Later we would all wander arm in arm up the white chalk road that led to the downs and lie there on the open hillside, our heads pillowed on the thyme-scented grasses. Tiny insects hummed about our ears, grass-hoppers chirruped their incessant songs around us and overhead myriad stars studded the deep impenetrable reaches of the sky. The light from a million stars and the tiny buzzing of a gnat's wing combined to emphasize the infinities of the universe and the sand-grain insignificance of our own existences.

We climbed together up the steep, homeward path, leaning well forward with our heads down watching our feet swish forward through the tall grass. We passed the chalk pit, winding on up to the calm, unruffled brow of the hill and stood there for a while. After the stiff climb, it seemed natural to pause, not only to regain our breath after the exertion of walking but also to lift our eyes and drink in the panoramic view of the village which had so suddenly appeared before us. The long, level line of the dark sea intersected by the smooth, swelling curve of Beacon Hill, the church and the windmill, the cluster of crooked roof-tops beneath which the village was slumbering so peacefully. It was all so familiar that memory filled in the detail obliterated by the shadows of night.

Then quite suddenly, as a ragged-edged continent of black cloud slid aside on the winds of the upper air, the moon, clearer and crisper now it was higher in the sky, burst through almost as bright as day and flooded the scene with brittle, silver light. Everything stood out in sharp relief drained of all colour like book-pressed flowers and with the ethereal quality of a photographic negative. '. . . Who has seen the rising moon break out of the clouds at midnight,' said Emerson, 'has been present like an arch-angel at the creation of light . . .' The psychological effect of this sudden surge of unexpected brightness seemed to bring a new awakening and reveal our homes and our lives in perspective for the first time.

Down in the valley our immediate past and the living present were clinging like smoke to the narrow street, the pond, the stables and farmyards, the flint cottages and the school. The more distant past and the roots to which we owed our very existence were firmly embedded in the churchyard and the fading volumes of written records in the vestry. The key to our futures lay somewhere under the great canopy of stars and beyond the horizons which fell away beneath us to all points of the compass.

The world was changing. On the parlour walls of our cottage homes, faded sepia photographs of our parents and grandparents emerging newly-wed from the village church reminded us how much modes of dress and hairstyles had altered over the years. Their cravats, winged collars and gold tie-pins seemed a world away from our open-necked shirts and Oxford bags and the girls wearing crinolines and buns seemed positively archaic. Yet from the hilltop we could see that the sea and sky, the downland, the church and mill, in fact the whole village, physically, had remained substantially the same. Perhaps the world wasn't changing so much as we, the people in it. We had not sought change, but had been picked up and carried along on the tide of events. We were lucky enough to have served our apprenticeship to life in the same place as our ancestors and had taken our place in the long line of continuity. But now we knew we were poised on the threshold, ready to step forward into the world.

Some never left the district, a few left never to return and some of us, after a sojourn in other parts, returned with an appreciation sharpened by comparison. We, who have come back, share with those who never went away a strong love of the vicinity which makes us singularly lacking in ambition to travel further afield in search of fame and fortune. We echo the sentiments of that local man who once said to a critical visitor, 'Look, if you dun't like it round these 'ere parts, there's plen'y on us as does—an' there's plen'y o' other parts f' they buggers as dun't!'

Part II

★　★　★

Old Songs from Rottingdean

Contents

When Shall We Get Married

When shall we get married?
When shall we get married?
When shall we get married?
Johnny, my own true love,

Why tomorrow morning to be sure, (3)
If that'll please you, my dear.

Oh, couldn't we get married sooner, (3)
Johnny, my own true love?

What the 'ell d'you wanna be married by moonlight for, (3)
Surely the girl must be mad.

What shall I wear to the wedding, (3)
Johnny, my own true love?

Why a nice clean print frock and blue apron, (3)
If that'll please you, my dear.

Oh, couldn't I have something better, (3)
Johnny, my own true love?

What the 'ell d'you want a lot of frills and furbilloes for, (3)
Surely the girl must be mad.

What shall you wear to the wedding, (3)
Johnny, my own true love?

Why, a nice clean smock frock and new 'bert-legs'[1] (3)
If that'll please you, my dear.

Oh, couldn't you wear something better, (3)
Johnny, my own true love?

What the 'ell d'you want a top hat and tail-coat for, (3)
Surely the girl must be mad.

What shall we have for the dinner, (3)
Johnny, my own true love?

Why bacon and beans to be sure, (3)
If that'll please you my, dear.

Oh, couldn't we have something better (3)
Johnny, my own true love?

What the 'ell d'you want duck and green peas for, (3)
Surely the girl must be mad.

Who shall we ask to the wedding, (3)
Johnny, my own true love?

Why father and mother to be sure, (3)
If that'll please you, my dear.

Oh, couldn't we have someone better, (3)
Johnny, my own true love?

What the 'ell d'you want a lot of dukes and duchesses for, (3)
Surely the girl must be mad.

[1] Boot-legs.

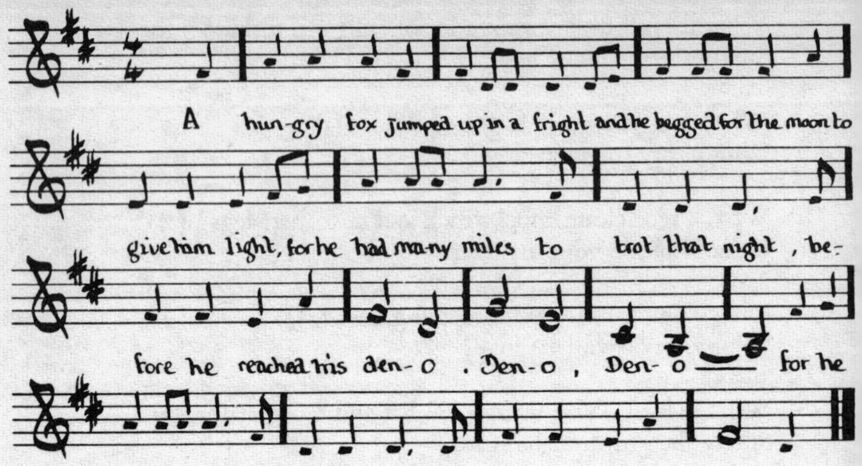

The Fox

A hungry fox jumped up in fright
And he begged for the moon to give him light,
For he had many miles to trot that night,
Before he reached his den-o.
Den-o, den-o, for he had many miles to trot that night
Before he reached his den-o.

So he cocked up his head and out went his tail
And off he went on the long, long trail
Which he done many times in calm and gale
But he always got back to his den-o.
Den-o, den-o, (*repeat last two lines*).

And soon he came to the old farm yard
Where the ducks and geese to him were barred
But he always got one by working hard
To take back to his den-o.
Den-o, den-o, (*repeat last two lines*).

He grabbed the grey goose by the neck
And slung him right across his back
And the old grey goose went quack, quack, quack
But the fox was off to his den-o.
Den-o, den-o, (*repeat last two lines*).

Ol' Mother Slipper Slopper jumped out of bed
And out of the window she poked her head,
Oh, John, John, the grey goose has gone
And the fox is off to his den-o.
Den-o, den-o, (*repeat last two lines*).

John went up to the top of the hill
And he blew a trumpet loud and shrill
Said the fox, that's very pretty music, still
I'd rather be in my den-o.
Den-o, den-o, (*repeat last two lines*).

At last he got back to his den
To his dear little foxes eight, nine, ten,
And they've had many fat geese since then,
And sometimes a good fat hen-o.
Hen-o, hen-o, (*repeat last two lines*).

The Parson and the Sucking Pig

Come maids and men and listen a while, I'll tell you of a rig,
Of the farmer and the parson and the little old sucking pig.
Of the farmer and the parson and the little old sucking pig.

Good morning sir, said the parson, good morning, sir, to you
I've come to get my little old pig, for you know it is my due,
I've come to get etc.

Now pick me one that's plump and fat for it is my design
This day to have a friend or two come round my house to dine,
This day to have etc.

The farmer he got into the sty and the little pigs they did squawl
And the one he picked for the parson was the smallest of them all,
And the one etc.

And when the parson saw the same how he did rant and roar,
He stamped his feet and shook his wig and he almost cussed and swore,
He stamped his feet etc.

All right then, said the farmer, if my offer you refuse
You're welcome in the sty, he said, yourself to pick and choose,
You're welcome in the sty etc.

The parson he jumped into the sty without any more ado.
The old sow she ran open-mouthed and at the parson flew,
The old sow etc.

The little pigs his stockings tore, his breeches tore in two,
The old sow got between his legs and into the mud him threw,
The old sow etc.

The parson he jumped out of the sty and off home he did run
You'da split your sides a-laughing to see how he was gone,
You'da split etc.

His wife was waiting at the door all for to let him in,
He said, get out you darned old bitch, I'm nearly dead with pain,
He said, get out etc.

I met with such cruel usage in that erratic sty
I'll never fancy sucking pig again until I die,
I'll never fancy etc.

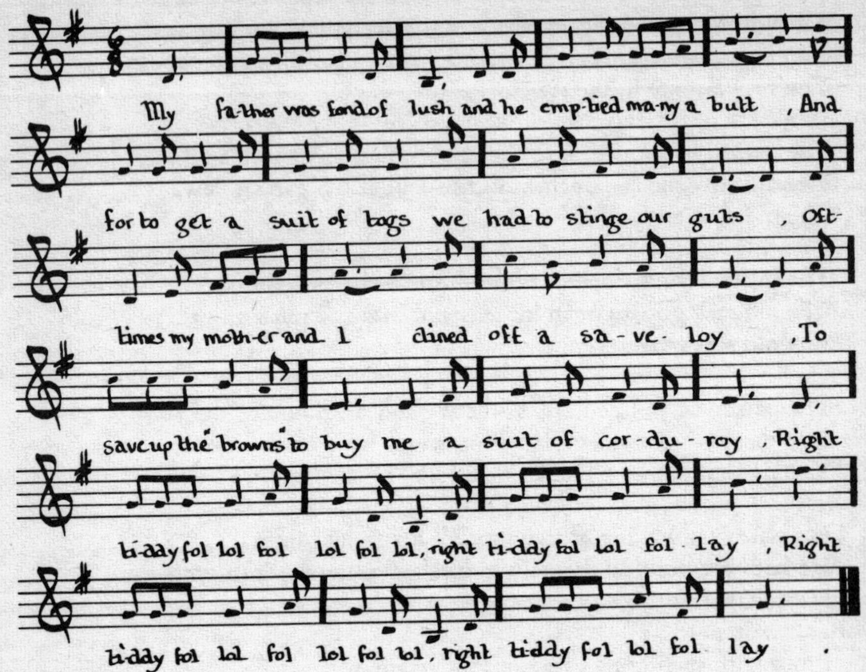

Corduroy

My father was fond of lush and he emptied many a butt,
And for to get a suit of togs we had to stinge our guts,
Oftimes my mother and I dined off a savaloy,
To save up the 'browns' to buy me a suit of corduroy,

Right tiddy fol lol fol lol fol lol right tiddy fol lol fal lay,
Right tiddy fol lol fol lol fol lol right tiddy fol lol fal lay.

When father came home at night and drunk we used him rob,
And after the course of a week or two we saved up seven bob.
One day my mother did say, Come along with me, my boy,
We will go to Moses and Sons for a suit of corduroy.

Right tiddy etc.

We soon picked out a suit, the best that we could find,
They fitted me very well but rather loose behind.
That's no fault said the man for he's a growing boy
And I'll warrant that his behind it will grow to the corduroy.

Right tiddy etc.

We quickly fitted them on and my mother she paid the blunt,
There were two pockets at the side and a little hole in front,
As we were walking along all the people they did cry,
How very nice he looks in his suit of corduroy.

Right tiddy etc.

My mother she used to scold because I had so many faults
And feeling rather queer one day she gave me a dose of salts,
Soon after I was taken short and the buttons did so annoy
And before I could get my trousers down I . . . my corduroy.

Right tiddy etc.

When I was out at play one day my pal said to me Jim
Let's go to Battersea Park and there'll we have a swim,
As we were swimming about me and this other boy
Some covey hooked it off with my suit of corduroy.

Right tiddy etc.

Now as naked as I was born I was taken home in a cart
And when my mother she heard the news it nearly broke her heart.
She said you've cooked my goose you very naughty boy,
I shall never forget the day when you lost your corduroy.

Right tiddy etc.

The Echoing Horn

The echoing horn sounds well in the morn
To call the brave sportsmen away (*repeat*)
With the cry of the hounds
Makes a musical sound,
So greatly enlightens the day, the day,
So greatly enlightens the day.

We'll away to some shaw to hear some brave noise
Our hounds they will open their throats (*repeat*)
When the fox he breaks cover,
Hark forward, High Over,
We will follow their musical notes, their notes,
We will follow their musical notes.

Hedges, gates and stiles cause us no denials,
Our horses they leap them so well (*repeat*)
With a High Tally Ho

And away we will go,
What pleasures can hunting excel, excel,
What pleasures can hunting excel.

While our hounds are at fault
We will hold hard our horse,
Till the scent of the fox we have gained (*repeat*)
With the crying Hark Forward
High Over, Hark Forward,
We will gallop him over the plain, the plain,
We will gallop him over the plain.

Over mountains he flies then afterwards dies,
He has led us an excellent chase (*repeat*)
We will take off his brush
Then home we will push
In order our spirits to raise, to raise,
In order our spirits to raise.

With our bottle and friend an evening we'll spend
We will crown the brave sports of the day (*repeat*)
Our wives will at night
Give us great delight
And solve all our sorrows away, away,
And solve all our sorrows away.

As I was a-walking one morning at ease,
Viewing the leaves as they fell from the trees, They we
all in full moti-on a-ppearing to be, And
those that were wi-thered they fell from the tree
What's the life of a man a-ny more than a leaf? A
man has his sea-sons, so why should he grieve? Although in this wide world hea-ppears fine and gay, Like a
leaf he shall with-er and soon fade a-way.

As I was a-walking one morning at ease,
Viewing the leaves as they fell from the trees,
They were all in full motion appearing to be,
And those that were withered they fell from the tree.
Chorus
   What's the life of a man any more than a leaf?
   A man has his seasons, so why should he grieve?
   Although in this wide world he appears fine and gay,
   Like a leaf he shall wither and soon fade away.

You should have seen the leaves but a short time ago
They were all in full motion appearing to grow,
Till the frost came and bit them and withered them all,
And the storm came upon them and down they did fall.
Chorus

Down in yonder churchyard many names you will see
They have fallen from this world as the leaves from the tree;
Old age and affliction upon them did fall,
And death and disease came and blighted them all.
Chorus

The Farmer in Cheshire

There was an old farmer in Cheshire,
To market his daughter did go,
And thinking that no-one would harm her
As she'd oft-times been that road before.
(*Repeat last two lines*)

Her business at the market being ended
And all her fine goods being sold,
Her journey back homewards she wended
Her pockets well lined with gold.
(*Repeat last two lines*)

She met with a rusty highwayman
Two pistols he held to her breast,
Saying deliver your money, your clothing,
Or else you shall die in distress.
(*Repeat last two lines*)

She being a buxom young damsel,
Dismounted as though unafraid,
One slash from her whip sent him sprawling
And his pistols she took as he laid.
(*Repeat last two lines*)

She put her foot in the stirrup
And mounted her horse like a man,
Then shouted back over her shoulder,
Catch me you old rogue if you can.
(*Repeat last two lines*)

The rogue he soon follow-ed after
But began for to puff and to blow,
Then seeing he could not overtake her
Sat down full of sorrow and woe.
(*Repeat last two lines*)

Her father being anxious about her
And finding 'twas getting quite late,
When hoof-beats he heard fast approaching
As she galloped up to the farm gate.
(*Repeat last two lines*)

Oh, daughter, oh, daughter, what's happened,
What kept you at the market so long?
Oh father, I fell in great danger,
But the rogue he has done me no wrong.
(*Repeat last two lines*)

She put her grey horse in the stable,
And laid a white cloth on the floor,
They counted her money a thousand,
A thousand, yes a thousand times o'er.
(*Repeat last two lines*)

verse 1
Lord Thomas he was a bold fo-rest-er And the
kee-per of our lord's deer Fair E-lean-or being a
young wo-man Lord Tho-mas he loved her so dear — Lord
Thomas he loved her so dear.
verse 2.
Come riddle me mother, Lord Tho-mas he said, Come
riddle me all at one, Whe-ther I shall have fair
E-lean-or, or bring the brown girl home — Or
bring the brown girl home

Lord Thomas he was a bold forester and the keeper of our Lord's deer
Fair Eleanor being a young woman Lord Thomas, he loved her so dear
Lord Thomas he loved her so dear.

Come riddle me, mother, Lord Thomas he said, come riddle me all at
    one,
Whether I shall have Fair Eleanor or bring the Brown Girl home
Or bring the Brown Girl home.

The Brown Girl she's got riches and land, Fair Eleanor she's got none,
And this I think to my blessing, bring me the Brown Girl home,
Bring me the Brown Girl home.

Lord Thomas he rode to Fair Eleanor's bower and boldly the bell did
    ring,
There was none so willing as Fair Eleanor to let Lord Thomas in
To let Lord Thomas in.

What news? What news, Lord Thomas? she said. What news has thou
    brought me?
I have come to invite thee to my wedding, and that's bad news for thee,
And that's bad news for thee.

She dressed herself all in milk white, and her merry men all in green,
And every town that she went through, they took her to be some
    queen.
They took her to be some queen.

Then she rode till she came to Lord Thomas' bower and boldly the bell
    did ring,
There was none so willing as Lord Thomas to let Fair Eleanor in,
To let Fair Eleanor in.

He caught hold of her lily-white hand and led her up the hall,
He set her above his own bride above the gay ladies all
Above the gay ladies all.

Is this thy bride, Lord Thomas, she said, I'm sure she looks wondrous
    brown,
When thou could'st have had me, as fair a lady as ever trod foot to
    ground,
As ever trod foot to ground.

Despise her not, Lord Thomas he said, despise her not unto me,
For better I love thy little finger than I do her whole body,
Than I do her whole body.

The Brown Girl had a little penknife that cut both keen and sharp,
And between Fair Eleanor's long and short ribs she plunged it into her
    heart,
She plunged it into her heart.

Then off he cut his own bride's head and dashed it against the wall:
He leaned his sword upon the ground and on the point did fall,
And on the point did fall.

Oh, dig me a grave, Lord Thomas he cried, both long and wide and
    deep,
And lay Fair Eleanor at my side and the Brown Girl at my feet,
The Brown Girl at my feet.

Lord Thomas was buried beneath the church wall, Fair Eleanor in the
    choir,
Out of Fair Eleanor grew a red rose and out of Lord Thomas a brier,
Out of Lord Thomas a brier.

They grew and grew to the chancel top till they couldn't grow any
    higher,
And there they entwined in a true-lover's knot for all the people to
    admire,
For all the people to admire.

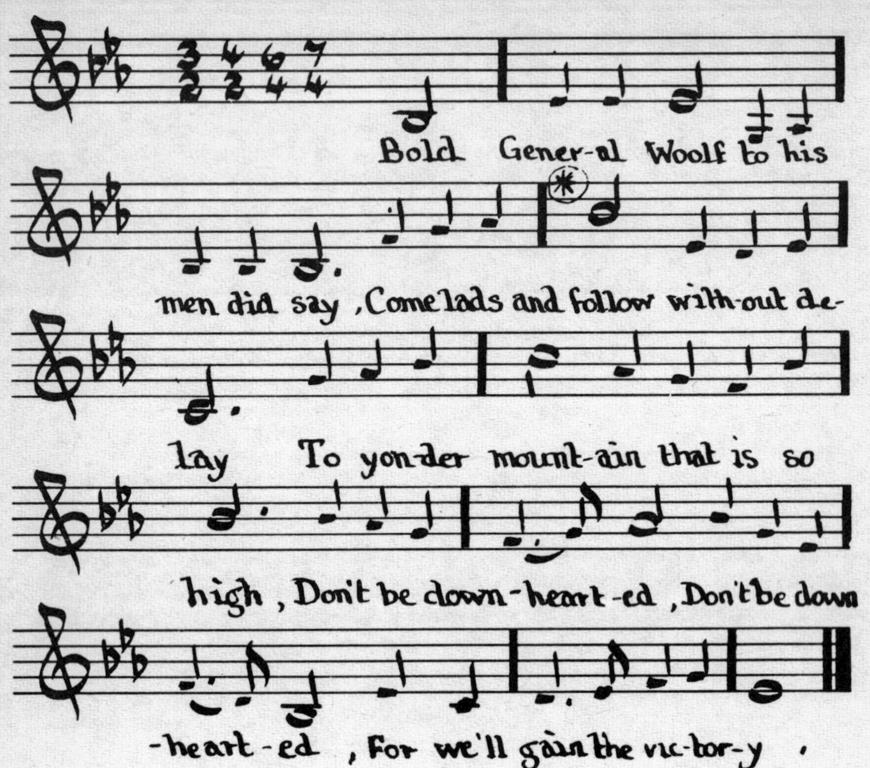

Bold Gener-al Woolf to his
men did say ,Come lads and follow with-out delay To yon-der mount-ain that is so
high , Don't be down-heart-ed ,Don't be down
-heart-ed , For we'll gain the vic-tor-y .

Bold General Wolfe to his men did say,
Come lads and follow without delay
To yonder mountain that is so high,
Don't be down-hearted, don't be down-hearted,
For we'll gain the victory.

There stand the French on the summit high,
While we poor souls in the valley lie.
We saw them fall like bots in the sun,
Through smoke and fire, through smoke and fire,
All from our British guns.

The first broadside that the French did give us
Did wound our General in the left breast,
Yonder he lie for he cannot stand,
Yet fight on boldly, yet fight on boldly
While I live I'll have command.

Here is my treasure lies all in gold,
Take it and part it for my blood runs cold,
Take it and part it brave Wolfe did say,
Ye lads of honour, ye lads of honour,
Since you have gained the day.

When to old England you do return
Tell all my friends I am dead and gone,
And bid my mother so kind and dear
No tears to shed for me, no tears to shed for me,
For our lads did gain the day.

Note: This song is clearly about Wolfe of Quebec, but the spelling of Wolfe's name often appeared as 'Woolf' in the Copper family songbook.

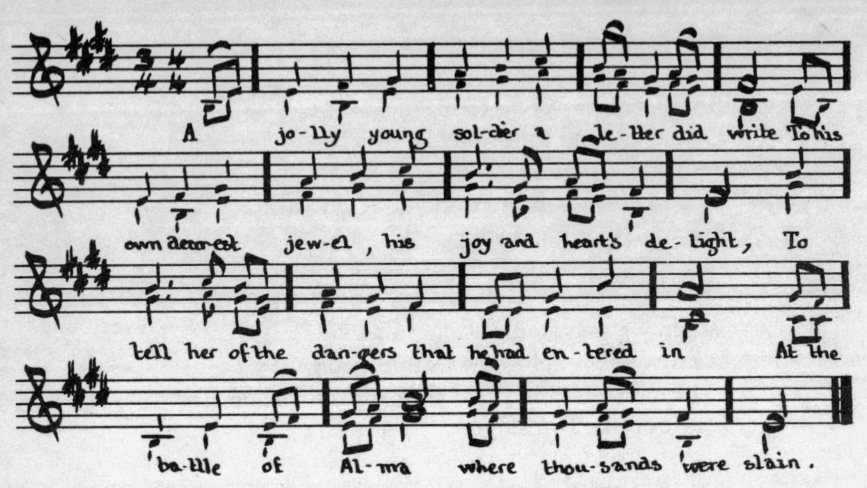

A jo-lly young sol-dier a le-tter did write To his
own dear-est jew-el, his joy and heart's de-light, To
tell her of the dan-gers that he had en-tered in At the
'ba-ttle of Al-ma where thou-sands were slain.

The Battle of Alma

A jolly young soldier a letter did write
To his own dearest jewel, his joy and heart's delight,
To tell her of the dangers that he had entered in
At the Battle of Alma where thousands were slain.

Our soldiers and sailors were all prepared for war
To fight those lofty Russians where thousands must fall,
They were commanded by Lord Raglan that man of courage bold,
They fought them sword in hand, my boys, and forced them to yield.

It was the bravest battle that did this world surprise,
To see our brave soldiers to stare them in the face,
They marched up to their guns, my boys, and soon they let them know,
They showed to them their needle work and forced them to yield.

The drums they did beat and the trumpets did sound
While thousands of soldiers lay dead on the ground.
There were rifle balls and musket came a-screeching by their ears
And the bomb shells a-bursting and loud cannon roar.

And now let us hope that these wars are all o'er,
While thousands of soldiers lie bleeding in gore.
May the Lord have mercy on them and save their poor souls,
May the sweet heavens protect them and God be their guide.

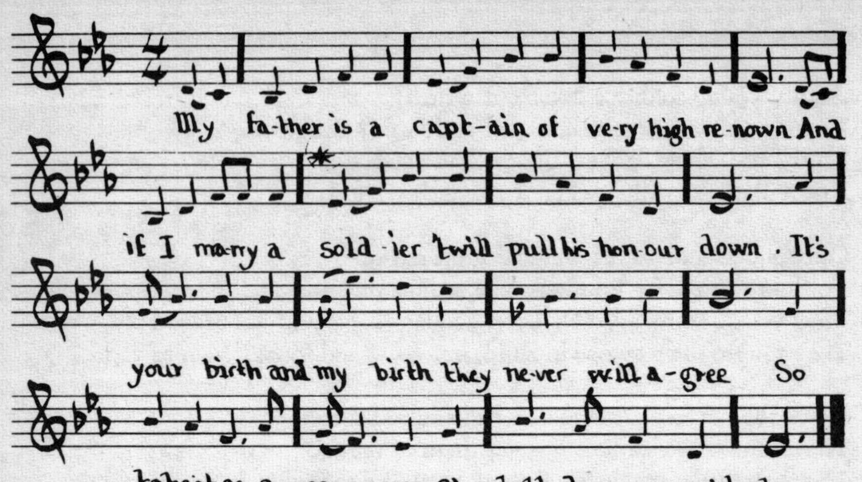

My fa-ther is a capt-ain of ve-ry high re-nown And
if I marry a sold-ier 'twill pull his hon-our down. It's
your birth and my birth they ne-ver will a-gree So
take it as a warn-ing, Oh bold dra-goon, said she.

My father is a captain of very high renown
And if I marry a soldier 'twill pull his honour down.
It's your birth and my birth they never will agree
So take it as a warning, oh bold dragoon, said she.

No warning, no warning I never mean to take,
I'll either wed or die, my love, all for your sweet sake,
And when the lady heard these words it caused her heart to bleed
So to the church they both went and were married with speed.

But when they were married and returning home again,
The lady spied her father with seven armed men.
I'm afraid, said the lady, we both shall be slain soon.
O, I fear nothing at all, said the jolly, bold dragoon.

There is no time to prittle, there is no time to prattle,
There are seven armed men just fitting for the battle,
For I will draw my broadsword and make their bones to rattle,
The lady held the horse while the dragoon fought the battle.

O, hold your hand, dear dragoon! Dear dragoon hold your hand,
And you shall have my daughter and ten thousand pounds in hand.
Fight on, says the lady, my portion is but small,
O, hold your hand, dear dragoon, and you shall have it all. .

So all you young ladies that have got gold in store
Never despise a soldier although he is so poor,
Although he is so poor he will fight for the crown—
Here's health to King George and his jolly dragoon.

The time pass-es o-ver more cheer-ful and gay, Since we've
learnt a new act to drive sorr-ows a-way. Sorrows a-
way —, So-rrows a-way ——, So-rrows a-
way —, Since we've learnt a new act to drive so-rrows a-way.

240

Thousands or More

The time passes over more cheerful and gay,
Since we've learnt a new act to drive sorrows away.
Sorrows away, sorrows away, sorrows away,
Since we've learnt a new act to drive sorrows away.

Bright Phoebe awakes so high up in the sky
With her red, rosy cheeks and her sparkaling eye,
Sparkaling eye, sparkaling eye, sparkaling eye,
With her red, rosy cheeks and her sparkaling eye.

If you ask for my credit you'll find I have none,
With my bottle and friend you will find me at home.
Find me at home, find me at home, find me at home,
With my bottle and friend you will find me at home.

Although I'm not rich and although I'm not poor
I'm as happy as those that's got thousands or more,
Thousands or more, thousands or more, thousands or more,
I'm as happy as those that's got thousands or more.

Old Adam

When Adam was first created
And Lord of the universe crowned,
His happiness was not completed
Until that a helpmate was found.
He had all things in food that were wanting,
To keep and support him in life,
He'd horses and foxes for hunting,
Which some men love more than a wife.

He'd a garden so planted by nature
Men cannot produce in his life,
But yet the all-wise Creator
Still saw that he wanted a wife.

Then Adam he lay in a slumber
And there he lost part of his side,
And when he awoke with a wonder,
He beheld his most beautiful bride.

In transport he gazed upon her,
His happiness now was complete,
He praised his beautiful donor,
Who had thus bestowed him a mate.
She was not took out of his head, sir,
To reign and to triumph o'er man;
Nor was she took out of his feet, sir,
By man to be trampled upon.

But she was took out of his side, sir,
His equal and partner to be,
But as they're united in one, sir,
The man is the top of the tree.
Then let not the fair be despised
By man, as she's part of himself,
For woman by Adam was prized
More than the whole world full of wealth.

[1]Man without woman's a beggar,
Suppose the whole world he possessed;
And the beggar that's got a good woman
With more than the world he is blest.

[1] Verse 5 starts where an asterisk is marked on the music.

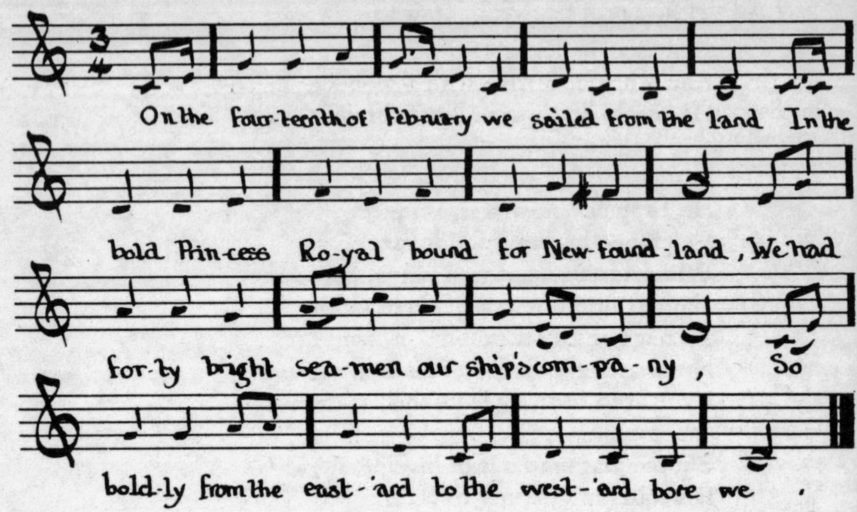

On the four-teenth of February we sailed from the land   In the
bold Prin-cess Ro-yal bound for New-found-land, We had
for-ty bright sea-men our ship's com-pa-ny ,   So
bold-ly from the east-'ard to the west-'ard bore we   .

Bold Princess Royal[1]

On the fourteenth of February we sailed from the land
In the bold Princess Royal bound for Newfoundland,
We had forty bright seamen our ship's company,
So boldly from the east'ard to the west'ard bore we.

We had not been sailing scarce days two or three
When a man from our top-mast a sail he did see,
Come bearing down on us to see where we bore
And under her mizzen black colours she wore.

Great God, cried our captain, what shall we do now?
Here comes a bold pirate to rob us I know.
Oh, no, cried our chief mate, that shall not be so
We will shake out our reef, my boys, and away from him we'll go.

It was the next morning at the dawning of day,
This lofty, large pirate shot under our lee.
Whence came you, cried the pirate, we answered him so,
We are out of fair London bound for Callao.

Then back your main top-sails and heave your ship to
For I have a letter to send down to you.
If I back my main topsails and heave my ship to,
It will be for some pilot—not alongside of you.

He chased us to the east'ard all that live long day,
He chased us to the west'ard but he couldn't make no way.
He fired shots after us but none did prevail
And the bold Princess Royal soon showed him her tail.

Oh, now, cried our captain, that pirate is gone,
Go down for your grog, my boys, go down every one.
Go down for your grog, my boys, and be of good cheer,
For while we've got sea room bold lads never fear.

[1] This version of *Bold Princess Royal* differs from that published in *Songs and Southern Breezes* by Bob Copper, and comes from Uncle John Copper, shepherd of Rottingdean.

The Mistletoe Bough

The mistletoe hung in the castle hall,
The holly branch hung on the old oak wall,
And the Baron's retainers were blythe and gay
All keeping their Christmas holiday.

The Baron beheld with a father's pride
His beautiful child, young Lovell's bride,
While she with her bright eyes seemed to be
The star of that goodly company
Chorus
Oh, the mistletoe bough,
Oh, the mistletoe bough.

I'm tired of dancing now she cried,
Here tarry a moment I'll hide, I'll hide,
And Lovell be sure thou'rt first to trace,
The clue to my secret hiding place.
Away she ran and her friends began
Each tower to search and each nook to scan
And young Lovell cried, Oh, where dost thou hide,
I'm lonely without you, my own dear bride.
Chorus

They sought her that night and they sought her next day,
They sought her in vain till a week passed away.
In the highest the lowest the loneliest spot
Young Lovell sought wildly and found her not,
And years flew by and their grief at last
Was told as a sorrowing tale of the past.
And when Lovell appeared the children cried,
See the old man weeps for his own dear bride.
Chorus

At length an old chest that had long lain hid
Was found in the castle, they raised the lid
And a skeleton form lay mouldering there
In the bridal wreath of a lady fair.
Oh, sad was her fate, in a sportive jest
She had hid from her lord in an old oak chest,
It closed with a spring, and a dreadful doom
The bride lay clasped in a living tomb.
Chorus

'Twas a cold winter's night and the wind Blew bitter a-cross the wild
moor, 'Twas then that poor Ma-ry re-turned with her child a-wand'ring
home to her own fa-ther's door. Cry-ing, Fa-ther, I pray, let me
in, Oh, come down and o-pen the door, Or the child that I hold at my
bo-som will die, As the wind blows a-cross the wild moor.

'Twas a cold winter's night and the wind
Blew bitter across the wild moor,
'Twas then that poor Mary returned with her child
Wandering home to her own father's door.
Crying, Father, I pray, let me in,
Oh, come down and open the door,
Or the child that I hold at my bosom will die,
As the wind blows across the wild moor.

O why did I leave that fair spot
Where I was happy and free,
Forever to roam without friend or a home,
Pray, father, take pity on me.
Her father was deaf to the cry
When the sound reached him over the door,
And the watch-dog he barked at the wind as it blew
Coldly across the wild moor.

You can't think what a father he felt
When he came to the door in the morn,
For Mary his daughter lay dead with the child
Clasped alive in a dead mother's arms.
With vengeance he tore his grey hair,
On his Mary he gazed from the door,
'Twas on that cold night that she perished and died
As the wind blows across the wild moor.

The father in grief pined away
And the child to its mother went soon.
There's no-one alive there to this very day
And the cottage to ruins has gone.
The villager points out the cot
Where the wild rose droops over the door
'Twas there Mary died, by the house of her pride
As the wind blows across the wild moor.

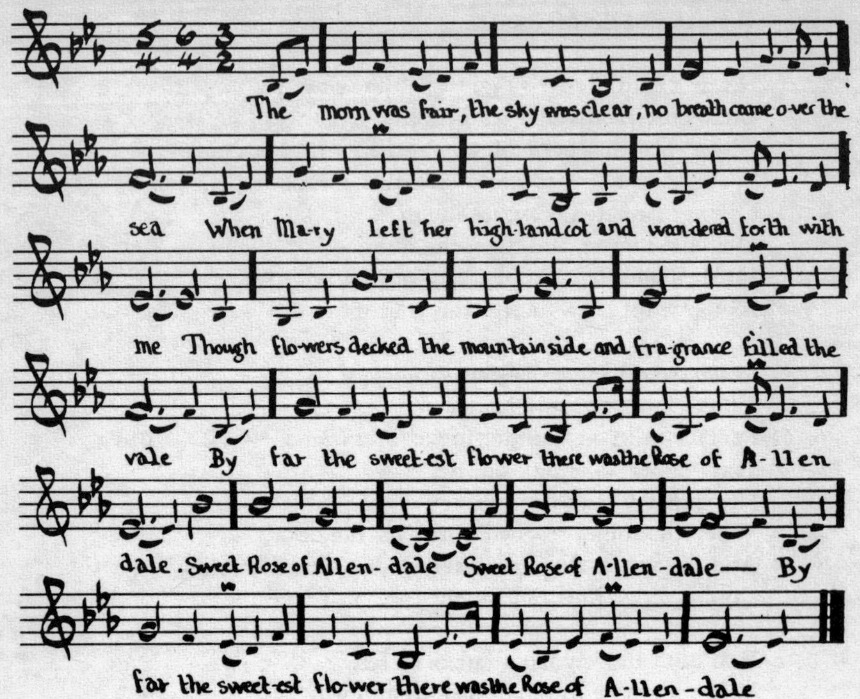

The morn was fair, the sky was clear, no breath came o-ver the
sea When Ma-ry left her high-land cot and wan-dered forth with
me Though flo-wers decked the moun-tain side and fra-grance filled the
vale By far the sweet-est flower there was the Rose of A-llen
dale. Sweet Rose of Allen-dale Sweet Rose of A-llen-dale—— By
far the sweet-est flo-wer there was the Rose of A-llen-dale

Rose of Allendale

The morn was fair, the sky was clear, no breath came over the sea
When Mary left her highland cot and wandered forth with me
Though flowers decked the mountain-side and fragrance filled the vale
By far the sweetest flower there was the Rose of Allendale.

Sweet Rose of Allendale, Sweet Rose of Allendale,
By far the sweetest flower there was the Rose of Allendale.

Where-e'er I wandered east or west though fate began to lour
A solace still was she to me in sorrow's lonely hour.
When tempests beat my lonely barque and rent the quivering sail
One maiden form withstood the storm, 'twas the Rose of Allendale.

Sweet Rose of Allendale etc.

And when my fevered lips were parched on Africa's burning sands
She whispered hopes of happiness and tales of distant lands.
My life has been a wilderness, unblest by fortune's gale
Had fate not linked my lot to hers, the Rose of Allendale.

Sweet Rose of Allendale etc.

As I walked out on a May morn-ing, On a
May morn-ing so early I ov-er-took a charm-ing
maid Just as the sun was a-ris-ing With my rue-dum day,
fol de ri-ddle day, Whack fal de rol de ri-ddle I-do.

As I walked out on a May morning,
On a May morning so early *(repeat)*
I overtook a charming maid
Just as the sun was a-rising
    With my rue-dum day, fold de riddle day,
    Wack fol de rol de riddle I-do.

Her shoes were black and her stockings white
And the buckles shown like silver. *(repeat)*
She had a black and a roving eye
And her hair hung down her shoulder
    With my rue-dum day etc.

Where are you going, my pretty dear?
Where are you going, my honey? *(repeat)*
She answered me right cheerfully
On an errand for my mummy
    With my rue-dum day etc.

How old are you, my pretty dear?
How old are you, my honey? *(repeat)*
She answered me right cheerfully,
I'm seventeen come Sunday
    With my rue-dum day etc.

And now she's with her soldier lad
Where the wars they are alarming. *(repeat)*
The drum and fife are her delight
And a merry man in the morning
    With my rue-dum day etc.

A law-yer bold the o-ther day came ri-ding thro' the
ci-ty , When he— be-held— a most —
hand-some fair So charm-ing sweet and pre-tty
Good morn-ing to you, my fair pre-tty maid And pray where are you
go-ing ? Down in yon-der green mea-dow, green mea-dow cried
she ——— , My fa-ther's there a-mow-ing

The Lawyer Bold

A lawyer bold the other day
Came riding through the city,
When he beheld a most handsome fair,
So charming sweet and pretty.

Good morning to you, my fair pretty maid,
And pray where are you going?
Down in yonder green meadow, green meadow, cried she,
My father's there a-mowing.

I'll take you up to London town
And honour you like a lady.
Fine dresses and gowns you shall put on
Fair ribbons and fine silken laces.

O, I want none of your London town
Nor any other such places,
Nor do I want your fine dresses and gowns,
Fair ribbons and fine silken laces.

And now she is a poor man's wife
And he does dearly love her.
She lives a sweet contented life,
No lady in town's above her.

On yon-der hill there lives a la-dy But her name I
do not know, I'll go and court her for her beau-ty,
Whether she ans-wers yes or no— No John no
No John no—, No John, No John, No John no

On yonder hill there lives a lady
But her name I do not know,
I'll go and court her for her beauty,
Whether she answers yes or no
   No John no, No John no, No John, No John, No John no.

She is a fair and handsome creature
And to woo her I will go.
I will ask her if she'll be my truelove,
Will she answer Yes or No
   No John no, etc.

If when walking in the garden
Plucking flowers all wet with dew,
Tell me will you be offended
If I walk and talk with you
   No John no etc.

Tell me one thing tell me truly,
Tell me why you scorn me so,
Tell me why, when asked a question,
That you always answer No
   No John no etc.

My father was a Spanish merchant
And before he went to sea,
He told me to be sure to answer
No to all you said to me,
   No John no etc.

And if when walking in the garden
I should ask you to be mine,
If I tell you that I love you
Would you then my love decline?
   No John no, No John no, No John, No John, No John no.

As I was a-riding a-long on the moor I saw the lawyer
on be-fore, I ride up to him these words I say, Have
you seen Tur-pin pass this way? For I'm the he ro, the
Tur-pin he-ro I am the great Dick Tur-pin ho.

Dick Turpin

As I was a-riding along on the moor
I saw the lawyer on before,
I ride up to him these words I say,
Have you seen Turpin pass this way?
   For I'm the hero, the Turpin hero,
   I am the great Dick Turpin ho.

No, I an't seen Turpin pass this way
Neither do I want to see him this long day
For he robbed my wife all of ten pounds
A silver snuff box and a new gown.
   For I'm the hero etc.

O, says Turpin, I'll play cute
I'll put my money down in my boot.
O, says the lawyer, he can't have mine,
For mine's sewn up in the cape behind.
   For I'm the hero etc.

As we were riding up Bradbury Hill
I bid the lawyer to stand still,
For the cape of his coat I must cut off
For my horse he wants a new saddle cloth.
   For I'm the hero etc.

I robbed the lawyer of all his store
And bid him to go to law for more,
And if my name is questioned in
You can tell him my name is Dick Turpin.
   For I'm the hero etc.

I am the last of Turpin's gang
And I am sure I shall be hanged,
Here's fifty pounds before I die
To give Jack Ketch for hanging I
   For I'm the hero etc.

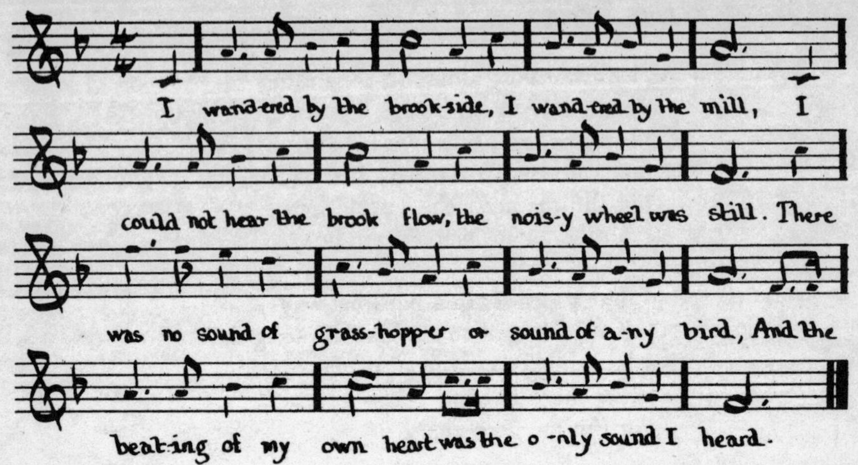

I wand-ered by the brook-side, I wand-ered by the mill, I
could not hear the brook flow, the nois-y wheel was still. There
was no sound of grass-hopper or sound of a-ny bird, And the
beat-ing of my own heart was the o-nly sound I heard.

I wandered by the brookside, I wandered by the mill,
I could not hear the brook flow, the noisy wheel was still.
There was no sound of grasshopper or sound of any bird,
And the beating of my own heart was the only sound I heard.

I sat beneath the elm tree and watched its long, long shade,
And as it grew still longer I did not feel afraid.
I listened for a footstep, I listened for a word,
But the beating of my own heart was the only sound I heard.

He came not, no, he came not, the night grew on alone.
The little stars sat one by one each on its silvery throne,
The evening winds passed by my cheeks, the leaves fell here and there,
But the beating of my own heart was the only sound I heard.

Fast silent tears were flowing as someone stood behind
A hand fell on my shoulder, I knew the touch was kind.
He drew me nearer, nearer, I could not speak one word
And the beating of my own heart was the only sound I heard.

The Bailiff's Daughter of Islington

'Twas of a youth, a well beloved youth,
And he was a squire's son,
He came a-courting a bailiff's daughter dear,
Who lived in Islington.

When his parents came for to know
Of his false and foolish mind,
They sent him up to London town,
Seven years to be confined.

When he had served seven long years,
And his lover he had never seen,
But many a tear had he shed for her
When little she thought of him.

I'll pull off my old attire,
Put on my rich attire,
And I'll go down to Islington Town
For my truelove to enquire.

As he was a-riding along the dusty road,
He met a pretty fair maid;
She stepped up to him and she said, Kind sir,
Can you ease me of one pain?

Oh, yes, my pretty fair maid, said he,
Can you tell me where you were born;
And if you know the bailiff's daughter dear
That was courted by a squire of Islington?

Oh, yes, kind sir, she then did say,
I knew her long I know,
But I must tell you, very kind sir,
She has been dead long ago.

Then I'll pull off my rich attire,
My bridle and my gold also,
And I'll go to some foreign country
Where no one does me know.

Oh, stop! Oh, stop! you well-beloved lord,
She is not dead but alive;
She stands by your horse's side
Ready to be your bride.

He kissed her and embraced her,
He kissed her o'er and o'er;
To think he should meet with his own truelove
Which he thought he would see no more.

The very next town that they came to
He gave her a golden ring;
The very next town that they came to
He gave her a grand wedding.

All you young maids take a warning by me,
And never your lover despise,
For if he's gone away he will soon return,
And will make you his lawful bride.

On the first day of Christ-mas my true love sent to me A
par-tridge in a pear tree . On the second day of Christ-mas my true love sent to me
Two tur-tle doves and a par-tridge in a pear tree . On the third day of Christ-mas
my true love sent to me . Three french hens, two tur-tle doves and a par-tridge in a pear
tree . On the fourth day of Christmas my true love sent to me, Four ca-na-ry birds,
three french hens, two tur-tle doves and a par-tridge in a pear
tree . On the fifth day of Christ-mas my true love sent to me
Five gold — rings — . Four ca-na-ry birds,
Three french hens, two tur-tle doves and a par-tridge in a pear tree .
On the sixth day of Christ-mas my true love sent to me Six geese a-lay-ing etc.
Five gold — rings — . Four ca-na-ry birds, three french hens,
two tur-tle doves and a par-tridge in a pear tree

On the first day of Christmas my truelove sent to me a partridge in a pear tree.

On the second day of Christmas my truelove sent to me Two turtle doves.

On the third day of Christmas my truelove sent to me Three french hens.

On the fourth day of Christmas my truelove sent to me Four canary birds.

On the fifth day of Christmas my truelove sent to me Five gold rings.

On the sixth day of Christmas my truelove sent to me Six geese a-laying.

On the seventh day of Christmas my truelove sent to me Seven swans a-swimming.

On the eighth day of Christmas my truelove sent to me Eight deers a-running

On the ninth day of Christmas my truelove sent to me Nine lads a-leaping.

On the tenth day of Christmas my truelove sent to me Ten ladies skipping.

On the eleventh day of Christmas my truelove sent to me Eleven bears a-baiting.

On the twelfth day of Christmas my truelove sent to me Twelve parsons preaching.

Sweep chim-ney sweep is the common cry I keep, If you
1st time - solo
2nd time - all.
can but right-ly un - der - stand me
all
With my brush, broom and my rake, With my brush, broom and my rake. See what
clean-ly work I make — With my hoe — hoe —
hoe — and my hoe and it's sweep, chim-ney sweep for me.

Sweep Chimney Sweep
Sweep Chimney sweep is the common cry I keep,
If you can but rightly understand me. (*repeat*)
With my brush, broom and my rake, with my brush, broom and my
    rake,
See what cleanly work I make
With my hoe, hoe, hoe and my hoe
And it's sweep, chimney sweep for me.

Girls came unto the door I look as black as any moor,
I'm as constant and true as the day (*repeat*)
Although my face is black, although my face is black,
I can give as good a smack,
And there's no one, no one, no one there's no one
And there's no one shall call me on hire.

Girls came unto the door I look as black as any moor,
Go and fetch me some beer that I might swallow (*repeat*)
I can climb up to the top, I can climb up to the top,
Without a ladder or a rope
And it's there you, there you, there you and there you,
And it's there you will hear me halloa.

Now here I do stand with my hoe all in my hand
Like a soldier that's on the sentery (*repeat*)
I will work for a better sort, I will work for a better sort
And kindly thank them for it.
I will work, work, work and I'll work
And I'll work for none but gentery.